SPA STYLE ASIA

SPA STYLE

ASIA

THERAPIES • CUISINES • SPAS

First published in the United Kingdom in 2003 by
Thames & Hudson Ltd, 181A High Holborn, London WC1V 7QX

British Library Cataloguing-in-Publication Data
A catalogue record for this book is available from the British Library

ISBN 0-500-28407-5

Printed and bound in Singapore by Tien Wah Press Pte Ltd

Contents

Introduction

More than just another decorative coffee-table tome, this user-friendly book has been designed with you in mind—whether you are an aficionado of spas or planning your first spa visit. The three main sections of this book, Spa Therapies, Spa Cuisine and Spa Digest, tell you what to expect of a spa experience in Asia, from the treatments offered to the cuisines served.

Spa Therapies

Deepen your appreciation of modern spa treatments as you read about their roots in Asia's traditional healing systems. This section provides a background, and a historical and cultural perspective to the treatments and therapies in Asia. Details of specific treatments, in particular, their beneficial effects, are provided to help you select which treatments might best suit your needs. In addition, there are also easy-to-follow recipes for treatments that you can try in the comfort of your home.

Spa Cuisine

In this section, you will find recipes for healthy and complete meals from top Asian spas and restaurants. Each chapter contains recipes of Asia's major national cuisines, and comprise an appetiser, soup, main course, dessert and drink, and a brief introduction to the cuisine served. The meals are low-fat, low-salt and low-cholesterol; calorie, protein, carbohydrate and fat counts are also provided for your information.

Spa Digest

An essential guide to Asia's top spas, Spa Digest contains information on the treatments, facilities and services offered by each of the 46 spas featured. Complete with images and a brief insight into the essence of each property, this guide will help you locate the spa that best suits your needs, personality and preferences. The spas are organised by country in alphabetical order.

ABOVE: The candle at the entrance of Asmara Tropical Spas at Mayang Sari Beach Resort remains lit throughout the day. The swirling pattern created by the candle represents the aromas that scent the air.

BELOW: *Jamu* ingredients at Jamu Traditional Spa at AlamKulKul Resort are mixed just minutes before the treatment to ensure their freshness.

A Spa Statistics panel located at the end of each feature helps you establish, at a glance, details about the spa—including its size, facilities, signature treatments, provision for special dietary needs, activities, services, admission criteria, and the spa's contact details.

If you're looking to share the spa experience with a partner, there's also information on couple-specific treatments and facilities, baby-sitting and other childcare services, and even discounts.

However, please note that the facilities, activities and services include those provided by the hotels or resorts that some of the spas are located in, and may only be available to in-house guests, health-club members or spa members, and not walk-in spa guests.

Spa Speak

The glossary explains frequently used spa, treatment and fitness terms.

Spa Directory

The directory provides a comprehensive listing by country of the spas in this book and their sister spas in Asia. Contact details are provided.

Index

The index helps you quickly reference information about a particular treatment, ingredient, activity, or healing method.

While *Spa Style Asia* primarily focuses on the spa traditions of Asia, it also includes New Asian and Cosmopolitan sections to give you a complete overview of the spa experiences available in Asia. The New Asian sections showcase traditional Asian treatments and recipes that have been updated with a modern twist, while the Cosmopolitan sections reflect the international flavour of therapies and cuisines embraced by the spa culture in Asia.

We hope you will enjoy this book, and your pursuit of wellness.

LEFT (CLOCKWISE FROM TOP): The spa pavilion at Banyan Tree Phuket incorporates Thai elegance within a natural setting for a traditional ambience; the deck at Soneva Gili Resort & Spa's Crusoe Villa overlooks the Indian Ocean; *tai ji* performed on the beach at Chiva-Som International Health Resort; a foot reflexology session at Amrita Spa will leave you feeling refreshed and rejuvenated.

BELOW: The spa ingredients at The Nautilus Spa at Coco Palm Resort & Spa add a touch of colour to the treatments.

Spa Therapies

Asia's healing traditions take a holistic approach of treating the body, mind and spirit as one, tackling the root cause of the problem and viewing the body as capable of healing itself. They are based on the fundamental principle of a 'life force' which flows through the body, an imbalance of which is believed to be the cause of illness.

The following pages give a background to Asia's ancient healing practices that form the basis of treatments and therapies offered by many spas in the region. 'New Asian' is devoted to traditional Asian treatments updated on a modern theme; 'Cosmopolitan' focuses on international treatments which are offered by Asian spas.

Each chapter also includes simple recipes for you to bring the spa into your home. Try them on yourself or a partner.

Yin-Yang and Qi

BALANCING THE CHINESE LIFE FORCE

W hen the World Health Organisation (WHO) first began endorsing traditional healing systems, traditional Chinese medicine (TCM) was placed on the top of their list. This is not surprising, as TCM's influence has spread further and wider than any other complementary therapy.

Many spa treatments you will enjoy in Asia have roots in Chinese healing philosophies. While the practices may vary slightly from country to country due to the availability of ingredients and therapists, the fundamental conceptual paradigms adopted are very much the same.

Therapists in spas adopting Chinese systems of healing are well-versed in the philosophical underpinnings of TCM. During your first visit, a practitioner of TCM will usually take some time to examine your state of well-being by the use of touch, sight and intuition. He may also ask you questions about your physical and emotional health. After getting a comprehensive picture of your medical background and present condition, he may suggest treatments such as acupuncture, massage or an exercise routine. In addition, you may be given suggestions on how to improve your lifestyle, and be introduced to herbal remedies or diet considerations to enhance your health. The heart of Chinese practice is its individuality and you will receive a unique combination of therapies according to your specific needs.

TOP: The *yin-yang* symbol demonstrates the mutually dependent nature of the two forces: when one increases, the other decreases; and at any one point, each contains a part of the other.

OPPOSITE: In the past, it was considered indecent to touch the body of a person of a different sex, so physicians developed the sophisticated diagnostic skill of pulse-taking to determine patients' conditions while they remained fully clothed. Reproduced by permission of The Wellcome Library, London.

Humans model themselves on earth,

Earth on heaven,

Heaven on the Way,

And the Way on that which is naturally so.

– Lao Zi in Dao De Jing

A Cultural Perspective

Chinese legend attributes the invention of early medicine to two emperors—Red Emperor Shen Nong, who originated herbal therapy; and Yellow Emperor Huang Di. Two of the ancient Chinese medical texts bear their names: *Shen Nong Ben Cao Jing* (Classic of Herbal Medicine) and *Huang Di Nei Jing* (The Yellow Emperor's Canon of Internal Medicine)—classics that are the foundation of TCM.

Archaeological evidence suggests that the roots of Chinese medicine date back almost 5,000 years. The most significant periods in the early history of medicine, however, are the Shang (1766–1100 BC) and early Zhou (1027–221 BC) dynasties which saw the development of pre-scientific supernatural medicine, and the late Zhou and early Qin (221–207 BC) dynasties which saw the foundation of scientific medicine, or what is now known as TCM.

The earliest medicine was based on ancestral worship, shamanism and magic practices. Through divination, the living consulted their ancestors on all issues. Their ancestors' displeasure resulted in illness and the cure was prayer and ritual sacrifices.

This early period of Chinese medicine also saw the beginnings of various schools of philosophical traditions which sought rational and scientific explanations based on empirical observation of nature. Their theories, brought together by Confucian theory, laid the foundation of scientific-based medicine.

Philosophy and religion play a large role in TCM, and living in harmony with the laws of the universe by following the path of Dao is important in the Chinese system of medicine. As with Ayurveda (see pp28–32), Dao advocates moderation, achieving balance and living in harmony with nature.

According to Daoist belief, the universe exists as a unified whole, and is made up of two opposing yet complementary forces known as *yin* and *yang*. The interplay between these forces changes the quality of *qi*, the energy that powers the universe and suffuses every living thing. The philosophy of *yin* and *yang* is further refined into the theory of the Five Elements. This theory is based on the interactions between the elements wood (*mu*), fire (*huo*), earth (*tu*), metal (*jin*) and water (*shui*), with the elements nurturing and supporting each other, or controlling and limiting each other. It explains the changes in the body that occur in cycles as a microcosm of the daily and seasonal cycles that occur in nature.

While Western practices have infiltrated much of China today, these ideas have been retained in the practice of TCM. From massage therapy to acupuncture, from herbal remedies to *tai ji*, the cultivation of these healing practices today is encouraged not only as clinical cures, but also as regular routines to ensure vitality, longevity and good health.

Qi

The concept of *qi*, the 'vital energy' or 'life force' within us all, is fundamental to the understanding of Chinese healing. While Western medicine revolves around the concepts of physical structures and components that work together to produce cause and effect, TCM considers 'process' as a fundamental principle that explains how we function. A Chinese practitioner sees your body as an energy system in

Yin and *yang* are the way of Heaven and Earth,

the great principle and outline of everything, the parents of change,

the root and source of life and death, the palace of gods.

Treatment of disease should be based upon the roots [of *Yin* and *Yang*].

– From the Huang Di Nei Jing

which various substances are interacting to drive the entire physical organism. The most important substance present is *qi*. *Qi*, together with *jing* (essence) and *shen* (mind or spirit), form what is termed the Three Treasures. *Qi* is the life force and the organising principle flowing through the body; *jing* governs vitality and longevity; and *shen* is responsible for consciousness and mental ability. Blood and body fluids are the other vital substances.

The Chinese believe that illness and ailment result when there is an accumulation or a blockage in the flow of these substances in the body. So when receiving therapies such as acupuncture, moxibustion, acupressure, reflexology and *tui na*, or practising exercise routines such as *qi gong* and *tai ji*, you are working towards removing these blockages and encouraging a better flow of *qi*.

Yin and Yang

When the concept of *yin* and *yang* originated in the 4th century BC, it introduced a marked shift away from the traditional Chinese belief that a person's life was at the whim of the gods, ancestors and demons, all of whom had to be pacified with rituals and sacrifices.

Yin and *yang* theory explains how *qi* differentiates the world we live in into opposing elements and how these elements interact. The Chinese character for *yin* translates as 'the dark side of the mountain', while *yang* means 'the bright side of the mountain'; everything that exists in the universe is believed to consist of both *yin* and *yang* properties.

The *yin* and *yang* symbol perfectly illustrates the principles of this theory. Like all entities that function as part of the universe, the human body comprises a combination of *yin* and *yang* elements. *Yin* is feminine, with cold, dark, quiet, static and wet properties; *yang* is masculine, with warm, bright, dynamic and dry properties. Without *yin* there is no *yang*, and vice versa. Their interdependent nature underscores the basic TCM principle that you can only achieve true balance and health when these two opposing forces are in balance. This principle of harmony and balance is central to all Chinese thought.

LEFT: A Chinese good luck talisman with the *yin-yang* symbol and the eight trigrams (*ba gua*). The three unbroken lines—the trigram for heaven—epitomises *yang*; the three broken lines—the trigram for earth—epitomises *yin*.

This equilibrium can be disrupted by influences within (emotional disturbances such as fear, grief, joy, shock, anger, sorrow or worry) and external environmental factors (caused by cold, fire, heat, wind, dampness and dryness). These act to disrupt the movement of the body's vital substances and the healthy performance of our organs.

The Chinese treatments used in spas today are modern adaptations designed to counter these internal and external factors so as to rebalance the *yin* and *yang* elements within us. This can be achieved by the manipulation of *qi* along the meridians through which the body's vital substances flow.

A Map of Meridians

Meridians are channels through which *qi* is circulated through the body. The meridian network, which is like a cobweb of crawling capillaries, comprises a system of 12 main channels spread throughout the body—six *yin* channels and six *yang* channels—and eight 'extraordinary channels'. Each channel corresponds to an organ whose name it carries. *Yin* channels are linked with corresponding *yang* channels and along them are vital points called acupoints that are used in acupuncture and its associated therapies.

It is at these strategic acupoints that *qi* accumulates, making it more easily located and manipulated. *Qi* is stimulated in various ways at these precise locations using needles, hands, fingers, or even the palms, elbows, knees and feet, depending on the treatment being administered.

There are altogether 300 acupoints in the body, but only some 57 are commonly used. Acupoints are located by proportional measurements called *cun*, the distance between the two creases on the middle fingers. Each acupoint is numbered according to its position along the meridian it is located on and may have a poetic name reflecting its use or the part of the body that it is linked to. For example, KD1 is the first acupoint on the Kidney Meridian; and ST1, appropriately named 'Containing Tears', is located on the lower eye socket and helps reduce excessive watering of the eye.

ABOVE: Detail from a reproduction of a painting by Li Tang of the Song Dynasty showing a village doctor treating a peasant with moxibustion. The moxa herbs are burnt around the body's acupoints to relieve pain.

RIGHT: A meridian map detailing the acupoints and the circulation of *qi* in the body.

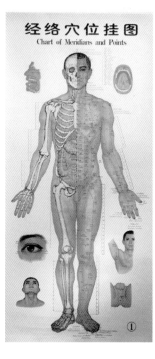

经络穴位挂图
Chart of Meridians and Points

A fine doctor acts even before there is anything wrong.

– From the Huang Di Nei Jing

TREATMENTS AND THERAPIES

Herbal Medicine

In ancient China, large prosperous households often retained their own herbalists. These herbalists were paid when the household was healthy, and not when there was illness. Herbalists were thus concerned just as much with preventing as with curing illnesses. This dual function of Chinese herbal medicine still holds firm today.

Chinese herbal medicine is thought to have developed from the Daoist alchemists' search for the elixir of life. It is one of the four main branches of TCM, its sister therapies being

LEFT: Herbs are processed in several ways before being administered. The processing is an important step as it modifies the herbs' therapeutic qualities.

BELOW (CLOCKWISE FROM TOP): Ingredients for Salvia Rose Tea, and Olive and Reed Tea: preserved black olives, American ginseng, rose buds, coix seeds, dried reed, hawthorn berries, rock sugar and salvia root.

OPPOSITE: Herbal medicine may be administered in many forms. Decoction, where herbs are boiled, steamed, or steeped in water or wine, is the most popular method.

acupuncture, *tui na*, and *qi gong*. Herbs are essential in maintaining health in Chinese philosophy as they help reorganise the body's vital substances and counter external elements such as heat, cold, dampness or wind.

Herbal medicine remains the prime orthodox medicine in China where hundreds of ingredients contribute to common cures. Chinese dispensaries stock herbs in their raw form, extracts and tinctures, oils and potions, and preparations ground to create ointments or poultices. The term 'Chinese herbs' is not limited to plants; animal and mineral elements, for instance dried geckos and pearls, are also important sources.

Herbs are classified according to their nature (hot, warm, cool or cold), taste (sour, bitter, sweet, pungent or salty), effectiveness and preparation. Each property influences the root cause of illness, thus effecting change in a person's condition.

Some spas may include herbal tonics in their menus to complement physical treatments prescribed to reinforce the *yin-yang* equilibrium. The following are herbal remedies from Yin Yang Spa, a member of the Eu Yan Sang group. Try this herbal tea to ease stress, relieve indigestion or chase menstrual pains and premenstrual tension fullness away.

SALVIA ROSE TEA

Ingredients	Metric	Imperial	American
American ginseng	10 g	½ oz	½ oz
Coix seeds	30 g	1 oz	1 oz
Hawthorn berries	15 g	½ oz	½ oz
Salvia root	5 g	¼ oz	¼ oz
Rose buds	10 g	½ oz	½ oz
Rock sugar	35 g	1 oz	1 oz
Water	800 ml	1 pt 11 fl oz	3½ cups

* Put all the ingredients except the rose buds into a pot and simmer until the water reduces to about half its original amount. Turn off the fire.
* Add the rose buds and let them steep for at least 12 sec with the pot covered, then serve hot.

Prepare this next tea and consume it throughout the day. It is the perfect solution for a sore throat.

OLIVE AND REED TEA

Ingredients	Metric	Imperial	American
Preserved black olives	4	4	4
Dried reed	30 g	1 oz	1 oz
Fresh reed	80 g	3 oz	3 oz
Water	1.5 litres	3 pts 3 fl oz	6½ cups

* Add the ingredients to the water and bring to the boil.
* Allow to cool before drinking.

Acupuncture (Zhen Fa)

The first recorded success of acupuncture (*zhen fa*) dates from about 400 to 300 BC when a Chinese physician, Bian Que, revived a dying man from a coma. The earliest needles date back to the Paleolithic age and were crafted out of stone. During the Neolithic period, needles were made out of bone, later, of bamboo, gold or silver, and today, most commonly of stainless steel. At the early stages of acupuncture, nine different needles (*jiu zhen*) were used, but today, many more needles, measuring from 2.5 cm (1 in) to 30.5 cm (1 ft) are used.

Stimulating or releasing *qi* at various acupoints along the body's meridians is the basis of acupuncture therapy. Acupuncture is widely accepted as an effective form of pain relief. A list of disorders that acupuncture treats effectively, published by the WHO, includes digestive complaints, gynaecological ailments, neurological problems and respiratory illnesses. Western medicine explains it as a method in which pain receptors are blocked, stimulating the nervous system, blood circulation and the production of endorphins. The overall effect can be numbing and comforting.

Needle insertion is quick and usually painless. Needles may be inserted into various acupoints in the area of pain or problem, or acupoints that lie on the associated meridian pathway. Various techniques will then be used to either sedate or disperse *qi*, and to supply and tone it. These techniques include rotating, lifting, lowering and even vibrating the needle, and they are sometimes synchronised with the patient's breath. The needles are removed immediately, or kept in place for a few minutes to half an hour to provide maximum relief.

Moxibustion (Jiu Fa)

Moxibustion (*jiu fa*), the burning of the herb moxa or *Artemisia Vulgaris* around acupoints, can be traced back centuries to Chinese peasants who burnt herbs around parts of the body to relieve pain. In an earlier form, heated rocks or hot sand wrapped in animal skin or tree bark were used in hot compresses to warm afflicted body parts.

Today, moxibustion is often applied using lit cylindrical moxa sticks that are filled with pressed *Artemisia* leaves mixed with other herbs and rolled in thin paper. These are moved at a short distance from the skin along the meridian lines, or rotated around affected areas to cause heat to enter the body. This encourages the circulation of blood and flow of *qi*.

Moxibustion is also applied using cones of moxa directly on the skin, or more commonly, indirectly with an insulating layer of other herbs. These insulators give an added effect to the treatment; ginger, for instance, releases warmth.

Acupuncture and moxibustion are often combined. In fact, the Chinese term '*zhen jiu*' (acupuncture and moxibustion) refers to both the insertion of needles and application of moxibustion on the skin to restore the body's energy to harmony. When used in conjunction with acupuncture, the moxa cones are placed at the ends of inserted acupuncture needles and lit, allowing the heat and curative effects of the herb to be conducted into the body without leaving a scar.

Moxa is thought to be *yang* in nature, and particularly effective when you are suffering from problems such as joint pain and stiffness caused by dampness and cold climates. It is not suitable for those suffering from heat.

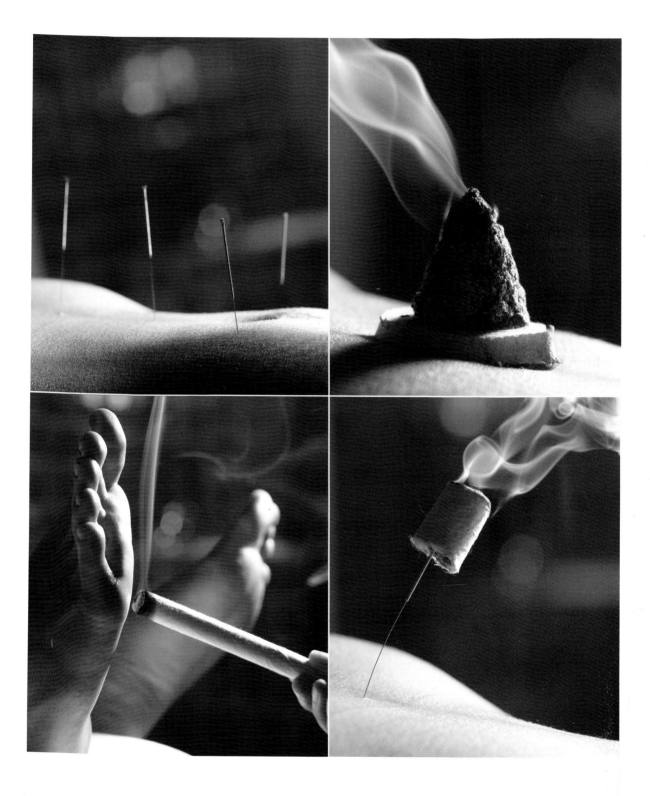

LEFT: Glass cups are the most commonly used type of jars in cupping. The transparency of the cups allows the practitioner to observe the effects of the local congestion, and so control the treatment.

Cupping (Ba Guan)

Cupping (*ba guan*) involves attaching small glass cups to the skin by creating a vacuum. Some practitioners also use metal jars or bamboo segments. The vacuum is created by placing a lighted match inside each cup to burn up the oxygen. The suction created increases the local circulation of *qi* and blood, and dispels cold and dampness from the body. Cupping is suitable for joint stiffness and pain, and for reducing swelling.

Acupressure

It is believed that acupressure predated acupuncture. At some point, it was considered an inferior form of treatment because it involved the practitioner actually touching the flesh of the patient—a practice that the upper classes regarded as disrespectful and unrefined. It only regained its status in modern times with China's encouragement of the revival of traditional medicine, and the West's interest in this traditional therapy.

Acupressure is essentially a massage therapy involving the stimulation of acupoints using the fingers, although the palms, elbows, knees and feet are sometimes used. Practitioners use firm finger pressure to stimulate acupoints, usually for a few minutes at a time. Acupressure is a highly effective way of relieving discomforts such as constipation, diarrhoea, insomnia, back pain, muscle pain and poor digestion. In spas today, therapists familiar with Chinese systems of healing may blend acupressure with other massage techniques.

Where congestion exists disease will result. ...

No one can deny the well-known fact that circulation is life; stagnation is death.

– Eunice Ingham in 'Stories the Feet Can Tell Thru Reflexology'
in The Original Works of Eunice D Ingham

Reflexology

Reflexology is said to have ancient origins in China, Egypt and Greece as a powerful healing tool. The principles of reflexology are that the feet—and to a lesser extent, the hands—are regarded as a microcosm of the body. Certain areas are mapped out on the palms, soles and top of the feet that correspond with organs, glands, limbs, senses and general functions such as speech and circulation. As the feet and hands are loaded with nerve endings, pressure placed upon a precise reflex area produces effects in another part of the body via the pathways of the nervous system.

Practitioners of reflexology refer to charts which indicate precisely how the body is reflected in the feet and hands. The big toe for instance is connected to the head, and stimulating it through massage may help ease a headache.

By putting pressure on a reflex zone of a foot or hand, a reflexologist can tell if there are problems in the corresponding part of the body, organs and glands, and help correct the imbalance. It is believed that reflexology removes blockages in the body's energy flow, resulting in a normalising of the blood and lymphatic flow, and promoting the oxygenation of tissues and removal of waste. Reflexology can also help improve circulation, ease pain, relax the body, and treat a wide range of acute and chronic illnesses. It is suitable for all ages.

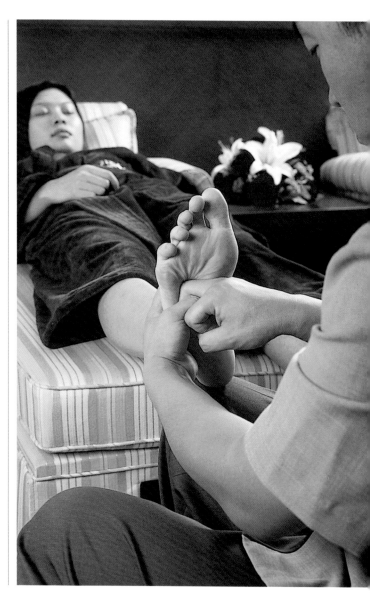

OPPOSITE (BELOW): Acupressure may easily be performed on yourself. Pressure on the acupoints shown stimulate mental functions (left); aids digestion and improves the complexion (centre); and strengthens the respiratory system and eases throat irritations (right).

RIGHT: There are 7,200 nerve endings on each foot, which are interconnected with all areas of the body.

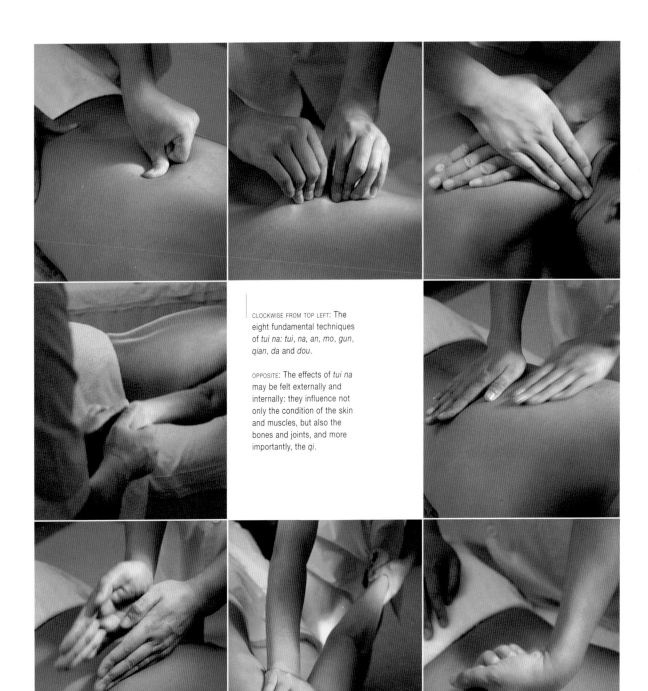

CLOCKWISE FROM TOP LEFT: The eight fundamental techniques of *tui na: tui, na, an, mo, gun, qian, da* and *dou.*

OPPOSITE: The effects of *tui na* may be felt externally and internally: they influence not only the condition of the skin and muscles, but also the bones and joints, and more importantly, the *qi.*

Tui Na

Archaeological digs reveal that *tui na* may have existed for over 3,000 years. Oracle bones carved with ancient inscriptions tell of a female shaman named Bi who healed people with massage manipulations. *Tui na* remains a significant form of massage in medical institutions today as it is used to treat specific illnesses of an internal nature and musculoskeletal ailments. It is believed to be the forefather of major bodywork techniques from shiatsu (see pp56–7) to traditional Thai massage (see p67).

If *qi* is not moving freely in the body, it is regarded as stagnating, and the practitioner will use several techniques to restore the smooth flow of or dissipate stagnant *qi*. Each technique has its own therapeutic effect on the body, and may be used repeatedly with a great deal of pressure, and for a few minutes up to half an hour each time. Eight fundamental techniques exist: *tui* (pushing), *na* (grasping), *an* (pressing), *mo* (rubbing), *gun* (rolling), *qian* (pulling), *da* (beating) and *dou* (shaking). Techniques are practised with one or two hands, and even with the arms, elbows and feet. *Tui na* may be applied on the whole body, although sensitive areas such as the face and neck may require gentler treatment.

Tui na is generally applied through clothes and with a concentrated amount of strength. It is common in China to wrap the area being massaged with an extra piece of cloth. Massage aids, such as rollers, and massage mediums, such as herbal preparations, are also used. Massage mediums can come in the form of ointments, oils or powders, and may be therapeutic even when used on their own. For instance, toasted sesame oil is commonly used on the abdomen and back, as it is slightly warming and beneficial in treating spleen *qi* deficiency that causes diarrhoea, tiredness and lack of appetite.

This recipe is recommended for treating the common cold and dispersing 'cold' from the abdominal region.

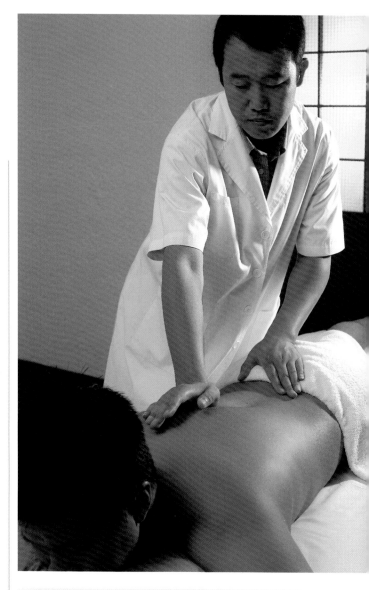

GINGER AND SPRING ONION TINCTURE

Ingredients	Metric	Imperial	American
Fresh ginger	30 g	1 oz	1 oz
Spring onion bulbs	30 g	1 oz	1 oz
White alcohol (vodka or white rum)	250 ml	8½ fl oz	1 cup

- Soak the ginger and spring onion bulbs in the alcohol for 2 weeks, then strain and store the tincture. Apply on to the skin when needed.
- If you're in a hurry, simmer the spring onion and ginger in water for 15 min before applying the tincture on to the skin.

If your energy is strong, no illness can befall you.

– From the Huang Di Nei Jing

Qi Gong and Tai Ji

The term '*qi gong*', which means working with or mastering *qi*, was coined in the 1930s to cover an extensive system of therapeutic breathing, and postural and moving exercises. Chinese arts such as *qi gong* and *tai ji* are based on the manipulation of *qi* through a system of exercises, and have been practised since ancient times as a way of improving fitness, managing health and ensuring longevity.

Qi gong methods vary according to the schools from which they originate. Shaolin *qi gong*, for instance, started as a form of martial arts for the Shaolin Temples. Some fascinating names for the exercises it propagates include 'Pushing Eight Horses Forward', 'Pulling the Golden Ring with One Hand' and 'Lifting up the Cauldron', which use 'scrubbing', 'shaking' and 'revolving' techniques respectively. If correctly executed on a regular basis, these exercises can help you develop a dynamic and powerful internal strength based on *qi*.

Tai ji (literally 'supreme ultimate fist') is a gentler and more graceful art form than *qi gong*, but it has a similar regimen of exercises designed to develop inner stamina and circulate energy. It consists of a series of movements called a 'form' and can take anything from five to 30 minutes to perform.

Tai ji exercises include those that help to regulate the body by means of both moving and stationary positions, the breath by means of breathing exercises, and the mind through visualisation and concentration techniques. Through these means, not only is the physical body exercised, but the energy systems of the body are also stimulated and mental functions enhanced, encouraging a higher level of consciousness, and resulting in an overall improvement in the quality of life.

LEFT AND OPPOSITE: The effects of *qi gong* (left) and *tai ji* (opposite) can be observed externally and felt internally. If practised diligently, the benefits will last a lifetime.

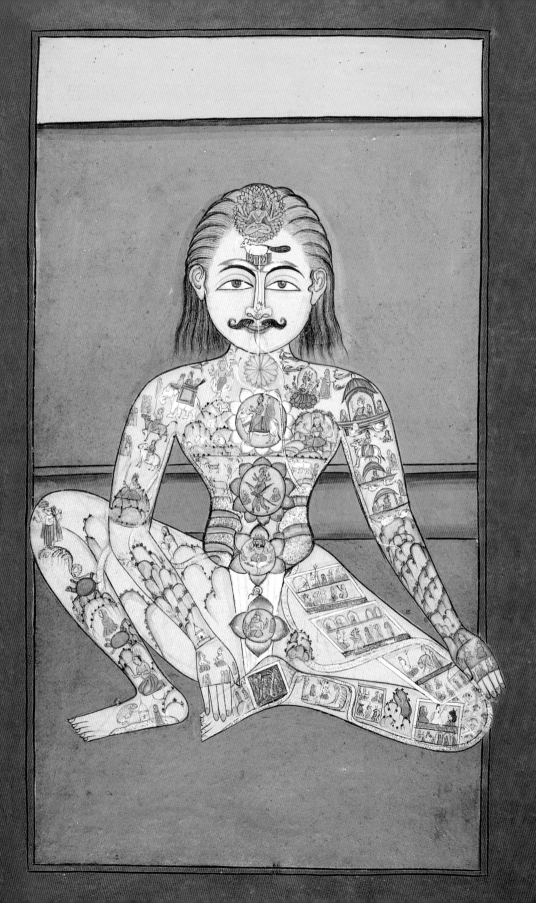

Ayurveda

INDIA'S KEYS TO HEALTH AND REJUVENATION

isit an Ayurvedic spa in India and take a step back in time. Translated from the ancient Indian language of Sanskrit as the 'Science of Life'—*ayur* (life), *veda* (knowledge)—Ayurveda is regarded by scholars as the oldest healing system in the world. And in many places in India, it is still practised in a charming, traditional way. Apart from sari-clad masseuses, fragrant incense burners, clay pots and *droni* (massage boards) are often the first welcoming images in the treatment rooms. In some cases, traditional heritage homes have been transported for miles and reconstructed on spa sites to form a village setting where guests receive the country's ancient therapies.

An Ayurvedic consultation begins the minute you walk through the door, with the practitioner observing your gait and general appearance among other things. Questioning and palpation, the other two forms of diagnosis, will enable the practitioner to determine your *dosha* type and the nature of your problem. Treatments range from external therapies, such as massage, to internal therapies, such as herbal medicine. In addition, the practitioner may make dietary and lifestyle recommendations.

Rituals start and end the Ayurvedic spa experience. The therapist begins by chanting a traditional prayer for your well-being, then slowly eases you into the treatment while keeping a hand protectively over your head. You may be anointed with vermilion on your forehead and a special herb powder may be applied on your head as a protective shield. Traditional Indian yogic chants are played according to the time of the day.

TOP: In Hindu mythology, Lord Vishnu guided the gods and demons to Lord Dhanvantari, the God of Ayurveda (pictured), to obtain the elixir of life. A grand battle ensued with the gods emerging victorious and saving mankind from perennial disease.

OPPOSITE: This illustration from an early 19th-century album shows the *chakras* or energy centres in our body.

The body is truly the support of one's well-being,

since humans are established in the body.

Leaving everything else one should take care of the body...

– From the Caraka Nidānasthāna

A Cultural Perspective

Legend has it that some three millennia ago, 52 *rishis* (wise old sages and religious leaders of ancient India) left their villages and gathered high in the Himalayas to seek enlightenment. Troubled by the problems of their people and widespread illness, they sought to learn from the creator god Brahma how to eradicate illness in the world. They were touched by divine inspiration while meditating and gathered their thoughts into a series of Vedic texts—ancient Sanskrit books that are today revered as the original Hindu tomes of knowledge. These volumes reveal a healing system steeped in Hindu philosophy on which the basic paradigm and practice of Ayurveda is based.

According to Ayurvedic belief, everything was 'one' in the beginning. Then the first sound, 'om', was heard. Its vibrations resulted in the creation of the Five Elements: ether or space, air, heat, fire and water—elements that make up everything in the universe. Although each of the Five Elements has its own characteristics and corresponds to specific senses and functions in the body, it does not act alone. The elements combine in pairs to form three forces called *tridoshas*—*vata* (air), *pitta* (fire) and *kapha* (earth)—and it is the balance of the *doshas* that gives us our individual constitutions, and form the basis for diagnosis, treatment and the maintenance of health in Ayurvedic medicine.

Ayurveda continues to be the prime healing tradition adopted by the peoples of India, Sri Lanka and Nepal today. Over the years, its secrets and health-enhancing properties have found their way into spas throughout Asia and are gaining immense popularity. The knowledge and practice today, especially those Ayurvedic elements pertaining to rejuvenation and longevity, have spread worldwide—thanks to the teachings of holistic lifestyle guru Deepak Chopra and the adoption of an Ayurvedic lifestyle by a clutch of celebrities including Demi Moore and Madonna. The Body Shop's line of products designed with Ayurvedic ingredients has also helped create a healthy following.

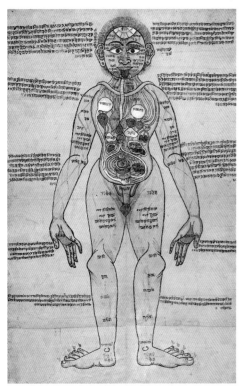

LEFT: India has an enormous number of medical manuscripts, yet no known tradition of illustrated medical texts. This Nepalese painting, an anatomical guide annotated in Sanskrit, is a rare example. Reproduced by permission of The Wellcome Library, London.

Ayurveda

At the heart of Ayurvedic philosophy is the concept that our bodies are a microcosm of the universe and that there are three universal governing forces at work inside us: *vata*, *pitta* and *kapha*. They are described as *doshas* (literally, the force that darkens or causes things to decay). And just as each of us has an individual face or thumbprint, we each also have a particular pattern of energy that corresponds with these three types, a combination of physical, mental and emotional characteristics that is our inherent constitution.

Broadly speaking, a *vata* type tends to be artistic, with a nervous or highly strung temperament. A *pitta* type, on the other hand, is the typical type 'A' personality—aggressive, driven and hot tempered, while a *kapha* type is the Mother Earths among us—charitable, loving and prone to weight gain. Still, diagnosing a *dosha* type is not as simple as it may seem.

It is believed that all individuals possess *vata*, *pitta* and *kapha* to certain degrees, but there is usually one *dosha* that is predominant. A spa's resident Ayurvedic practitioner will first determine your constitution or combination of *tridoshas* before prescribing the treatments that you may need. Unlike Western diagnoses that attempt to identify illness through common symptoms, the Ayurvedic system is highly individualised and holistic in

ABOVE: The 19th-century palace of the Maharaja of Tehri Garhwal forms the backdrop of Ananda-In the Himalayas Destination Spa. Its quiet elegance mirrors the tranquillity within.

approach. An examination of the pulse, eyes, tongue and overall physical appearance is incomplete without a thorough assessment of your emotional and spiritual well-being. The Ayurvedic practitioner's task is to re-balance your body, mind and spirit according to your unique personal 'pattern' so that they can resume harmony once again with the universe.

We are said to be in good health when all three *doshas* are properly balanced. The proper amount of *vata* promotes creativity and flexibility, *pitta* generates understanding and analytical ability, and *kapha* engenders stability, affection and generosity. Imbalances in the *doshas* are thought to disrupt the flow of *prana* (the equivalent of *qi* in TCM), the 'life force' that enters the body through food and breath; and impede *agni*, the fire that provides energy for digestion, metabolic processes, the immune system, and the processes of thought and feeling. The key to Ayurveda is treating the body, mind and spirit as a unified entity to ensure total harmony is achieved. So 'illness' is just a reflection of an imbalance of *doshas*, and it is believed that once the *doshas* are balanced again, all symptoms of disease will disappear.

At the spa, your prescription to help increase or decrease each *doshic* property usually entails a combination of treatments, usually in seven-day cycles. A typical regime could include a series of luxurious massages, oil therapy, vegetarian diet, consumption of healthy herbal tonics and a daily routine of yoga and meditation. For those who are in perfect health, preventive treatments that revitalise the body may be prescribed.

Therapies are generally divided into curative or preventive treatments, but all follow the essential self-healing philosophy and promote self-care techniques. Those who practise Ayurveda understand it to be a long-term lifestyle choice, with the full benefits reaped only if its principles are followed in every respect.

ABOVE: A 19th-century Indian painting depicting an Ayurvedic practitioner examining a patient.

BELOW RIGHT: Ayurvedic vessels were once made of gold, silver, wood, leather and clay. Today, brass and copper are more commonly used. The old-style vessels pictured here for Ayurvedic treatments are made from pure brass; copper is not used for holding oils as it oxidises easily.

Health is known as Happiness while Disorder Unhappiness.

– From the Caraka Saṃhitā

TREATMENTS AND THERAPIES

Ayurvedic Massage

Ayurvedic massage is performed using herbal oils selected to suit your constitution. The massage is done directly on the skin, and is aimed at loosening the excess *doshas* and directing them towards the organs of elimination. It also promotes circulation, increases flexibility and relieves pain and stiffness.

Massages may be performed by one or more therapists, and on the whole body or specific parts of the body, such as the head, or the neck, shoulders and hands. Techniques range from kneading to rubbing and squeezing, and are generally executed with the hands. The feet are sometimes used in *chavutti pizhichil*, a specialised form of massage where a therapist suspends himself by a string from the ceiling to apply extra pressure with his feet to undo stubborn aches in the body. Massage aids such as wooden rollers are also used.

HERBAL OIL MASSAGE
Ingredients
Vata   Calming oils: almond, castor, olive, sesame and wheat germ
Pitta   Cooling oils: almond, coconut, sandalwood and sunflower
Kapha   Invigorating oils: canola or corn and mustard

- Warm 125 ml/ 4 fl oz/ ½ cup) of your favoured oil in the microwave (taking care that it is not too hot, as this changes its properties).
- While standing in the bath, massage it all over your body, rubbing it gently into the skin from head to toe for at least 15 min.
- Once the oil is fully absorbed, turn on your shower and blast your skin with hot water. The effect is invigorating.

Purvakarma

Purvakarma is performed to ensure that the body is ready for *panchakarma*. It comprises two preparatory treatments, *snehana* and *svedana*, which soften and cleanse the skin.

Snehana (Oil therapy): A mixture of herbs, oils and natural ingredients is carefully blended together based on your *dosha* to enhance or depress certain properties. It is gently massaged on to your body to stimulate or soothe, using several massage techniques. These include massages for the body, face and neck. The oils may also be taken orally or introduced in enemas.

Svedana (Sweat therapy): A cross between a steam bath and sauna, *svedana* is a method of body purification that leaves you relaxed and deeply cleansed. After your massage, step into a giant steam box. Through perspiration, your body automatically removes the toxins that have been brought to the upper layers of the skin during the massage. Apart from the elimination of wastes, *svedana* also warms up the muscles, helps relieve heaviness due to bloating and improves the radiance and condition of the skin. A combination of herbs and oils may be added to the water to flavour the process.

HERBS FOR SVEDANA
Vata   Bala or dashamala
Pitta   Camomile or comfrey
Kapha   Rosemary or sage

LEFT: Indian head massage has become so popular in recent years that it is now offered as a therapy on its own. It is particularly effective in relieving headaches, stress and tension.

FAR LEFT: *Nasya* is the recommended treatment for diseases of the head.

LEFT: The basil plant is considered sacred in India. It is a common sight at the entrance to homes, and is believed to bring prosperity, good luck and longevity.

OPPOSITE: The 'third eye', centred on the forehead, receives restorative pampering with the healing oils of *shirodhara*.

Panchakarma (Internal Detoxification)

This common Ayurvedic regime is also the most intense, and is not suitable for those suffering from anaemia or weakness, pregnant women, or the very young and very old. The full detoxification therapy has several steps and may be given individually or as a combination of treatments depending on a person's *dosha* and needs. *Panchakarma* involves the removal of toxins at the deepest internal levels. It helps dislodge and flush the body of its toxins using the organs of elimination that the body uses naturally to cleanse itself.

Vamana (Emetic vomiting): The *rishis* believed that it was beneficial to consume certain potions to induce vomiting. *Vamana* gets rid of excess *kapha*, and is recommended for treating bronchitis, and for throat, chest and heart problems.

Virechana (Gentle purging): A herb tea, which acts as a safe and mild laxative, is consumed to help flush out any elements that may be clogging up the digestive track. *Virechana* cleanses the *pitta*, and is recommended for the treatment of conditions such as skin diseases, fevers, intestinal worms and irritable bowel syndrome.

Vasti (Enema): *Vasti* is recommended for treating disorders arising from an imbalance of *vata*. *Anuvasana vasti* (oily enemas) are used to treat skin dryness and digestive imbalance, while *asthapana vasti* (decoction enemas) are used to treat nervous problems and fatigue.

Nasya (Nasal scenting): Nasal drops are applied to clear the nasal passages and help alleviate *kapha*-oriented problems, such as headaches, allergies and nasal congestion. A few drops of medicated oil are introduced into the nose, after which the mucous membrane is gently massaged.

Raktamokshana (Blood-letting): *Raktamokshana* is used for *pitta* diseases, such as skin problems, boils and abscesses, and is carried out using surgical instruments or leeches.

Shirodhara (Heavenly Compress)

Shirodhara, sometimes referred to as the 'massage of the third eye', is considered as one of the most powerful Ayurvedic treatments available. A steady stream of medicated oil is directed on the forehead in a unique therapy designed to relieve mental tensions and provide a calm state of mind. The regular rhythm has a restorative effect on the senses.

Herbal Medicine (Samana)

Herbal medicine is used to correct imbalances in the *doshas*. They usually come in liquid form or as dried herbs, although powders or tablets are now available. Herbal remedies are prescribed individually to suit your constitution, and have the effect of increasing or decreasing the levels of *doshas*.

This basil-leaf tea, a common home remedy in India, is recommended for easing coughs and sore throats.

BASIL-LEAF TEA			
Ingredients	Metric	Imperial	American
Basil leaves	7	7	7
Clove	1	1	1
Ginger juice	1½ tsp	1½ tsp	1½ tsp

• Steep the ingredients in hot water for a minute, and drink while hot.

Ageing is 'a mistake of the intellect ...

this mistake consists of identifying oneself solely with the physical body'.

– Deepak Chopra in Perfect Health

Yoga (Union or 'Oneness') and Meditation

Therapies that pamper the mind and spirit are just as important in Indian philosophy as physical treatments. Meditation is described as the highest form of yoga. During meditation, the pulse slows, the blood pressure reduces and the brain relaxes, eliminating stress and providing a sense of peace and tranquillity.

Yoga, the Hindu method of body-mind integration, was originally practised by ancient Hindu sages to help achieve enlightenment. These days, it is no longer guru-oriented or religion-based, so it has become a mainstay of the routines of many seeking a more centred lifestyle. Its system of promoting health and preventing disease makes it highly popular.

Much of what is known of yoga today is derived from the translations of Sanskrit texts by the Indian yogi Pantanjali, who lived around 300 BC. His *Yoga Sutras* provides a framework for the practice of yoga: *yamas* (moral codes), *niyamas* (daily observances), *asanas* (postures), *pranayama* (breath control), *pratyahara* (withdrawal of the senses), *dharana* (concentration), *dhyana* (meditation) and *samadhi* (spiritual union). To reach the bliss and peace of *samadhi* is the ultimate goal.

There are several ancient methods that promote inner strength and happiness. Two of the more popular branches are *hatha* yoga, which uses *asanas*, *pranayama* and relaxation techniques; and *mantra* yoga, which uses the repetition of a sound or phrase to focus the mind.

Asanas, the sequences of physical postures that develop a healthy body and mind, are what most people associate with yoga. Stretching the body in various positions enables the individual to grow strong physically and removes toxins while putting the mind and willpower to the test. Regular sessions of yoga and meditation are recommended for a more disciplined body and a better focused mind.

There are many forms of *asanas* but standing and sitting postures are most frequently practised. Here are some simple standing postures that you may practise at home:

Tadasana: *Tadasana* is used as a beginning posture for many other *asanas*. It is an excellent *asana* for those with bad posture as it helps to extend the vertebrae, strengthen the spinal muscles and align the skeleton correctly.

Begin by standing tall with your feet together, arms by your sides. Bring your awareness to the base of your feet while distributing your weight evenly.

Without lifting your feet, lift your calves, kneecaps and thighs towards your hips so that your leg muscles are tightened.

Draw your buttocks under and your abdomen in slightly. You will feel your spine extending up above your hips.

LEFT AND OPPOSITE: Yoga and meditation are important components in the holistic system of Ayurveda. Some of their many benefits are vitality and rejuvenation.

Relax your shoulders backwards and downwards so that your chest expands. Inhale and exhale using deep, slow breaths to expand your chest completely.

Now focus on your arms in the same way, extending your energy focus through the arms and fingers.

Vrksasana: *Vrksasana* stretches and strengthens the feet and leg muscles and helps you develop balance. Besides improving concentration, it also soothes your mind and nervous system.

Stand in *tadasana*. Bend your right foot so that it is placed on your left thigh and locked in. Open up your hip so that your right knee is moved as far back as is comfortable.

Centre your body weight and place your hands together, as if in prayer, before your heart. Drop your shoulders and hold them back, relaxing your face and opening your chest.

Breathe deeply and hold for 10 breaths. Exhale and release your right leg, then repeat on the other side.

Virabhadrasana: *Virabhadrasana* is a dramatic posture that helps lengthen and tone your spinal muscles while developing your nervous system.

Stand in *tadasana*. Place your feet 1.2 m (4 ft) apart. Turn your left foot out 45 degrees and your right foot out 90 degrees. Inhale, lifting your arms above your head and lifting your waist.

Turn your body and hips to the right so that you are facing the same direction as your right foot. Exhale while bending your right knee at a right angle to the foot. Your left foot should be extended straight behind you.

Rotate your left hip forward so that it is parallel to your right foot. Bring your palms together above your head and focus on the extension of your spine above your hips. Keep your eyes up, focus on your hands, and slow down your breathing.

Breathe deeply and feel your chest expand. Relax, hold for five breaths and release. Repeat on the other side.

J a m u

INDONESIA'S ANCIENT ELIXIR

A tropical paradise comprising some 17,000 islands and populated by an estimated 200 million people, Indonesia is home to some 200 spas. Over the past decade, Indonesia has seen a rapid growth in its spa industry and is now second only to the United States in the number of spas in any one country.

Most of the spas in Indonesia are located in Bali, and they offer a myriad of pampering treatments—scrubs, floral baths, crème baths, massages and wraps—amid scenic landscapes. A spa experience in Indonesia is said to nurture, calm, relax, detoxify and rejuvenate your body and soul all at once.

Herbs are often used in spa treatments—the traditional *lulur* involves the use of a herbal paste as a body scrub, while *jamu,* loosely translated as traditional herbal medicine, is served as a tonic drink. *Jamu* is made from herbs and roots and is believed to preserve inner beauty while traditional massages and other body treatments enhance outer beauty—spas are also known as beauty and health centres in Indonesia.

Despite the range of treatments, spas in Indonesia all share the same fundamental belief that the inner and outer harmony of a person must be balanced for good health. This concept of maintaining harmony and balance between man and nature is not unlike those of traditional Chinese medicine (TCM, see pp12–7) and Indian Ayurveda (see pp28–32). Maintaining equilibrium seems to be the key to good health.

TOP: A Batak text on medicine and antidotes against poison. The Batak people of North Sumatra kept records of medicinal information.

OPPOSITE: *Datu* (herbalists) are believed to be able to treat diseases, foretell the future and keep people invulnerable to charms. Shown here are some of the recipes and methods used, as inscribed in the *Pustaha Laklak*.

Nature has been sent by God for humankind to exploit and use for its good purpose ...

God sent down a treatment for every ailment.

– From the Koran

A Cultural Perspective

According to the World Health Organisation (WHO), plants and other natural products are still tapped for their medicinal value by about 70 per cent of the world's population today. Out of all the tropical plant species in the world, an estimated 30,000 or 75 per cent can be found in Indonesia. It is no wonder then that Indonesian traditional medicine is largely herbal.

Although written records of traditional medicine in Indonesia are extremely rare, evidence of the use of herbal remedies and body massages can be found etched on the walls of Borobudur, the famed Buddhist monument in central Java. Religious, scientific and cultural records of ancient Indonesia found in the famous 18th-century *Serat Centhini* (Book of Centhini) also list an impressive 1,700 medical remedies, many of which are still being used today in some form or other. As with many other remedies, they were exclusive to people of royal status for a long time.

In line with the belief that balance between inner and outer harmony maintains health, a remedy in traditional healing must be, in principle, an attempt to restore equilibrium between man and nature rather than treating only the afflicted part (as in Western medicine). Treatment methods used by local healers include massages and herbal medicines. A massage is commonly given after childbirth and also used to set bone fractures; massage ointments are derived from coconut or ginger. Where the cause of an illness is unknown, *dukun* (healers) sometimes invoke ancestral spirits for aid.

Traditional remedies have been derived largely by trial and error. However, medicinal uses of certain plant species still persist across cultures. For example, the *dukun* use the same plant to treat malaria as the tribal healers of the Philippines.

Within Indonesia itself, healing traditions differ from region to region. However, one tradition that has remained constant is the use of *jamu*. From the days when it was first used, *jamu* has permeated all levels of society. Today it is fast gaining popularity outside Indonesia.

LEFT: Traditional Balinese medicine holds that the human body contains an intricate and complex system of humours that circulate within the body.

Jamu

Jamu is synonymous with Indonesian traditional medicine and is touted as an ancient elixir of life. Despite the lack of scientific proof supporting its wonders, many Indonesians swear by its effectiveness. An estimated 70 to 80 per cent of the Indonesian population drink a glass of *jamu* daily, but not without a prayer first—*jamu* is supposedly ineffective without it.

As many as 150 ingredients are used to produce *jamu*, although only a few are usually used at any one time. Raw ingredients include the leaves, bark and roots of spices such as ginger, turmeric and cinnamon. Sweeteners such as palm sugar are usually added for the flavour. If the *jamu* drink is bitter, a sweet drink will be offered to counter its unpleasant flavour.

Jamu has four basic functions: to cure illnesses, prevent diseases or maintain health (by promoting blood circulation and increasing metabolism), relieve aches and pains (by reducing inflammation and aiding digestion), and correct malfunctions (such as infertility and menstrual irregularity).

Jamu is available in many different forms. It may be consumed as a tonic, brew or juice; used in body wraps or as a facial mask; and as a massage ointment. Simply put, *jamu* is an extremely versatile remedy. Modern scientists do not yet know what its active ingredients are, but they do not discourage its consumption as long as its effects are identified and qualified, and most importantly, there are no side-effects. Today, it is common to find *jamu gendong* (ladies selling *jamu*) in the streets of Javanese towns. With bottles of *jamu* in a basket slung over the neck and shoulders with a *slendang* (carry cloth), the *jamu gendong* goes from door to door in the villages, helping to keep the age-old tradition alive.

RIGHT: The preparation of *jamu* is largely intuitive— neither recipes nor reference books are available.

OPPOSITE: 'Bread feeds the body, indeed, but flowers feed also the soul.'
– *From the* Koran

TREATMENTS AND THERAPIES

Jamu (Herbal Medicine)

Recipes for *jamu* preparation are passed down from generation to generation by oral tradition. Mothers frequently prepare *jamu* for their daughters as a gesture of their love. Traditionally, the mother of the bride presents the newly-married couple with a box containing several kinds of seeds, rhizomes, spices and dried cuttings of traditional medicinal plants. They are to be used on the first day of marriage, and more importantly, to be planted in the garden of the couple's home. This symbolises the mother's last effort to ensure her daughter's good health.

Jamu has been used since the 17th century, when princesses in the Central Javanese courts of Surakarta and Yogyakarta began experimenting with plants, herbs and spices to concoct beauty potions. Since then, the use of *jamu* has extended considerably—an entire beauty regime can be created just on jamu alone, from facial masks to hair conditioners to hand creams. No spa experience in Indonesia would be complete without *jamu*.

Below is a recipe for a *jamu* herbal drink from Jamu Traditional Spa at AlamKulKul Resort. This recipe makes 20 glasses and is best taken during the menstrual cycle.

KUNYIT ASEM

Ingredients	Metric	Imperial	American
Water	1 litre	2 pts	4 cups
Limes	3	3	3
Tamarind	100 g	3½ oz	3½ oz
Turmeric, freshly grated	80 g	3 oz	3 oz
Honey	2 tbsp	2 tbsp	2 tbsp
Palm sugar	10 g	½ oz	½ oz
Sugar	70 g	2½ oz	⅓ cup
Pandan leaf, 15 cm/6 inches	1	1	1

- Bring the water to the boil. Extract juice from the limes, then boil it with the remaining ingredients for about 10 min.
- Strain the drink through a fine-mesh sieve and refrigerate before serving.

Mandi (Baths)

Mandi Susu: The legendary fame of Queen Cleopatra's beauty, in particular her smooth skin, has often been attributed to her fondness for immersing herself in moisturising goat's milk. In Indonesia, Javanese princesses were also known to indulge in milk baths, especially goat's, sheep's or cow's milk. A *mandi susu*, literally translated as milk bath, is one of the treatments offered for softer, smoother skin.

Modern science has revealed the secret behind this: the lactic acid in milk naturally dissolves the 'glue' that holds dead skin cells together. So in effect, a *mandi susu* removes dead skin to reveal new skin below.

Treat yourself to Maya Ubud Resort and Spa's *mandi susu* in the comfort of your home with the following instructions. The best time for a soak is before a meal.

MANDI SUSU
- Fill the bath with 5 tsp of yogurt-based milk for every 100 litres of warm water. Soak for about 20 min then rinse with cool or warm water.

Floral Bath: Not quite regarded as a treatment on its own, a floral bath is often the finishing touch to body massages, wraps and other treatments. A long soak amid fragrant blooms brings about a sense of tranquillity, allowing the spa experience to end on a relaxing note.

At the Maya Ubud Resort and Spa, a floral bath also includes the use of fragrant bath salts.

FLORAL BATH
- Fill the bath with hot water and dissolve 25 ml/1 fl oz/5 tsp of aromatherapy bath salts for every 100 ml/3½ fl oz/½ cup of water. For a refreshing bath, try orange rosehips or bergamot lime bath salts.
- Add your favourite fresh flowers and soak yourself in the bath for 10 to 15 min. Then rinse with cool or warm water.

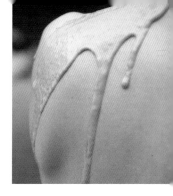

ABOVE: Jasmine, rose frangipani and other aromatic blooms are often used in a *lulur* treatment. The treatment also includes a *jamu* drink during the floral bath and lasts about 2 hours.

Traditional Lulur

The *lulur*, Javanese for 'coating the skin', is most often associated with the luxurious pre-wedding ritual of Indonesian women. The treatment traditionally lasts for over 40 days, during which the bride-to-be is kept in confinement. These 40 days are also a time of female bonding, where personal stories are exchanged. Today, modern brides opt for a seven-day treatment without the confinement, rather than the traditional 40.

One of the most pampering treatments available in spas, the *lulur* is today no longer a privilege only for brides-to-be. It generally comprises an aromatic massage, an exfoliating scrub, and a relaxing floral bath. The treatment may vary slightly between spas—an additional massage to moisturise, soften and hydrate the skin sometimes follows the exfoliating scrub; a brief shower to rinse off all ingredients may precede the floral bath. But these variations do not in the slightest affect the enjoyment of the *lulur*.

This recipe for a luxurious *lulur* from Pita Maha Spa A Tjampuhan Resort & Spa restores the natural pH balance of your skin and moisturises it.

TRADITIONAL LULUR

Ingredients	Metric	Imperial	American
Rice powder	2 tsp	2 tsp	2 tsp
Sandalwood, ground	½ tsp	½ tsp	½ tsp
Turmeric	2 tsp	2 tsp	2 tsp
Jasmine essential oil	3 drops	3 drops	3 drops
Yogurt	500 ml	1 pt	2 cups
Water	a little	a little	a little

- Combine the rice powder and sandalwood with the turmeric and jasmine essential oil to make the *lulur* paste.
- Massage your body with your choice of massage oil, then apply the *lulur* paste generously over yourself. Once it dries, gently rub the paste off to exfoliate your skin.
- Apply the yogurt to your skin.
- Finally, rinse and dip into a floral bath.

FAR LEFT: Some people choose to give the *lulur* treatment a miss as the turmeric used might leave a yellowish stain.

CENTRE: Balinese coffee beans are used in scrubs to cater to the taste of spa-goers.

LEFT: Ingredients used in the Balinese *boreh*.

Scrubs

Reflecting Indonesia's love for nature, many of the ingredients used in body scrubs are natural, and, interestingly, found in the kitchen. Coffee, coconut, honey and avocado are but some of the ingredients commonly used. Coconut oil is a natural skin cleanser while honey works to moisturise the skin.

Body scrubs work by removing the dead layers of skin, revealing the soft, supple skin below. There are scrubs for all skin types and certain scrubs are not suitable if you suffer from rashes, acne, or are pregnant or sunburnt.

Bali Coffee Scrub: The Bali Coffee Scrub, as its name suggests, uses grains from finely ground Bali coffee beans. This scrub is a treat for all coffee-lovers, who will undoubtedly savour the rich aroma while enjoying a body scrub at the same time. It is offered at The Spa at The Chedi by Mandara, which uses the following recipe.

BALI COFFEE SCRUB

Ingredients	Metric	Imperial	American
Coffee beans	200 g	7 oz	2 cups
Kaolin clay or cosmetic clay	3 tbsp	3 tbsp	3 tbsp
Ground pumice stone	a pinch	a pinch	a pinch
Carrots, blended	220 g	8 oz	8 oz
Gelatin, already set	1 tsp	1 tsp	1 tsp

- Ground the coffee beans finely and mix with the kaolin clay and pumice stone. Add a little water so that the mixture becomes a paste.
- Rub the paste all over your body, taking time to thoroughly exfoliate the skin. Remove the excess scrub with a damp cloth.
- Mix the carrot with the gelatin. Apply to your body and leave it on for a short while. Rinse off and moisturise.

Balinese Boreh: The Balinese *boreh* (scrub) is a traditional village remedy originally used by rice farmers in Bali. It is believed that the *boreh* stimulates body warmth and relieves aching muscles and joints, especially during the cold and rainy season. Hand-crushed spices were applied on the farmer's legs after a day's work in the *padi* fields. Because it encourages body warmth, the *boreh* scrub is also good for relieving fevers and headaches, and preventing colds. This scrub is not recommended for pregnant or nursing women and is not suitable for use on sunburnt skin.

Jamu Traditional Spa at AlamKulKul Resort shares its version of the Balinese *boreh* below.

BALINESE BOREH

Ingredients	Metric	Imperial	American
Babakan powder (*Kulit Kayu*)	20 g	1 oz	1 oz
Rice powder	1 tbsp	1 tbsp	1 tbsp
Clove powder	1½ tbsp	1½ tbsp	1½ tbsp
Ginger root, grated	1 slice	1 slice	1 slice
Cinnamon powder	1 tsp	1 tsp	1 tsp
Water	as required	as required	as required

- Blend all the ingredients with water to make a thick paste. Spread the paste over your body. (If you feel it necessary to reduce the intensity of the heat, mix a greater proportion of rice powder to the spices.)
- Leave the paste on until it dries then exfoliate your skin by rubbing the paste off. Rinse off.

Tongkat Ali Scrub: Before the Western drug Viagra made headlines, the *Tongkat Ali* scrub was already used in Indonesia and Malaysia to increase sexual potency. This scrub is offered at Jamu Nature Spa at The Andaman Datai Bay in Langkawi, Malaysia and only to men.

TONGKAT ALI SCRUB

Ingredients	Metric	Imperial	American
Tongkat Ali leaves	10	10	10
Water	450 ml	15 fl oz	2 cups
Mangir body scrub	1 tbsp	1 tbsp	1 tbsp
Carrot, finely grated	2 tbsp	2 tbsp	2 tbsp

- Boil the *Tongkat Ali* leaves in water until the water reduces to half its original amount.
- Combine the *mangir* body scrub and carrot with the *Tongkat Ali* water until it becomes a paste. Apply thoroughly to the body and massage.

Beauty and ethics and aesthetics serve the good of the world.

– An old Javanese saying

Crème Bath

Before commercial shampoo was available, Indonesian women used sticky gel from crushed hibiscus leaves and coconuts to keep their locks soft and shiny. The coconut provided thick milk for conditioning, washing, and massaging while its lighter milk was suitable for rinsing and conditioning.

In a *Mandi Kepala* (crème bath hair treatment), the therapist first applies conditioner liberally before massaging the hair section by section. Different ingredients may be used to treat different hair conditions—for instance, henna is used to nourish dry or treated hair, avocado for dry strands, and candlenut to achieve glossy locks. The shampoo treatment may sometimes include a stress-relieving head and neck massage to stimulate the scalp and soothe sore shoulders. This treatment is guaranteed to soften locks, strengthen follicles and give extra shine.

The following crème bath remedy by Thalasso Bali at the Grand Mirage Resort is particularly suitable for dry hair.

THALASSO BALI CRÈME BATH

Ingredients	Metric	Imperial	American
Fresh aloe vera	150 g	5 oz	5 oz
Moisturising cream with Vitamin E	100 ml	3½ fl oz	½ cup
Jasmine essential oil	3 drops	3 drops	3 drops
Camomile essential oil	3 drops	3 drops	3 drops

- Peel the aloe vera and discard the skin. Blend the aloe vera until it becomes a thick paste. Transfer it to a bowl and add the moisturising cream and essential oils. Mix thoroughly by hand.
- Apply the crème bath to the roots of the hair and massage in hard circular motions. Slowly move to the tips and continue to massage. If possible, steam the hair to help it absorb the crème bath.

BELOW: Even distribution of the crème bath—from the roots to the tips—is important to ensure the best results. The therapist may plait your hair or fashion it into a bun to allow your hair to better absorb the crème.

LEFT AND BELOW: Every ingredient in the Papaya, Kemiri, Mint Body Wrap has a specific purpose. The papaya has a cooling effect and softens the skin; the kemiri nuts (left) exfoliate and moisturise; and mint is a stimulant and a natural antiseptic.

Indonesian Wrap

Most women in Asia have heard of this Indonesian beauty remedy. Indonesian women are famed for regaining their slender figure shortly after childbirth, and this is widely attributed to the *bengkung* treatment (herbal wrap). The *bengkung* is a long abdominal sash that is bound tightly round the abdomen and hip areas, and is believed to help rid the body of excess wind, restore muscle tone, flush toxins and strengthen the new mother. It is also said to stimulate the body's lymphatic system, thus quickening the process by which the new mother sheds the extra weight put on during her pregnancy.

The traditional treatment takes about a month and is usually carried out by an *ibu pijat* (female masseur). A hot bath and herbal oil massage is given each morning to restore muscle tone. A herbal paste is then applied to the stomach before a corset of 8 to 15 metres of cotton fabric is tightly wound around the body from hips to rib cage. Ingredients for the paste vary, and typically include *sirih* (betel leaves) for its antiseptic properties and ability to combat odour, lime juice to flush toxins, eucalyptus to aid the digestive process, and crushed coral for its high mineral content and ability to keep the body warm. This paste is also believed to 'cleanse' the womb while firming and shrinking the stomach.

The *bengkung* is tightly wound to increase its effectiveness in contouring the figure and reducing the excess flab. It is left overnight and only removed when the *ibu pijat* visits the next morning for the day's massage and herbal wrap.

In comparison, a body wrap in an Indonesian spa is less complex. As with the *bengkung* treatment, the paste applied is also herbal and may include ingredients such as aloe and lavender. At the Jamu Traditional Spa at AlamKulKul Resort, a Papaya, Kemiri, Mint Body Wrap is offered after a traditional massage. This treatment is usually followed by a floral bath.

PAPAYA, KEMIRI, MINT BODY WRAP

Ingredients	Metric	Imperial	American
Papaya, medium, mashed	1	1	1
Kemiri nuts, grated	20 pcs	20 pcs	20 pcs
Peppermint leaves	10	10	10
Water	as required	as required	as required
Banana leaves	as required	as required	as required

- Blend all the ingredients until you get a fine paste. Apply the paste generously over your body, especially over the drier areas. Wrap the body with banana leaves and secure with a sarong.
- Allow sufficient time for the body to soak in the paste, then remove the leaves and rinse off the ingredients with warm water.

Rupasampat Wahya Bhiantara—the balance between inner and outer beauty,

between that which is visible and that which lies within.

– An ancient Javanese expression

Indonesian Massage

Practitioners of traditional Indonesian medicine have used massages effectively for centuries and often complement them with herbal brews and other treatments in traditional healing. Traditional Indonesian massage can be classified into two main types: *urut* and *pijat*—*urut* is the Indonesian word for massage and *pijat* is the Javanese word for massage. The word '*pijat*' is also used to refer to an Indonesian masseur.

The *urut* is more frequently used to treat medical conditions, such as bone fractures and chronic backaches. This massage works on muscles and nerve pathways to encourage blood circulation and aids the removal of toxins by way of stimulating the lymphatic system. Therapists who practise *urut* often possess some knowledge of acupressure, acupoints and nerve pathways. In this respect *urut* is influenced by TCM as it uses Chinese meridian networks to seek out acupoints (see p17).

The therapist may use his fingers, palm, knuckles, fist and even his entire body during an *urut*. Hence, some people find it uncomfortable, even unbearably painful, but the results of the massage make it all worthwhile.

A *pijat*, on the other hand, is much gentler and more relaxing. It does not require as much technical knowledge and thus is widely practised in villages. The massage comprises simple repetitive squeezing movements between the palm and fingers. The therapist generally works to relax tensed muscles and it is up to the masseur to judge how much strength should be used in the kneading and squeezing.

Specially blended massage oils are used for both massages. The effects of a massage are usually immediate: your face will glow and you feel wonderfully relaxed. Only a few sessions are needed to help you completely relax, or, as the Indonesians believe, attain a balanced inner harmony.

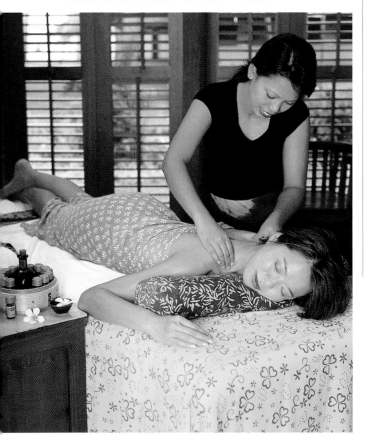

LEFT AND OPPOSITE: Traditionally, Indonesian healers used massages to treat all sorts of medical conditions—from aches, pains and fractures to indigestion and heartburn.

K i

HOLDING THE JAPANESE HEALING BOWL

 pas in Japan are largely centred around bathing—a reflection of the importance of purity to the Japanese. *Onsens* (natural hot spring baths) and *rotenburos* (outdoor baths) now dot the volcanic islands that make up Japan.

Unlike other spas in Asia where the healing experience is essentially a private ritual involving only the therapist and recipient, Japanese *onsens* offer a communal atmosphere. The Japanese take this ritual as seriously as sipping their tea—it is done regularly, leisurely and sometimes with company.

Many spas are found around the volcanic areas in Japan as the Japanese believe the mineral-enhanced waters found there are beneficial to health. The baths are usually divided into two sections, one catering to men and the other to women. Sometimes, only a screen separates one section from the other. In larger spas, you may even find a section set apart for families. You'll be expected to disrobe before you enter the main bath area where you can have a quick rinse and scrub using a wash towel and a jar or bucket of water, before stepping into the piping hot waters.

Unlike the bathing ritual, which has its roots in Japanese culture, most of Japan's other therapies are influenced by theories and literature from China, Korea and Europe. In fact, *kanpō*, Japan's traditional medical system, literally means 'Chinese method', and is the Japanese adaptation of traditional Chinese medicine (TCM, see pp12–7).

TOP: *Inros* or medicine boxes have been in use since the 16th century. Medicine is stored in the different compartments, which are suspended by a silk cord and a toggle from a sash on the kimono. The use of *inros* was originally a privilege belonging to the samurai warrior class.

OPPOSITE: Coloured late-19th-century woodblock print of an advertisement for Wakyogan, a proprietary remedy for intestinal problems.

A Cultural Perspective

According to the *Kojiki* (Record of Ancient Matters), an official account of Japanese history compiled in AD 712, the Shintō deity Opo-namudi-no-kami prescribed this treatment for the white rabbit of Inaba who lost his fur to the sharks while attempting to return to his homeland across the ocean:

> *Go quickly to this river-mouth and wash your body with its*
> *water. Then take the pollen of the Kama grass of the*
> *river-mouth, sprinkle it around, and roll on it.*
> *If you do this your skin will certainly heal as before.*
> – From the Kojiki

The three native Japanese healing methods—exorcism, purification and herbal therapy—are employed in this famous Japanese myth. Opo-namudi-no-kami, as the Shintō deity who determines the cure for illnesses, is the archetype of the ancient shamans or medicine men who performed exorcisms; the bath in the waters of the river-mouth purifies the white rabbit of Inaba; and the *Kama* grass pollen sprinkled around and rolled on represents herbal therapy.

Traditional Japanese belief held that disease was the result of possession by vengeful spirits (*kami*), and so the cure was purification rites (*harai*), or exorcism performed by shamans. In fact, purification was important more for its preventive rather than for its curative properties, and even today, bathing, purification rituals and careful attention to personal hygiene are an intrinsic part of Japanese culture. The earliest source to mention herbal therapy is the *Kojiki*, which details native herbs used for healing such as *Kuzu* (arrowroot), *Momo* (peach), *Kaba* (birch) and *Suzuki* (pampas grass).

The principles of the Japanese healing system as we know it today were derived from TCM. Monks and travelling physicians were the first bearers of Chinese cures to other parts of Asia. A Korean physician, Kon-mu, who became the Japanese emperor's personal physician, first introduced

TOP: A water basin for ritual cleansing is found at the entrance to every Japanese shrine. Before entering a shrine, the Japanese first purify themselves by using the bamboo or metal cups to pour water to wash their hands and rinse their mouths.

LEFT: In the 5th and 6th centuries, medical knowledge was passed on through itinerant monks visiting from Korea and China.

Chinese medicine to the imperial court of Japan in the 5th century. Around AD 560, the Chinese physician Zhi Cong brought detailed medical documents, including texts on *materia medica*, acupuncture and moxibustion, to Japan, and these were studied avidly at court.

From the 6th century, diplomatic exchanges between the two countries increased, and this led to the introduction of many important medical and scientific findings into Japan. By the 7th century, Chinese medicine began to be systematically adopted by the Japanese.

European medical information made its way to Japan in the second half of the 16th century, and started competing with Japanese medicine. It became the dominant system with the end of the feudal era in 1868 and the start of the Meiji period (1868–1912), when the Japanese government favoured Westernisation, even in the field of medicine. All medical practitioners were required by law to study Western medicine, and medical licences were issued only to those who passed the national examination which was based on Western medicine. Japanese medicine steadily declined. Traditional practices such as acupuncture lost their status and became mainly the realm of blind practitioners. Some of the schools set up to train blind practitioners still exist, although sighted practitioners now outnumber blind ones.

After the Meiji era, a classical revival began which saw the rise and establishment of Japanese medicine in modern Japan. The Japan Society

ABOVE: A blind practitioner massaging the arm and back of a woman. These *anma-san*, as they were known, walked through the streets blowing high-pitched whistles to alert their clients. When summoned, they would go into their clients' homes to give them a massage.

All that's visible springs from causes intimate in you

While walking, sitting, lying down, the body itself is complete truth.

– Dogen (1200–83 BC) in Moonlight in a Dewdrop

of Oriental Medicine was established in 1950, and went on to become officially approved as one of the Japanese Associations of Medical Sciences in 1991. Some *kanpō* formulations were officially approved for administration through health insurance in 1967.

Today, the Japanese adaptation of the Chinese system of healing still exists and is known as *kanpō*, although the term is now more commonly used when referring to herbal therapy in particular. Although heavily influenced by Chinese ideology and methods, the Japanese have developed distinct features in their own healing practices, including the development of shiatsu and reiki to promote health. Distinctively Japanese diagnostic techniques, manipulative therapies and folk remedies have also evolved.

While Western medicine dominates the Japanese medical scene, Japanese traditional medicine has retained a firm place in the country's modern healing system. And despite the many scientific influences Japan has been exposed to, spiritual rituals such as prayers to deities and the use of talismans from temples and shrines are still popular today when treating illnesses.

Ki

The concepts employed in Japanese medicine are strongly linked with TCM and similarly advocate living in harmony with nature. *Qi*, or the life force that sustains the body in TCM, is known as *ki* in Japan, and its manipulation is an essential part of many Japanese healing techniques. TCM's philosophy can be applied to the understanding of Japanese healing—the Chinese *yin-yang* theory of balance (see pp16–17) corresponds to the balance between *in* and *yo* in Japan; the network of 12 main meridians and 8 'extraordinary channels' in TCM (see p17) are the same as those in the Japanese system.

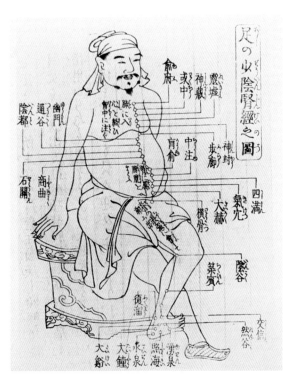

LEFT: A medical illustration depicting the acupuncture points on the body.

RIGHT: A late 19th-century woodblock print showing women gathering medicinal herbs.

BELOW: A late-19th-century *netsuke* showing a physician diagnosing through *setsu-shin* or pulse-taking. Pulse-taking enabled physicians to gather information about patients' conditions while they remained fully clothed.

Illness is believed to result when there is a disruption of normal processes caused by *ki* that is in a state of either *kyo* (deficiency) or *jitsu* (excess). When *ki* is deficient, it is said to be more *in* (yin) in nature; when it is in excess, it is more *yo* (yang).

Bo-shin (observation diagnosis) and *setsu-shin* (palpation diagnosis) are the two primary ways a Japanese practitioner determines your state of *ki* and thereby your state of health. In *bo-shin*, various visual indicators, including your gait, skin, nails, hair, facial features, and body size and proportions are used. *Setsu-shin* is a sophisticated diagnostic technique that requires considerable experience and skill. It entails taking your pulse at the wrist, with the practitioner diagnosing your state of health by analysing your pulse patterns, which reveal the patterns of *kyo* and *jitsu* in your organs and meridians. It was particularly useful in the past when modesty prevented a patient from disrobing before a physician.

Ampuku (abdominal diagnosis), which originated in the early 17th century, is another popular diagnostic technique, and one that is unique to the Japanese. It is based on the premise that different areas of the abdomen correspond to specific organs. Through gentle pressure, a practitioner may detect conditions of *kyo* or *jitsu*, and, some believe, even life expectancy.

Once a practitioner has determined the amount of *ki* in the different meridians and organs, he is able to determine the root cause of the imbalance and disease, and recommend an appropriate treatment. The primary aim of treatment, whether through acupuncture, massage or herbal therapy, is *kyo-jitsu-ho-sha*, which means replenishing a deficiency of *ki* and dispersing excess *ki*, in order to regain balance.

In Japan, we call shiatsu the echo of life. ...

The receiver becomes the giver and the giver becomes

the receiver as their breathing becomes one.

– Ohashi

TREATMENTS AND THERAPIES

Acupuncture (Hari) and Moxibustion (Kyu)

Acupuncture (*hari*) and moxibustion (*kyu*) are imported from China, and the principles behind both treatments are the same as those of TCM (see pp20–1). However, the application of both treatments and the equipment used are different in Japan. The Japanese techniques are generally more subtle, and they use finer equipment. It is believed that the insertion of needles and the burning of moxa herbs at precise acupoints will stimulate the flow of *ki*, and replenish or disperse it.

Acupuncture in Japan has evolved to become an almost painless therapy: the needles used are generally finer than Chinese ones; shorter needles are preferred and guide tubes are used to tap the needles in quickly. Unlike the Chinese treatment, where a strong needle sensation is felt both by the practitioner and recipient, Japanese acupuncture treatment is gentle and the needling is much more superficial, so the patient may not feel anything at all.

The use of moxibustion is widespread in Japan for the relief of pain and common ailments. Self-help packaged moxa is readily available. The most popular moxibustion technique involves direct contact with the skin. Tiny rice-sized moxa pieces are placed on appropriate acupoints and lit. They are then allowed to burn right down to the skin, or extinguished just before, with the process repeated until there is a feeling of warmth. Indirect moxibustion is also practised, and the techniques used are similar to those used in TCM.

Shiatsu

The term 'shiatsu' is a Japanese word made up of two characters, '*shi*' (finger) and '*atsu*' (pressure). It refers to the gentle form of Japanese massage that originated from *tui na* (see pp24–5), and despite its name, the palms and heels of the hands, forearms, elbows, knees and feet are also used to apply pressure. It is a relatively modern system, popularised just a century ago by Japanese physician Tokujiro Namikoshi.

Shiatsu is holistic in nature and helps to improve the well-being of the entire body instead of only treating specific symptoms. It borrows principles from acupuncture and incorporates techniques from osteopathy, physiotherapy and other healing traditions. A shiatsu therapist applies gentle pressure to acupoints in order to restore a balanced flow of *ki* within the meridians; pressure is also applied over a larger area than just at the acupoints. The treatment also includes a series of body stretches along meridian passages.

Specific areas or the entire body may be treated at one time and each session may last from 60 to 90 minutes. With manipulation and pressure, areas in the body may feel sensitive at first but this eases quickly as the treatment progresses.

Unlike other massage methods, pressure is sustained and stationary rather than vigorous and moving, which allows the muscles targeted and soft tissues to relax. Designed to boost stamina, and improve digestion and concentration, shiatsu is also well-known for relieving stress and calming nerves.

LEFT: In direct moxibustion, refined moxa 'wool' is rolled into tiny rice-sized pieces and placed on appropriate acupoints. The moxa pieces are then lit with the lighted ends of incense sticks.

OPPOSITE: Shiatsu is traditionally performed with the receiver lying on the floor. This permits the practitioner to allow his full body weight to sink into the receiver, which provides a deeper level of pressure.

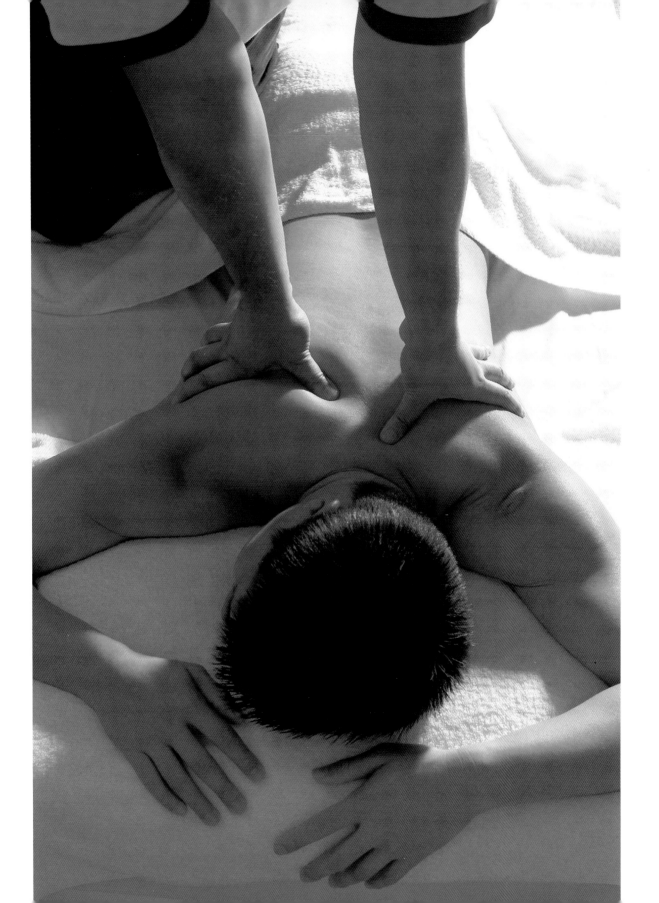

LEFT (CLOCKWISE FROM TOP LEFT):
Herbal remedies: kidney tonic
pills; dried herbs for coughs
and colds; *Lithospermum*
added to formulations intended
for auto-immune disorders;
Minor Bupleurum for relief of
fevers, bronchitis and asthma;
and a combination of cinnamon
and ground-up fossilised
bones for the liver.

Kanpō (Herbal Medicine)

The Japanese system of herbal medicine, adapted from TCM, is commonly referred to as *kanpō*. Some of the first *kanpō* recipes can be found in Japan's oldest medical text, the *Ishinpō*, compiled by Yasuyori Tanba in the 10th century. Today, there are some 150 *kanpō* recipes listed on the Japanese National Health Insurance Drug Price Tariff. These formulae are often complex and use a wide variety of ingredients. They are gentler than the Chinese recipes, and differ in the finer and smaller quantities used, but are just as effective.

The aim of the *kanpō* practitioner is to balance your *ki* and in doing so address ailments in all areas of your body. *Kanpō* may not have any visible effect unless your natural equilibrium is lost; the medicine then acts to re-balance and strengthen your physical system, and activate its self-healing potential—*kanpō* does not attack the pathogen directly.

Kanpō medicine is highly individualised, and the combination of herbs will depend on your constitution, strength, symptoms and resistance to disease. A *kanpō* formula is tailored to you, not the disease, and designed not only to relieve the symptoms of disease, but to bring you back to health. The herbal remedies are consumed orally, and come in the form of teas or decoctions, or most commonly as pills or granules.

Kanpō ingredients may be derived from plants, minerals or animals, although plant ingredients are the most common. They are classified according to their side effects and toxicity: *shang pin* (upper-class) drugs may not have a strong effect, and have no adverse side effects; *zhong pin* (middle-class) drugs have weak side effects in small doses or taken over a period of time; and *xia pin* (lower-class) drugs have strong effects, often accompanied by adverse side effects. The drugs are carefully combined based on long-standing formulations so that each acts to create a synergistic effect.

The concept of balance in Japanese cuisine has been influenced by the principles of *kanpō*. Here's a simple *kanpō* recipe you may like to try at home using aubergines. Traditionally, aubergines are said to be effective in eliminating fever or loss of appetite. Chilling and serving them with a slightly sour sauce helps increase the appetite. This recipe is recommended for those suffering from high blood pressure or constipation:

STEAMED AUBERGINES IN SOUR SAUCE

Ingredients	Metric	Imperial	American
Seasoning			
Soy sauce	3 tbsp	3 tbsp	3 tbsp
Sake (Japanese rice wine)	2 tbsp	2 tbsp	2 tbsp
Sugar	1 tbsp	1 tbsp	1 tbsp
Vinegar	1 tbsp	1 tbsp	1 tbsp
Hot water	3 tbsp	3 tbsp	3 tbsp
Steamed Aubergines			
Spring onion (white portion), finely chopped	½ stalk	½ stalk	½ stalk
Ginger, grated	¼ pc	¼ pc	¼ pc
Parsley, finely chopped	a pinch	a pinch	a pinch
Japanese aubergines, medium	7	7	7

- Mix the seasoning ingredients together, then add the spring onion, ginger and parsley. Chill in the refrigerator.
- Remove the stems and skin of the aubergines, then steam (preferably in a bamboo steamer) for 15 min.
- Remove the aubergines from the steamer and while hot, squeeze all the liquid from the aubergines. You may wish to put the aubergines on a chopping board and use a tea towel for this purpose, or use a rolling pin to squeeze out the liquid initially, but eventually the finishing touches are best applied by hand.
- Separate what remains of the aubergines into bite-sized portions using your fingers, length-wise, along the natural fibrous grooves of the aubergines. Squeeze dry once more.
- Roll each piece into a ball, and while the aubergines are still hot, blend in the prepared seasoning sauce. Do this while the aubergines are hot to ensure that the seasoning is absorbed well.
- Allow the aubergines to cool down to room temperature then put them into the refrigerator. Serve chilled.
- Make sure the aubergines are well-chilled before serving. Serve in a chilled serving dish.

Just for today, do not worry.

Just for today, do not anger.

Honour your parents, teachers, and elders.

Earn your living honestly.

Show gratitude to everything.

– Dr Mikao Usui in The Five Ethical Principles of Reiki

Reiki

The term 'reiki' is a Japanese word that comes from two characters, '*rei*' (universal) and '*ki*' (life force), and refers to the universal life force that is in and around everything, and which can be used to help the body, mind and spirit heal itself. Reiki is primarily perceived as a method of curing the physical body, but is also regarded as an effective means of healing the mind and spirit. It aims to promote health and well-being.

Reiki is believed to have been rediscovered in ancient Tibetan Sanskrit *sutras* (Buddhist teachings) in the late 1880s by Dr Mikao Usui, who was given an understanding of the meanings of the symbols and sounds in the ancient texts after an intense period of fasting. The ancient symbols and sounds are believed to activate the universal life energy for healing. Dr Usui went on to practise reiki in Japan, and introduced it to other 'masters'. Today, it is fast becoming one of the most popularly taught and practised therapy in the West.

Reiki is an extremely calming form of touch therapy. A person who practises reiki is thought to have harnessed his ability to control *ki* to heal others. Although *ki* is found in everyone, it is believed that a person needs to be 'attuned' according to the ancient symbols before he can use it to heal. 'Attunement' is achieved in three stages over years.

Reiki practitioners use primarily two techniques: they place their hands over or on key areas of your body where the principal organs and glands are located. When a reiki practitioner channels this life force through his hands to you, it is believed to rebalance and replenish areas where *ki* is depleted, and activate your body's natural ability to heal itself. *Ki* channelled into you reaches the deepest levels of your body, where illness originates, and helps initiate recovery by releasing blocked energies and cleansing toxins that may have accumulated. *Ki* released in this manner works where your body needs it most.

During a reiki session, a practitioner transmits the energy from his own body to you by placing his hands over or on the areas that need attention, starting with the head. He may place his hand on your abdomen to cure a digestive problem or ease menstrual cramps, for instance. Some reiki practitioners are said to be able to transmit healing energy from a distance. Treatment sessions last about an hour, and you will feel relaxed or invigorated after the treatment.

Reiki is said to be effective in relieving many illnesses including arthritis, insomnia and migraine. Apart from treating others, reiki is also considered an effective form of self-healing.

RIGHT: An important aspect of reiki is that you take an active role in your treatment by drawing in energy as needed. An open and positive mind also helps to ensure that you will benefit from reiki.

RIGHT: 'Modesty' towels are usually issued by the *obasans* (old women) who man the *onsens*. Once safely in the water, you may wet it, wring it outside the bath and place it on your head. It is believed to prevent you from passing out.

Baths

Baths play a central role in the health regime of all Japanese. Cleansing the spirit and warding off disease are the main benefits thought to be derived from some 2,500 *onsens* or hot spring baths spotted throughout the islands. The term '*onsen*' can refer to a single bathing facility, or to an entire town or hot spring area. *Onsens* range in size from small tubs for one person to enormous pools that can accommodate over 100 bathers. Baths are traditionally measured in *tatami* mats, a traditional Japanese unit based on the size of the straw mats that are used in houses. There is a wide variety of springs in Japan, and these include *uchi-buros* (indoor baths), *rotenburos* (outdoor baths) and *mushi-yus* (steam baths).

In the Japanese style of bathing, your body is washed and scrubbed clean before entering the bath. Sit on one of the stools provided, rub soap into your *tenugui*, a small towelling cloth, and soap yourself all over. This leaves the skin soft, smooth and invigorated as dead cells are removed and the blood circulation stimulated. Briskly rinse off the soap before immersing yourself in the bath to enjoy a relaxing soak.

Hot baths are believed to have remedial qualities because they often contain essential minerals that rejuvenate and promote cures. Bathing in mineral-enhanced waters is believed to cure illnesses such as nervous disorders, bad circulation, skin irritations, aches and fatigue.

Seasonal Baths: The Japanese enjoy different ' bath flavours' in different seasons. Mandarin orange peel baths are used in the late autumn while warming ginger baths are used in winter.

AUTUMN OR WINTER BATH
Put Mandarin orange peel or freshly chopped ginger into little muslin bags and toss them into your bath to infuse the water with their scent and healing properties. This aromatic bath aids digestion and clears phlegm.

Sên

THAILAND'S HEALING LEGACY

 hailand, also termed the land of *wats* (temples), is one of Asia's best destinations for a spa getaway. Thai spas are well-known for their luxurious surroundings and can be found throughout the kingdom—from the city of Bangkok to the hilly northern region of Chiang Mai and southern beach paradise of Hua Hin.

Of all the treatments offered in the spas, the most popular and famous one is the Thai massage. People have been so intrigued by the wonders of Thai massage that they seek professional training in it before introducing the art to their home countries. The *Nuat bo'rarn* (Thai massage) was developed in the ancient kingdom of Siam some 2,500 years ago. '*Nuat*' means 'to touch with the intention of imparting healing' while '*bo'rarn*' is derived from the Sanskrit language and means 'ancient, sacred and revered'. Put together, '*nuat bo'rarn*' literally means 'ancient massage'.

No visitor to Thailand should leave without experiencing a Thai massage. If done well, a Thai massage will soothe aches and pains, loosen joints and ease muscle tension, leaving you feeling completely refreshed.

TOP: The *saan chao te* (spirit house) is a home for spirits believed to inhabit the earth. In return for good health and success in their undertakings, the Thais offer flower garlands, joss sticks, candles and edible food to please the spirits.

OPPOSITE: According to Buddhist doctrine, *tam boon* (merit-making) brings happiness, peace and other good things, and helps one attain advancement in the next life. A mural from the Suan Pakaad Palace shows people earning merit by giving alms to Buddha. The act of healing is also a sign of compassion and is another way of earning merit.

When any person is sick in Siam he begins by causing

his whole body to be moulded by one who is skilful herein,

who gets upon the body of the sick and tramples him under his feet.

– Simon de la Loubere, leader of the French embassy to Ayutthaya in 1687

A Cultural Perspective

Buddhism is the dominant religion in Thailand and an estimated 95 per cent of Thais are Theravada Buddhists. Temples found on almost every street in Thailand bear testimony to the Thais' religious devotion. Many locals, and even tourists, can be found offering incense in the temples at all times of the day.

Theravada Buddhism is a form of Buddhism that originated in India and spread through Southeast Asia, including Sri Lanka, Myanmar, Laos, Cambodia and Thailand. Not surprisingly, traditional Thai medicine began in the cultural and historical context of Theravada Buddhism, and like many other traditional medical systems, was influenced by Indian Ayurveda (see pp28–32) and traditional Chinese Medicine (TCM, see pp12–7). The earliest practitioners of Thai medicine were Theravada Buddhist monks who underwent years of strict discipline, intense practice and meditation before they could be considered well-versed in the healing methods. The meditation and prayers reflect how steeped the Thais were in their religious belief. Today, masseurs are encouraged to recite a prayer before beginning their work.

Historically, Buddhist temples were centres of learning, not only of religion, but also of worldly matters such as astrology and medicine. The monks were what we would term today doctors and pharmacists, for they were also herbalists who knew of the curative and preventive properties of herbs. Indeed, monks were respected both for their religious authority and their ability to heal.

Like most medical traditions in Asia, traditional Thai medicine is holistic and emphasises harmony—within your body and with nature—as the key to good health. An illness is viewed as an imbalance in the body, mind and spirit. A healing session therefore seeks to correct the balance within your body as well as with nature. Diagnosis is done by evaluating pulse and heartbeat and by examining skin colour and texture, body temperature, abnormal physical symptoms and bodily excretions of patients.

LEFT: An artist's impression of Wat Po, the oldest temple in Thailand. Formerly known as Wat Phra Chetupon, it was the most important temple in providing education for the Thais. Numerous stone slabs depicting a wide range of subjects, from botany to history and geography, made the temple an accessible source of reference for many.

Four principal methods of traditional healing are generally used by the monks: *wai khruu* (prayers and meditation based on Theravada Buddhist tradition), herbs (taken internally and applied externally), diet and massage. If taken internally, the herbs are infused, boiled or rendered into some other consumable form. For instance, piper roots provide relief for stomach ailments and various *yaa hawm* (fragrant medicine) are used as balms for muscle aches and headaches. These herbal medicines are readily available at traditional medicine shops even today. Dietary advice is also provided to aid in the healing process. For instance, eating sour foods in moderation is supposed to help relieve throat irritation and prevent illness.

These healings methods were handed down from one generation to the next as oral tradition. Written records are few, as much of Thailand's archives, including medical texts, was destroyed when the Burmese sacked Ayutthaya in 1767. Only two medical texts, the *Scripture of Diseases* and the *Pharmacopoeia of King Narai*, survived, and much of traditional Thai medicine today conforms to these texts.

In 1832, the rising popularity of traditional Thai massage inspired King Rama III (1824–51) to have all available knowledge on the subject carved on stone slabs. These slabs were later set into the walls in Wat Po, Thailand's oldest and largest temple. Today, the School for Traditional Medicine is located at Wat Po, which is also the national headquarters for the teaching and preservation of traditional Thai Medicine. Wat Po is also reputed to be the best place to receive a traditional Thai massage.

ABOVE: Wat Po is also known as the Temple of the Reclining Buddha. Its 45 metre-long Reclining Buddha is covered entirely with gold leaves.

LEFT: A stone *rishi* (hermit) found in the outer courtyards of Wat Po. The *rishi* figures demonstrate yoga positions and self-massage techniques for relieving physical and mental complaints.

RIGHT: Two of the epigraphs found at Wat Po. There are 60 epigraphs in all, 30 showing the front of the body, 30 showing the back.

Previously banned in Thailand for being unscientific, traditional Thai medicine has only been recently recognised by Thai medical authorities. It is practised in villages and rural areas, and also in urban areas where clinics and healers specialising in traditional Thai medicine can found. Some Thai doctors offer a complementary blend of traditional and international medicine.

Sên

The influence of Indian Ayurveda and TCM is evident in traditional Thai medicine—practitioners of traditional Thai medicine believe in the presence of a basic energy life force that runs throughout an intricate and complex network of energy channels within the human body. *Sên* are acupressure points that are found along these energy lines. The human body is believed to have 72,000 *sên* points, and each has its own specific function. Practitioners of Thai massage only focus on ten, believing that these are sufficient to treat illnesses of every kind, in every part of the body.

Medical systems based on this theory of energy channel and acupoints stress that ill health is the result of an imbalance or disharmony of energies within the body. Consequently, the way to address this is via external stimulation by way of massage or other means. Any blockage of energy along the channels must be removed and an evenly distributed free flow of energy encouraged within the body. This will help restore balance and in turn ensure the well-being of the person.

Many Thais today still apply this belief and seek a massage as a tool for relaxation and disease prevention. Applying appropriate pressure on *sên* points is believed to release the body's natural healing energies and redirect them to areas that need healing. It also promotes blood and lymphatic circulation, helping to eliminate harmful toxins within the body.

... we pray for the one whom we touch,

that he will be happy and that any illness will be released from him.

– Part of the prayer recited by a therapist before a massage

TREATMENTS AND THERAPIES

Thai Massage (Nuat Bo'rarn)

It is only when a masseur performs his 'art' in a meditative mood that he can be considered a truly good practitioner of Thai massage. Traditionally, a Thai massage begins with a meditative prayer called a *puja*. It is recited in the original Pali language and seeks to remind the therapist of the Four Divine States of Mind according to Buddhist teachings: compassion, loving kindness, vicarious joy and mental equanimity. These four states of mind, if attained, help the therapist provide a healing experience for the recipient.

One of the four healing methods in Thai medicine, traditional Thai massage has been practised for over 2,500 years and is based on acupressure points according to Indian Ayurveda and TCM, and yoga. To the uninitiated, a Thai massage is associated with being contorted into all sorts of unimaginable body positions while being painfully kneaded by a therapist at the same time. While it is true that a Thai massage does not seek to relax the body (unlike most Western massages), it still remains popular among both the locals and visitors to Thailand.

Specific anatomical knowledge and massage techniques are not deemed as important as attaining a meditative state of mind. Therapists are taught to focus on their breathing and the purpose of their work they are about to perform, that is, the massage. It is believed that the meditative state they are in can be imparted via their touch to the recipient.

RIGHT: There are generally four positions for a Thai massage: front or prone, back or supine, side and seated. The majority of the massage is received in the front position with a focus on the legs. A massage on the legs is very beneficial for relieving lower back problems.

Thai massage is given very slowly to facilitate the tendency toward mindfulness, so that any resistance or discomfort resulting from a particular yoga position can be quickly detected, thus minimising the risk of injury. The massage is given on a floor mat to allow for the therapist to use his body as leverage and allow for movements otherwise impossible on a table.

During the massage, the therapist uses his hands, thumbs, fingers, elbows, forearms, knees and feet to apply pressure on *sēn* points. He will also pull, twist and manipulate your body in ways that have been compared to 'passive yoga'. All these movements aim to create a smooth energy flow within the body.

Oil or lotions are rarely used and the recipient is advised to wear loose and comfortable clothing. A Thai massage is believed to help loosen joints, stretch muscles and even tone internal organs. Its after-effect should be one of deep relaxation. A typical massage lasts two hours, although it is not uncommon to have one lasting as long as three.

Thai Herbal Wrap

A Thai herbal wrap is different from other wraps in that it uses mineral-rich mud found in many parts of Thailand. A herbal wrap both pampers and moisturises your skin at the same time.

The herbs used are chosen for their natural properties; for instance, turmeric is a natural antioxidant. The ingredients are mixed into a paste and massaged on to your body. A plastic sheet is then used to wrap you for some 20 minutes. Alternatively, strips of cloth are soaked in a herbal solution and then used to wrap your body. It is believed that toxins and other impurities will be removed as you perspire.

The Six Senses Spa at The Evason Hua Hin shares its recipe for the following Thai Herbal Wrap, guaranteed to rejuvenate even the most weary. Adjust the quantities according to your body size. If you are doing the wrap at home, you could leave the herbs on as a mask rather than a wrap for convenience.

THAI HERBAL WRAP

Ingredients	Metric	Imperial	American
Ginger	20 g	1 oz	1 oz
Turmeric	80 g	3 oz	3 oz
Rice	a handful	a handful	a handful
Water	as required	as required	as required

- Ground the ginger and turmeric and mix them with the rice and warm water to make a thick paste. Massage the paste over your body using circular motions. Be sure to pay special attention to the drier areas such as your knees, elbows and feet, or areas with fatty deposits such as the thighs, bottom and upper arms.
- Leave the paste on for 20 min, then rinse off (with a loofah if you prefer) and moisturise.

ABOVE: Fresh ginger is traditionally used in Thai healing treatments—it is believed to moisturise, stimulate circulation and impart warmth to your body.

Scrubs

Traditionally, scrubs and masks are used to exfoliate and nourish the skin and improve circulation. In a Thai spa, natural ingredients are used—the most popular being honey. Harvested in the northern part of Thailand, honey is a natural moisturiser and has traditionally been used to treat open cuts and wounds by encouraging the growth of new skin.

Devarana Spa at The Dusit Thani Hotel has, with the support of Spa of Siam, created the following scrub to promote silky smooth skin. This scrub promises to stimulate circulation, and cleanse, exfoliate and tone even the most sensitive skin. Simple yet effective, it can be easily done at home.

RICE BODY POLISH

Ingredients	Metric	Imperial	American
Rice meal	1 tbsp	1 tbsp	1 tbsp
Ochna	1 tbsp	1 tbsp	1 tbsp
Tamarind paste	3 tsp	3 tsp	3 tsp
Honey	3 tsp	3 tsp	3 tsp
Your choice of body lotion			

- Pound the rice meal using a pestle and mortar to a desired consistency—finer for sensitive skin and coarser for normal skin. Transfer to a bowl and combine all the ingredients (including your favourite body lotion) together to form a paste.
- Apply the polish on your body in light circular motions, paying special attention to your knees, elbows and feet. Rinse off, preferably only with water and no soap, and moisturise.

Thai Herbal Bolus Treatment

In traditional Thai medicine, herbs are used to complement massages that treat illnesses. Herbal *bolus* (pack) treatment, also known as herbal heat revival, is believed to calm nerves and redirect energy vital for health. Typically, a herbal *bolus* consists of herbs and spices that are wrapped tightly in muslin or cotton, and then infused in hot water or steam.

A herbal *bolus* is used in a few ways. Instead of using hands, your therapist may use the *bolus* to apply soothing strokes to massage you. This type of massage is said to be particularly good for muscle aches and pain resulting from excessive sport. Alternatively, the herbal *bolus* may be placed on various parts of your body to relieve sore muscles, stimulate circulation and refresh your skin.

When infused in hot water, the resulting steam from the *bolus* is absorbed by your skin and inhaled. It is believed that toxins are removed from the body via the perspiration caused by the heat. Many Thai women in rural areas still swear by this treatment, which is especially popular as a post-natal therapy.

Many of the ingredients used in a herbal *bolus* are commonly found in our home kitchens. For instance, lemon grass, kiffir lime and turmeric are all common ingredients used in Thai cooking. In particular, lemon grass has both antibacterial and antifungal properties, and its aroma is also a relaxant.

New Asian

ASIA'S PARADIGMS REVAMPED

Many of the therapies known as New Asian are based on traditional oriental healing systems that have been practised throughout history. Often, the founders of these therapies are trained in traditional oriental healing methods which they later modify. Not surprisingly, many New Asian therapies maintain the principle of balance within the body and with nature.

Examples of New Asian therapies include watsu, *marma* point massage and macrobiotics. Watsu is based on shiatsu, *marma* point massage has its origins in Indian Ayurveda (see pp 28–32), and macrobiotics is partly derived from traditional Chinese Medicine (TCM, see pp12–7). The macrobiotics approach recommends a diet based on your *yin-yang* balance and making adjustments to your lifestyle. For instance, you are encouraged to adopt more natural ways of cooking by using gas and wood stoves instead of microwave ovens, and to use products that do not contain toxic ingredients.

Many New Asian therapies combine different traditions within a treatment. So instead of having a strictly Thai or Indonesian massage, you might enjoy a massage that borrows from many different massages—the four-handed massage is one such example. Another form of treatment, equilibropathy, combines acupuncture with stretching and breathing exercises.

TOP: Crystals have been known to calm, relax and heal, and are viewed by some as a doorway to an alternative lifestyle of spiritual growth, natural healing and holistic living.

OPPOSITE: The notions of fitness, wellness and a healthier lifestyle have led to renewed interest in massages and meditation as methods of stress reduction and relaxation.

Those who desire longevity ... should place the utmost faith in the teachings of Ayurveda

– From the Vāgbhata Sūtrāsthana

TREATMENTS AND THERAPIES

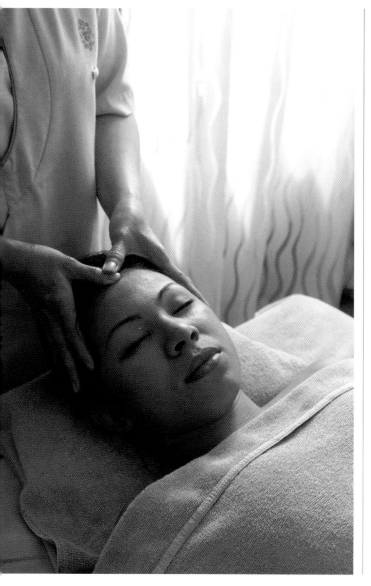

Marma Point Massage

Marma point massage has its origins in Indian Ayurveda, which is the oldest healing system in the world. The use of *marma* points in a massage is based on the belief that the human body contains a basic energy life force (*prana*) which accumulates at numerous energy points or centres. *Marma* means secret, hidden and vital, and *marma* points are essentially vital energy points in the body.

Ancient treatises on Indian Ayurveda states that the human body contains 107 *marma* points, which, when struck or massaged, may either injure or heal. For example, the *lohit*, a *marma* point on the leg, may be massaged to treat paralysis. Conversely, if the same point is struck, it can cause paralysis.

Today the *marma* point massage is most frequently practised in South India. It is believed to work best for *vata* types (see pp30–32), and serves to heal and increase flexibility.

You may get a therapist to do a *marma* point massage on you, or you may do it yourself. A *marma* point massage is done with the thumb or index finger. Beginning with small clockwise circles, the therapist will gradually increase the circular motion and the pressure used. A *marma* point that is believed to be blocked or out of balance will cause some discomfort when massaged. Traditionally, medicated oils made from Ayurvedic herbs were used in the massage; today essential oils such as lavender, eucalyptus or peppermint are used.

LEFT: *Marma* point massages usually focus on the face, neck, scalp and shoulders. It is believed that massaging the *marma* points relieves anxiety, aids hearing and improves your vision.

OPPOSITE: The four-handed massage is one of the most luxurious massages offered at spas today. It has been likened to a choreographed dance, where the masseurs work in perfect coordination.

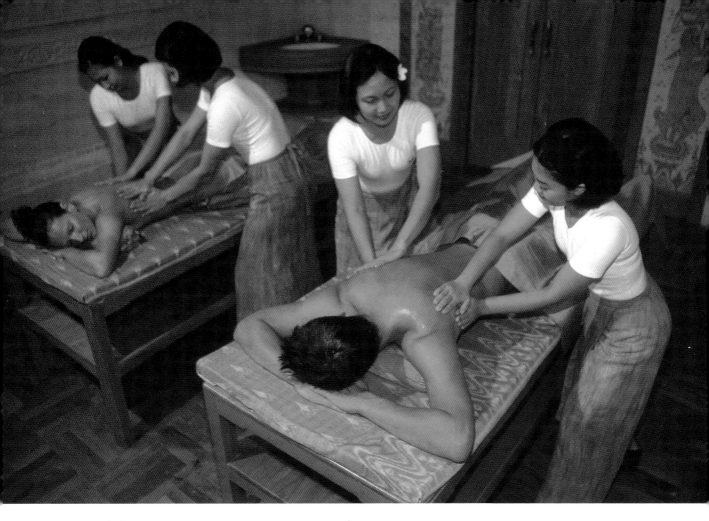

Four-handed Massage

If there's anything that doubles the pleasure of a massage, it's having two therapists massaging you simultaneously. When they are perfectly synchronised, the effect is that of a massage by one therapist with two pairs of hands. To help achieve this effect, many spas try to partner therapists who match each other in terms of physique and disposition.

The four-handed massage is believed to have originated from Hawaii's Lomi Lomi (see p84). The first therapist is also called the lead therapist or 'mother' while the second therapist acts as a 'mirror' of the mother. The presence of the second therapist is discreet—he or she may enter the room only after the first has invited you to lie face down on the bed.

Traditionally, a four-handed massage might comprise an Ayurvedic massage performed simultaneously by two therapists. Modern four-handed massages are more likely to blend Eastern and Western techniques. For instance, one of the most famous four-handed massages, the Mandara Massage, uses a blend of shiatsu (see pp56–7), traditional Thai massage (see p67), Indonesian massage (see pp48–9), Swedish massage (see p82) and Hawaiian Lomi Lomi (see p84) styles with aromatherapy oils (see pp80–1).

In a Mandara massage, the therapists stand on either side of your body and begin by placing their palms together over you—this is called 'balancing' and serves to synchronise their energies. Next, each therapist places one hand below the shoulder blade and the other above the hipbone, and with synchronised breathing, simultaneously stretch your upper body. They do the same with the lower body, with one hand at the heel and the other below the hipbone. After these stretching movements, the massage begins with one therapist at your feet and one at your head. Throughout the massage, their smooth movements along the length of your body create the illusion of one therapist rather than two.

Watsu is as unlimited as the water it is done in ... the relaxing effects of warm water and the therapeutic nature of Watsu's moves and stretches create a bodywork modality of extraordinary depth which has both specific therapeutic results and healing on many levels.

– Harold Dull, founder of Watsu

Watsu

Watsu, derived from the words 'water' and 'shiatsu', is a water-based form of shiatsu—a Japanese massage that balances and stimulates energy flow in the meridians (see pp56–7).

Devised by Harold Dull in 1980, watsu is essentially shiatsu conducted in chest-high warm water. After training in the techniques of shiatsu in Japan, Dull had returned to his home in California where he began conducting the first watsu sessions in hot springs.

Watsu is more than just a massage in water—it also involves gentle cradling and exercises. Because it is carried out in water, you will enjoy greater flexibility and be able to move into different massage positions that might have been virtually impossible had the massage been done on a floormat or a bed. The water also serves to support your body weight as you lie floating on your back. Indeed being in water has the effect of 'reducing' your body weight by as much as 90 per cent, which in turn eases pressure on the spine. Exercising in water is also beneficial as the buoyancy effect of the water protects your joints from injury while the water pressure creates resistance, making your muscles work harder.

Watsu is particularly suitable for pregnant women and people suffering from muscular dysfunction and joint problems such as arthritis. Today, teachers and practitioners of watsu can be found in many countries and are certified by the Worldwide Aquatic Bodywork Association.

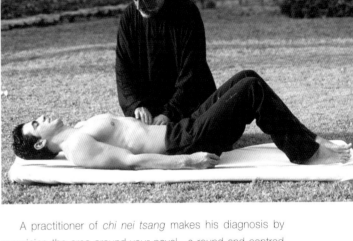

Chi Nei Tsang

Chi nei tsang—*chi* (or *qi*) meaning energy and information and *nei tsang* meaning viscera or internal organs—roughly translates into 'working the energy and programming of the internal organs'. It is a term loosely used to describe a massage that is concentrated on the abdominal area, called *tan tien* in Chinese, and is also sometimes called an 'internal organ massage'. *Chi nei tsang* was developed by Chinese Daoist monks in mountain monasteries a long time ago as a method by which they sought to detoxify, strengthen and refine their bodies to attain the highest levels of spiritual practices.

Chi nei tsang is based on the belief that the abdominal area, specifically the lower abdomen around the navel, is the structural centre of gravity of the body and also the centre for metabolic processes such as digestion, detoxification and energy processing. The *tan tien* is also where stress, tension and negative emotions accumulate and congest, leading to a blockage of the body's energy, and consequently a weakening of the internal organs. Most importantly, it is the body's centre of energy, where vital energy sustaining life originates. Whereas other massages work from the periphery of the body towards the centre, *chi nei tsang* does the opposite, working from the centre to affect other areas of the body.

A practitioner of *chi nei tsang* makes his diagnosis by examining the area around your navel—a round and centred navel is considered ideal. Among the things he notes are the quality of the skin around the navel, whether it is thick, thin, hard or soft, and how its shape changes as he lightly pushes or pulls the area clockwise and counterclockwise.

Focusing on the abdominal area alone, *chi nei tsang* is said to bring about healing from within. It detoxifies, improves circulation, stimulates the lymphatic system and eliminates toxins. The massage also addresses visceral structures and the positioning of internal organs. In particular, it is believed to help correct misalignment of the feet, legs and pelvis, and relieve chronic pain in the back, neck and shoulders. Emotions are 'balanced' as negative emotions believed to be stored in the digestive system are channelled away.

OPPOSITE: Watsu is sometimes conducted with a partner, described as a giver, rather than with a therapist. The gentling cradling and exercises involved have been said to stimulate the feeling of being in your mother's womb, and hence evoke a sense of security and warmth.

ABOVE RIGHT: Providing a suitable environment for healing is important in *chi nei tsang* as it is believed to facilitate the healing process.

RIGHT: *Chi nei tsang* is mostly done with the thumbs and forefingers although the elbow may sometimes be used.

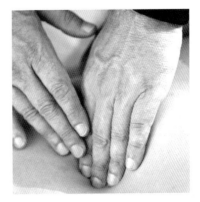

Consciously or unconsciously, every being is capable of healing himself or others.

– Inayat Khan

Equilibropathy (Dullayaphap Bumbud)

A therapy that combines principles of traditional oriental healing systems with modern medical science, equilibropathy (*dullayaphap bumbud*), devised by Dr Taworn Kasomson, M.D., aims to balance the body, mind and spirit.

In equilibropathy, a diagnosis is made from an examination of your spine and associated muscle groups along the spine. Through look and touch, the practitioner detects both symptomatic and asymptomatic problems and determines their causes and effects. Next he uses acupuncture to ease muscle tension and, more importantly, to clear any blockage of energy within the body. This is believed to improve circulation as well as nerve signal transmission in the body.

Equilibropathy also includes breathing, balancing and stretching exercises. Instruction on maintaining proper posture is also given, as it is believed that proper posture will prevent the body from going further out of balance. Regular practise of these exercises is recommended to maintain health and improve the body's own natural healing capabilities.

Macrobiotics

The term 'macrobiotics' comes from the Greek word *markos,* meaning long or big, and *bios,* meaning life. Macrobiotics is more a way of life than a therapy, and is based on the view that we are the products of and are continually influenced by our environment. It is often used with both conventional and alternative medical treatments.

Proper dietary and lifestyle habits are of utmost importance. Every individual is believed to have a personal tendency towards *yin* or *yang.* If you're more of a *yin* person, then consuming *yang* foods will help address any imbalance and thus help you achieve harmony with the environment. Organic foods are highly recommended while processed and treated food are to be avoided. Ideally, a macrobiotic diet should comprise mainly brown rice and whole grains. Fresh beans and vegetables are to be included while meat, dairy products and other items are to be taken in moderation or completely avoided. A complete macrobiotic approach to diet extends even to the way food is prepared—traditional gas or wood stoves are preferred over microwave ovens; earthenware or stainless steel cookware are preferred over aluminium or teflon-coated pots and pans.

Other basic macrobiotic practices include regular exercise, using products made from natural, non-toxic ingredients, and maintaining a positive outlook on life.

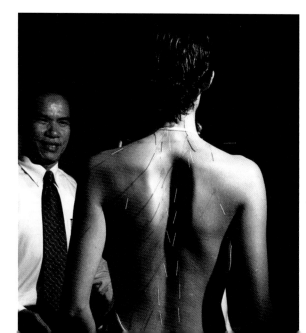

LEFT: Equilibropathy has been used to treat medical conditions such as asthma, migraine, sinus congestion and any others in which there is lowered immunity.

OPPOSITE (CLOCKWISE FROM TOP LEFT): According to *yin-yang* theory, foods can be classified into four categories: very yin, moderately yin, moderately yang and very yang.

Cosmopolitan

A KALEIDOSCOPE OF INTERNATIONAL CURES

 he word 'spa' literally means *'solus per aqua'* or 'health by water'. It is taken from the town of Spa in Belgium, which was one of the first places to recognise the healing properties of mineral-rich water. Hippocrates, father of Western Medicine, was an advocate of regular bathing and other water applications to strengthen the constitution and treat medical complaints. In addition, many early healthcare systems also viewed water as the basis of health. For instance, the ancient Egyptians believed water had both physical and sacred properties. In traditional Chinese medicine, water is central to restoring harmony within the person as it is the carrier of *qi* (life energy). Similarly in Indian Ayurveda, water is a medium by which *prana* (life force) travels within the human body.

Hippocrates was also a firm advocate of massage as a healing technique. Some of the greatest Western physicians, including Celsus and Galen, recommended using massages as therapy and to prevent illness. Another famed physician, Avicenna (AD 980–1037), also wrote about massage in his Canon of Medicine, a work considered the authoritative medical text in Europe for several centuries.

Today the term spa is used to refer to a place you visit to relax, recharge and refresh yourself. A spa treatment almost always involves water, in the form of thalassotherapy, flotation or even a simple floral bath, and includes a massage. Given that an estimated 85 per cent of all illnesses are stress-induced, massage is increasingly utilised both as a preventive and therapeutic treatment, to combat the effects of stress as well as to increase relaxation.

TOP: Making herbal medicine in ancient Egypt in the 4th century BC. A large alabaster pot is first filled with flowers, herbs and water, and then heated. The aromatic vapour saturates the animal skin that is stretched across the pot. The skin is later squeezed as shown to obtain herbal medicine. A similar method is also used to make perfume.

OPPOSITE: A Greek stone relief from the 4th century BC showing the physician Aesculapius treating a patient's arm injury by 'rubbing' (the ancient Greeks and Romans referred to massage as rubbing) as recommended by Hippocrates.

Volatile essences have healed people since the dawn of time ...

– René-Maurice Gattefossé

TREATMENTS AND THERAPIES

Aromatherapy

The properties of aromatic plants have been recognised and used for health purposes for many centuries. The Egyptians in particular, have a rich history of using aromatic plants—for instance as perfumes and to embalm their dead. Furthermore, Imhotep, the Egyptian God of Medicine, is said to have recommended fragrant oils for bathing and massaging.

Much of aromatherapy as we know it today began with René-Maurice Gattefossé, a French chemist. In 1910, a laboratory explosion caused his hands to be badly burnt. After immersing his hands in lavender oil, he found the oil not only healed his hands quickly, but also left it without scar or infection. Following the incident he devoted his life to the study of essential oils, and is credited with coining the term 'aromatherapy', which literally means 'therapy through aroma or scent'. However, research on aromatherapy waned until World War II when a French doctor, Dr Jean Valnet, recognised the antibiotic and healing properties of essential oils when treating injured soldiers. He later documented his findings in his book, *Aromathérapie*.

In the late 1950s, Madame Marguerite Maury introduced the use of aromatics in massages. Trained as a biochemist, she was unable to dispense essential oils as medicine and so sought a way to use them for therapeutic and cosmetic benefits.

Today, aromatherapy is used in many different ways although essential oils remain the basis for all traditional aromatherapy. Essential oils, which are aromatic essences extracted from plants, flowers, trees, fruit, bark, grasses and seeds, are believed to contain therapeutic, psychological and physiological properties. These properties are mostly antiseptic, with other properties being antiviral, anti-inflammatory, pain-relieving, anti-depressant and expectorant.

About 150 essential oils have been identified thus far. They may be inhaled, used in massages or added to baths. Depending on what is needed, an aromatherapist may select an essential oil or blend a few for use. For instance, muscle pain may be caused by stress or some other mental pressure. In such a case, the blend of essential oils created should relieve not only the muscle pain, but also the stress.

ESSENTIAL OIL	USES
Lavender	For stress-related disorders such as nervousness, insomnia, depression and skin complaints
Tea Tree	Has anti-viral, antiseptic, fungicidal and immune-stimulant properties. Also good for skin complaints such as acne, rashes, dandruff as well as respiratory disorders such as asthma, bronchitis and sinusitis
Rosemary	Has stimulant properties, particularly to the central nervous system, helps strengthen mental clarity and aid concentration. Also an expectorant and a tonic to the entire system
Roman Chamomile	A mild relaxant and anti-inflammatory agent, good for stomach, intestinal or menstrual problems and headaches. Also especially suitable for children
Peppermint	For digestive complaints such as nausea or indigestion, for respiratory problems and for treating colds, flu and fevers

A maximum of three oils in a blend is recommended lest the individual qualities of the oils are lost. Because essential oils are highly concentrated and extremely volatile, they are usually diluted with base oils such as almond, walnut or evening primrose oil. This inhibits the evaporation of the essential oil and encourages better absorption into the skin.

While it takes a skilled aromatherapist to truly understand the properties of essential oils, it is generally possible to treat common ailments using only up to five oils (see table opposite). However, essential oils must never be taken internally except on the advice of a trained physician. Because of its relative ease of use, aromatherapy is one of the fastest-growing fields in complementary medicine and is widely used for pain relief.

Inhalation: There are several ways in which essential oils may be inhaled. You could add a few drops of essential oil to a handkerchief and directly inhale its vapour, or add a few drops on to your pillow before sleeping to combat insomnia.

Steam inhalation is another method commonly used. Using water as a medium, add a few drops of essential oil to a shallow tub of hot water. Place a towel over your head and breathe deeply. Although highly effective for treating respiratory problems such as congested sinus, throat and chest infections, steam inhalation is not recommended for asthmatics.

Inhalation is an effective form of aromatherapy as essential oils are extremely volatile and are easily absorbed into the blood stream via the lungs and the nose. The vapour travels to the limbic system of the brain, which is the area of the brain responsible for the integration and expression of feelings, learning, memory, and physical drives. Each essential oil may contain as many as 100 chemical components, which when combined together, exert a strong effect. It is still not yet known exactly how essential oils work, but what is certain is that they affect our minds and emotions and leave no harmful residue.

Aromatherapy Massage: Before an essential oil can be used as massage oil, it must first be diluted with a base oil. Care must be taken to maintain a correct proportion of oils, for the concentration differs according to the purpose for which the oils are used and the condition of the recipient. For instance, pregnant women and those with sensitive skin should only use diluted oils. More concentrated oils would be required for complaints of a physical nature such as muscle aches as compared to emotional complaints.

In an aromatherapy massage, the essential oil is absorbed through the skin and carried to the muscle tissue, joints and organs. However, the main effect of the oil still lies in its scent.

OPPOSITE: Steam inhalation is used in facials and saunas—for instance, adding tea tree oil to the water can help unblock pores and clear the complexion of blemishes.

ABOVE: An aromatherapy massage is essentially a lymphatic massage that uses essential oils to stimulate blood flow and lymph fluid.

The physician must be experienced in many things, but assuredly also in rubbing ...

For rubbing can bind a joint which is too loose and loosen a joint that is too hard.

– Hippocrates, father of Western Medicine

Swedish Massage

The most popular of all traditional European massages, the Swedish massage is probably the most widely practised massage in Western countries. It was introduced by Per Henrik Ling (1776–1839) in the 1700s, who merged Western and Eastern healing techniques and exercises to form what has been long thought of as the first organised and systematic method of modern therapeutic massage in the Western world.

Generally a Swedish massage uses five main strokes, all of which are done on the more superficial layers of the muscles and generally in the direction of the blood flow toward the heart.

Effleurage or 'touching lightly' comprises long gliding strokes from the neck to the base of the spine, or from the shoulder to the fingertips. Done with the entire hand or the thumb pads, these strokes help the therapist examine the texture and quality of your muscle tissues and also relax them.

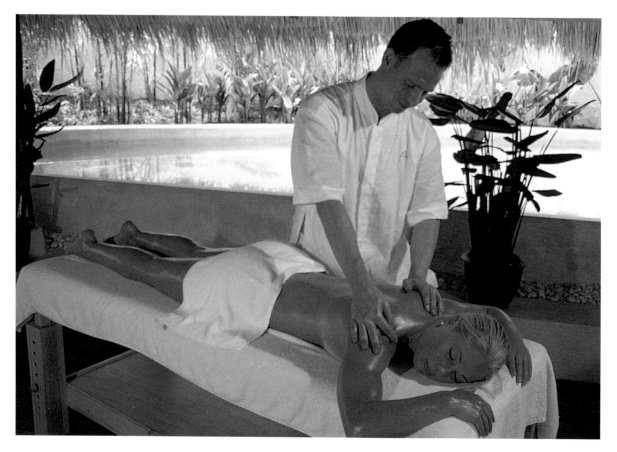

LEFT: It is said that the Swedish massage was developed by Per Henrik Ling in his bid to cure himself of rheumatism, which had been crippling him for many years.

Pétrissage or 'kneading' follows effleurage, and involves the therapist kneading, rolling or squeezing the muscles to encourage deeper circulation in the veins and lymph vessels. This stroke is believed to remove toxins from the muscles and bring nutrients to cells to aid growth and repair.

The next stroke, friction or 'rubbing', is applied near joints and other bony areas and is used to break down adhesions— knots of muscle fibres formed after any muscular trauma or strain. It consists of deep circular or transverse movements made with the thumb pads or fingertips.

In the fourth stroke, tapotement or 'tapping', the therapist taps the muscles to release tension and cramping. The stroke is applied with the edge of the hand, tips of the fingers or with a closed fist. If done correctly, this stroke first invigorates the muscles, then relaxes them. An important use of this stroke is to stimulate circulation in an area of atrophy.

Vibration or 'shaking' is done at the end of the massage and is not considered a stroke by some. Basically it entails the therapist pressing his hands on your back or limbs and rapidly shaking them for a few seconds. This stroke is particularly helpful for relieving lower-back pain.

Oil, lotion or baby powder is used as a lubricant to facilitate the massage strokes. A typical Swedish massage lasts 30 minutes to an hour, although the massage is usually shorter for children, the elderly and the ill.

Lymphatic Massage

The lymphatic massage was first developed as a treatment for lymphedema disease. The lymph, a milky fluid in which our organs and muscles are bathed, delivers nutrients, antibodies and other immune constituents to the tissue cells and drains impurities and wastes away. These wastes are a by-product of metabolism and are normally drained by muscular contractions when we exercise. A lymphatic massage not only serves to stimulate the movement of lymph, but also helps to strengthen our immune system. Of late, it has also become increasingly popular to use a lymphatic massage for cosmetic benefits—it is believed the massage gets rid of stretch marks.

Sports Massage

Developed only in the recent years, the sports massage is essentially a form of Swedish massage which specially caters to athletes. It is used before, during or after events to enhance an athlete's performance, as part of an athlete's training regime or to speed up recovery from injuries.

Generally, a sports massage is slow and thorough; the therapist begins with superficial strokes to identify any problem areas and detect overused muscles, the most common cause of sports injuries. These muscles are hard and tense compared to the surrounding tissues. A sports massage is usually given through clothing and lasts 30 minutes to an hour.

OPPOSITE: Like most massages, the Swedish massage aims to improve circulation, relieve muscle tension and induce general relaxation. It is also believed to shorten recovery time from muscular strain.

RIGHT: The sports massage generally focuses on muscles relevant to the particular athletic activity so as to prevent injury. The optimal frequency for a sports massage is once a week.

The way to health is a scented bath and an oil massage every day.

– Hippocrates, in the 5th century BC

Lomi Lomi

Also known as a 'temple style' massage because it used to be performed only in temples, the Lomi Lomi is in fact more than a massage—it is a way of healing that has its roots in ancient Hawaiian traditions. A traditional Lomi Lomi session comprises prayer, fasting and a massage. Traditional Hawaiian healers believed that illness is the result of suppressed emotions, mental disturbances, spiritual disharmony and tension brought about by blocked energy within the body. Thus, restoring health involves physical, emotional and mental healing.

Today a Lomi Lomi session is more associated with a massage, done either by one therapist or two in perfect synchronisation. The massage focuses on dispersing energy blockages by way of moving the palms, thumbs, knuckles and forearms in rhythmic, dance-like motions.

The massage has both physical and emotional benefits. It is believed to improve circulation, increase the rate of nutrients brought to the muscles, stimulate the lymphatic system to drain waste products and is especially useful to aid recovery from injuries to the ligaments and tendons. On the emotional front, a Lomi Lomi massage is believed to release you from any anxiety, worry, fear and other negative thoughts.

Warm Stone Massage

Also known as hot stone massage or *la stone* therapy, the warm stone massage entails the use of smooth warm stones in long, flowing strokes on your body. The stones are also placed on strategic energy points to ease away tension. These warm stones may also be used in Swedish massages, Lomi Lomi and other traditional massages.

In ancient times, the Hawaiians used lava stones in the Lomi Lomi, believing that the heat emitted by the stones would warm the body, relax the muscles and soothe the soul. These smooth volcanic rocks are naturally plentiful in Hawaii and they are believed to enhance therapeutic treatments.

In a variation of the warm stone massage, *la stone* therapy uses smooth stones in contrasting temperatures. The contrast between heat and cold is believed to stimulate relaxation and deep circulation, which will, in turn, stimulate the lymphatic system to detoxify the body. These smooth stones are massaged on the body as in the Lomi Lomi, and are also placed on, under and around strategic points on the body. Typically lasting 90 minutes, the *la stone* therapy begins with heated stones to relax and relieve muscle tension, followed by cool stones to strengthen the immune system and induce relaxation.

LEFT: The *kahuna* Lomi Lomi, revered masters of healing massages, believed that our bodies come from our thoughts, which contain *mana* (energy). As pain and tension is massaged away, it will become easier for us to choose patterns of thinking that will lead to healthier bodies.

OPPOSITE: Massage oil is sometimes used to facilitate movement of the stones against your body. Following the massage, the warm stones are placed on energy points.

LEFT: Because your body is freed from gravitational forces by the buoyancy of water, your muscles can fully relax, allowing for deep relaxation.

Flotation

Flotation is a treatment not recommended if you are claustrophobic or lygophobic (afraid of the dark), for it involves floating in an enclosed tank or pool of water about 25 centimetres/ 10 inches deep in complete darkness or very little light. A two-hour flotation session is equivalent to eight hours of deep sleep.

The first flotation tank was designed in the 1950s by Dr John C Lilly, an American neuro-physiologist and psychoanalyst who wanted to prove that neural activity ceases in the absence of external stimuli. Contrary to his belief, Dr Lilly found that the brain functioned at a higher level than normal in the absence of external stimuli.

Today flotation tanks can be found in spas, bio-fitness institutes as well as hospitals. Each tank contains some 800 pounds of Epsom salts to make the water buoyant. The water is heated to an average skin temperature of 34°C/93.5°F to reduce the sensation between body and water. Fresh air circulates inside the tank, and for those who fear solitude and absolute silence, soft soothing music can be played during the session. There is also an intercom system which allows you to speak with your therapist at any time of the treatment.

Before a flotation session, eat only a light meal as digestive discomforts could interfere with the floating experience. Avoid stimulants such as caffeine and alcohol, and cover all cuts and scratches with lotion. After a session, drink lots of water to rehydrate yourself as Epsom salts are strong detoxifiers.

A flotation experience is said to heighten awareness of your senses and emotions. It is best for relieving chronic pain such as arthritis, headaches and back pains, and is also often used to enhance meditation. The effects can last from a few hours to a few days, and are prolonged with subsequent sessions. Flotation is not recommended for people who suffer from epilepsy, schizophrenia, kidney conditions or skin disorders.

The sea heals man's illnesses.

– Euripides, 480 BC

Thalassotherapy

The word *'thalassa'* is Greek for sea. What distinguishes thalassotherapy from other forms of therapy is its use of seawater and seaweed. The French have been practising thalassotherapy for over a century on their Atlantic coast; the Egyptians used seawater and seaweed to heal skin burns while the ancient Greeks sought hot seawater as a cure for all ills.

Commonly found in European spas, thalassotherapy is now available in Asian spas such as Thalasso Bali in Indonesia. It is believed to relieve allergies, and lift depression and irritability.

Minerals found in seawater, in particular salts, are believed to have innate healing properties as a result of having come into contact with beneficial substances. These minerals are believed to be absorbed through the skin, so rather than using his hands to massage you, your therapist might spray jets of seawater at you while you stand in a shower. Alternatively, you could sit in a whirlpool and be lifted or sucked by the water, or soak in a bath of warm seawater.

There are also minerals found in seaweed, for example, iodine, which encourages perspiration and thus the removal of toxins from the body. Seaweed is often used in body wraps as it helps to cleanse and tone the skin. It is also used in other ways in thalassotherapy—it can be added to a bath (also known as a kelp bath) or used as a poultice on specific areas of the body to soothe aches and pains.

Even the air above seawater is said to be beneficial—it contains a greater proportion of negative ions compared to air over land. These ions help reduce the levels of histamines which are produced during allergic reactions. Fresh sea air also supposedly stimulates the immune system and helps you combat modern-day stresses and strains.

Instead of heading to a spa for a thalassotherapy massage, some spa-goers have invested in jacuzzis, which are believed to achieve similar effects. Home thalassotherapy kits are also available in the form of lotions to add to your bath, seaweed wraps and kelp extract tablets to be taken. Alternatively, you could make your own salt scrub to try at home. The following is one such example from Thalasso Bali in Indonesia.

THALASSO BALI SALT SCRUB

Ingredients	Metric	Imperial	American
Beach sand	50 g	2 oz	2 oz
Coarse sea salt	10 g	½ oz	½ oz
Unscented base cream	15 g	½ oz	½ oz
Water	4 tsp	4 tsp	4 tsp
Your choice of aromatherapy oil	5–10 drops	5–10 drops	5–10 drops

- Grind the beach sand and sea salt into a rough powder. Add the base cream and stir until it is well-mixed. The resulting mixture should look somewhat crumbly.
- Add 5–10 drops of your favourite aromatherapy oil to the mixture. Lastly, add the water and mix it in thoroughly.
- Apply the mixture generously over your body (excluding your face) in circular motions until the scrub begins to crumble off your skin. Rinse off with warm water and moisturise.

FAR LEFT: Jets of seawater are sometimes sprayed on specific parts of the body to relief pain

LEFT: Thalassotherapy products range from lotions to soaps and mud scrubs.

ABOVE: As with most massages, a thalassotherapy massage boosts blood circulation and relaxes your muscles.

Spa Cuisine

The Asian love for food and attention to well-being come together in spa cuisine—meals that are low-fat, low-salt and low-cholesterol, but rich in taste. Spa cuisine is well-balanced and designed to be easily digested while providing your body with an optimum amount of energy, and encouraging a healthier way of eating and living.

Many spas provide calorie, protein, carbohydrate and fat counts, and cater to special dietary requests. Some use organic produce, often with herbs and vegetables from their own gardens.

In the following pages, chefs from top Asian spas and restaurants share their recipes for you to try out in your own kitchen.

The Chinese Kitchen

BALANCING YIN-YANG AND QI

hinese food varies widely even in China itself. However, an ideal Chinese meal remains one that balances the elements of *yin, yang* and *qi. Yin* and *yang* are broadly described as two opposites of a central life force, and these opposites extend to food as well: certain foods have a cooling effect on the human body—*yin*; while other foods have a warming effect—*yang*. For instance, bamboo shoots and cucumbers are considered *yin* foods, while chicken and ginger are considered *yang* foods. In between are the so-called 'neutral' foods such as white rice. As healthy individuals tend to have a tendency toward *yin* or *yang*, a balanced meal can serve to either correct an existing imbalance or maintain the balance already present in the body.

A balanced meal is also believed to strengthen and balance your *qi* (see pp15–6). The Chinese believe that foods have a directional effect on the *qi*. A specific direction might be needed when you are ill: for instance, an outward energy flow can help reduce a fever by encouraging perspiration.

The Hilton Shanghai shares with us some of its recipes for a healthy Chinese meal. These dishes contain a blend of *yin* and *yang* ingredients and herbs such as *mai dong, dang gui* (Chinese angelica) and *ren shen* (ginseng). Chinese angelica and ginseng are both commonly found in tonic remedies— Chinese angelica is believed to nourish the blood and stimulate the liver while ginseng, a potent *qi* tonic, combats fatigue and is especially beneficial to the lungs, spleen and heart.

CHINESE VEGETABLE SALAD

Serves 4 • 59.3 Calories per serving • Protein 1.5 g • Carbohydrate 6.1 g • Fat 3.5 g

INGREDIENTS	Metric	Imperial	American
Vegetable Salad			
Bamboo shoots, finely cut	10 g	⅜ oz	⅜ oz
Bean curd sheets, finely cut	10 g	⅜ oz	⅜ oz
Bean sprouts, finely cut	10 g	⅜ oz	⅜ oz
Black fungi, finely cut	10 g	⅜ oz	⅜ oz
Carrots, finely cut	10 g	⅜ oz	⅜ oz
Celery, finely cut	10 g	⅜ oz	⅜ oz
Chinese celery, finely cut	10 g	⅜ oz	⅜ oz
Coriander leaves	10 g	⅜ oz	⅜ oz
Cucumber, finely cut	10 g	⅜ oz	⅜ oz
Dried fried bean curd, finely cut	10 g	⅜ oz	⅜ oz
Enoki mushrooms, finely cut	10 g	⅜ oz	⅜ oz
Green capsicum, finely cut	10 g	⅜ oz	⅜ oz
Red capsicum, finely cut	10 g	⅜ oz	⅜ oz
Preserved radish, finely cut	10 g	⅜ oz	⅜ oz
Preserved Chinese cabbage, finely cut	10 g	⅜ oz	⅜ oz
Snow peas	10 g	⅜ oz	⅜ oz
Turnip, finely cut	10 g	⅜ oz	⅜ oz

INGREDIENTS	Metric	Imperial	American
Seasoning			
Powdered chicken stock	½ tsp	½ tsp	½ tsp
Olive oil	2 tsp	2 tsp	2 tsp
Sesame oil	½ tsp	½ tsp	½ tsp
Salt	½ tsp	½ tsp	½ tsp
Sugar	½ tsp	½ tsp	½ tsp

PREPARATION

- Except for the snow peas and coriander leaves, cut all the vegetables into thin strips. Bring a pot of hot water to the boil and blanch the vegetables over medium heat for 3 min. Scoop out the vegetables, drain, and put into a mixing bowl. Place the mixing bowl with the vegetables into a basin of hot water. Then add the seasoning and toss until the vegetables are evenly coated.

- Let the salad cool, then chill it in a refrigerator before serving.

DOUBLE-BOILED GUINEA FOWL SOUP
WITH AMERICAN GINSENG AND CHINESE HERBS

Serves 4 • 116.2 Calories per serving • Protein 13.7 g • Carbohydrate 0.5 g • Fat 6.3 g

INGREDIENTS	Metric	Imperial	American
Supreme Soup			
Chicken	½	½	½
Air-dried ham	750 g	1 lb 10 oz	1 lb 10 oz
Beef	1 kg	2 lb 3 oz	2 lb 3 oz
Lean pork	2 kg	4 lb 6½ oz	4 lb 6½ oz
Dried longans	50 g	2 oz	2 oz
White peppercorns	50 g	2 oz	2 oz
Water	15.2 litres	4 gal	4 gal
Ginger, sliced	100 g	3½ oz	3½ oz
Spring onions, sliced	100 g	3½ oz	3½ oz
crosswise into quarters			
Salt	to taste	to taste	to taste
Double-boiled Guinea Fowl			
Guinea fowl	1	1	1
American ginseng	20 g	¾ oz	¾ oz
Mai dong (Chinese herb)	20 g	¾ oz	¾ oz
Supreme soup	3 litres	6 pts 5 fl oz	12½ cups
Seasoning			
Powdered chicken stock	½ tsp	½ tsp	½ tsp
Salt	½ tsp	½ tsp	½ tsp

PREPARATION
Supreme Soup

- Wash the chicken under cold running water. Put the chicken breast side down in a large saucepan together with the ham, beef, pork, longans and peppercorns, and cover generously with cold water. Bring the water to the boil over moderate heat.
- Skim the top layer off the stock and add the ginger, spring onions and salt. Then half-cover the pan. Turn the heat down to low and leave the stock to simmer for 7 to 8 hr.
- Turn the chicken over from time to time and continue to skim the top layer off the surface.
- Remove the chicken, then boil the stock for 30 min to reduce and concentrate it slightly. Strain the stock through a muslin-lined sieve and leave to cool.
- Refrigerate overnight. Skim the top layer off before using.

Double-boiled Guinea Fowl

- Remove the internal organs of the guinea fowl, trim off the fat and wash thoroughly. Cut the fowl into small pieces and blanch in boiling water for 5 min. Remove the fowl, then rinse and drain.
- Put the fowl into the steamer, add the American ginseng, *mai dong* and supreme soup. Cover the steamer and double-boil the soup for 4 hr before serving.

STIR-FRIED SHRIMPS WITH HONEY BEANS, FRESH LILY BULBS, FRESH GINSENG AND CHINESE WOLFBERRIES

Serves 4 • 75.2 Calories per serving • Protein 7.1 g • Carbohydrate 12.1 g • Fat 0.7 g

INGREDIENTS	Metric	Imperial	American
Chinese wolfberries	2 tbsp	2 tbsp	2 tbsp
Fresh ginseng, sliced	30 g	1 oz	1 oz
Fresh lily bulbs	200 g	7 oz	2½ cups
Honey beans	250 g	9 oz	9 cups
Shrimp, shelled and deveined	300 g	10½ oz	10½ oz
Water	as required	as required	as required
Seasoning			
Salad oil	2 tsp	2 tsp	2 tsp
Salt	½ tsp	½ tsp	½ tsp
Sugar	1 tsp	1 tsp	1 tsp

PREPARATION

- Bring a pot of water to the boil and add a little oil, salt and sugar. Blanch the Chinese wolfberries, ginseng, lily bulbs and honey beans for less than 1 min. Drain and put aside.
- Boil the shrimp, drain and put aside.
- Heat some oil in a wok, then stir-fry everything.

DOUBLE-BOILED SWEETENED SNOW FROG JELLY AND ALOE VERA IN COCONUT SHELL

Serves 4 • 253.6 Calories per serving • Protein 1.7 g • Carbohydrate 25.7 g • Fat 17.2 g

INGREDIENTS	Metric	Imperial	American
Coconut	1	1	1
Aloe vera	100 g	3½ oz	3½ cups
Snow frog jelly	100 g	3½ oz	3½ cups
Coconut milk	1 tsp	1 tsp	1 tsp
Sugar water	240 ml	8 fl oz	1 cup

PREPARATION

- Slice open the top of the coconut, wash and drain for later use.
- Blanch the aloe vera and snow frog jelly for 1 min. Remove and rinse before transferring into the coconut shell.
- Add coconut milk and sugar water to the mixture, stir and serve.

GINSENG SODA

Serves 4 • 174.1 Calories per serving • Protein 0 g • Carbohydrate 44 g • Fat 0 g

INGREDIENTS	Metric	Imperial	American
American ginseng	25 g	1 oz	1 oz
Water	30 ml	1 fl oz	⅛ cup
Angelica root	25 g	1 oz	1 oz
Honey	1 tsp	1 tsp	1 tsp
Chilled club soda	1 can	1 can	1 can
Ice (optional)	as required	as required	as required

PREPARATION

- Slice the ginseng diagonally. Add water to the ginseng and Angelica root and bring the mixture to the boil. Leave it to boil until it reduces by half.
- Strain the concentrate to remove any residue.
- Mix the concentrate with honey and top with chilled club soda. Serve with or without ice and garnish with a few fruit slices.

The Indian Kitchen

SPICE DELIGHT

Indian cuisine is well-known for its rich curries, *dals* (lentil preparations that accompany nearly every meal), breads and especially for its generous use of spices. The ability of an Indian chef to blend and use his spices well, be it to tenderise, colour or enhance the flavour of his dish, is a measure of his skills.

Ayurvedic texts dating back some 3,000 years recorded the use of spices for their curative properties. Since then, spices have also been used to preserve food, aid digestion and balance the tastes and properties of food. For instance, it is believed that garlic lowers cholesterol levels and hypertension, turmeric provides relief from stomach ulcers and ginger aids digestion.

Spices are also blended to give what is more commonly known as *masala*, literally a blend of several spices. *Garam masala* (hot *masala)* is the most important and is considered essential to Indian cuisine, although the blend differs from region to region.

The Ananda-In the Himalayas has its own herb garden to ensure a steady supply of rare herbs and spices and its spa cuisine is centred around locally available fresh organic produce. Organic brown rice, baby potatoes or whole-wheat pastas are served as staples. A wide range of soya products such as soya yogurt and tofu, along with organic mountain lentils fulfil the protein requirements of vegetarians. *Jhangora*, a mountain grain known for its therapeutic properties, is used in desserts and main courses.

TANDOORI LOTUS STEM

Serves 4 • 75 Calories per serving • Protein 3 g • Carbohydrate 17 g • Fat 0 g

INGREDIENTS	Metric	Imperial	American
Kuchumber Salad			
Lime	1	1	1
Beet	20 g	¾ oz	¾ oz
Onion	20 g	¾ oz	¾ oz
Radish	20 g	¾ oz	¾ oz
Carrot	20 g	¾ oz	¾ oz
Chaat masala	1 tsp	1 tsp	1 tsp
Tandoori Lotus Stem			
Lotus stem, peeled	400 g	14 oz	14 oz
Turmeric powder	½ tsp	½ tsp	½ tsp
Water	1 litre	2 pts 2 fl oz	4 cups
Soya yogurt	60 ml	2 fl oz	¼ cup
White pepper powder	1½ tsp	1½ tsp	1½ tsp
Garam masala	1½ tsp	1½ tsp	1½ tsp
Lime juice	½ tsp	½ tsp	½ tsp
Saffron, soaked in warm water	a pinch	a pinch	a pinch
Salt	to taste	to taste	to taste
Garnish			
Mint chutney (see recipe on p115)			
Paprika			

PREPARATION

Kuchumber Salad

- Extract the lime juice. Slice the beet, onion, radish and carrot very finely, then combine them with the lime juice and *chaat masala*. Toss well.

Tandoori Lotus Stem

- Slice the lotus stem, then boil it in turmeric water (turmeric powder dissolved in water) until it is partly cooked. Combine all the other ingredients, then add the lotus stem and leave it to marinate for 1 hr.
- Skewer the lotus stem, then grill it in a *tandoor* (charcoal-fired clay oven). Serve hot with the *kuchumber* salad and garnish with mint chutney and *paprika*.

BROWN RICE AND SUBZI SHORBA

Serves 4 • 111 Calories per serving • Protein 3 g • Carbohydrate 21 g • Fat 2 g

INGREDIENTS	Metric	Imperial	American
Clear Vegetable Stock			
Onions	200 g	7 oz	7 oz
Leeks, sliced	50 g	2 oz	¼ cup
Celery stalks	50 g	2 oz	¼ cup
Carrot	150 g	5 oz	5 oz
Ginger, crushed	½ tbsp	½ tbsp	½ tbsp
Coriander, stem and roots	1 tbsp	1 tbsp	1 tbsp
Peppercorns	5 pcs	5 pcs	5 pcs
Bay leaf	1 pc	1 pc	1 pc
Water	1.3 litres	2 pts 12 fl oz	5½ cups
Brown Rice and Subzi Shorba			
Brown rice	80 g	3 oz	⅓ cup
Water	500 ml	1 pt	2 cups
Onion	30 g	1 oz	1 oz
Garlic	5 g	⅛ oz	⅛ oz
Carrot	20 g	¾ oz	¾ oz
French beans	20 g	¾ oz	¾ oz
Sunflower oil	1 tbsp	1 tbsp	1 tbsp
Cauliflower	20 g	¾ oz	¾ oz
Green peas, shelled	1½ tsp	1½ tsp	1½ tsp
Salt	1 tsp	1 tsp	1 tsp
White pepper powder	1½ tsp	1½ tsp	1½ tsp
Garnish			
Coriander leaves, chopped	2 tsp	2 tsp	2 tsp

PREPARATION

Clear Vegetable Stock

- Combine all the ingredients in a pot and bring it to the boil. Then reduce the heat and allow to simmer for 40 min. Strain the stock, discard any residue and allow to cool.

Brown Rice and Subzi Shorba

- Cook the brown rice with the water and then purée it. Set aside.
- Chop the onion, garlic, carrot and French beans. Set aside.
- Heat the sunflower oil in a saucepan then sauté the onion and garlic until they turn light brown. Add the chopped vegetables, cauliflower and green peas. Adjust the taste with salt and pepper and sauté for another 1 min over low fire.
- Next add the puréed brown rice and vegetable stock. Simmer until the vegetables are fully cooked.
- Transfer to a serving bowl, garnish with coriander leaves and serve hot.

PAHADI KEBAB WITH LACCHA PARATHA

Serves 4 • 360 Calories per serving • Protein 32 g • Carbohydrate 46 g • Fat 6 g

INGREDIENTS

	Metric	Imperial	American
Laccha Paratha			
Wheat flour	200 g	7 oz	2 cups
Sunflower oil	1 tbsp	1 tbsp	1 tbsp
Salt	1 tsp	1 tsp	1 tsp
Water	110 ml	4 fl oz	⅓ cup
Pahadi Kebab			
Chicken breast, deboned and skinned	4 pcs	4 pcs	4 pcs
Sunflower oil	1 tbsp	1 tbsp	1 tbsp
Garlic	20 g	¾ oz	¾ oz
Ginger, chopped	20 g	¾ oz	¾ oz
Coriander leaves, chopped	2 tbsp	2 tbsp	2 tbsp
Mint leaves, chopped	2 tbsp	2 tbsp	2 tbsp
Yogurt	2 tbsp	2 tbsp	2 tbsp
White pepper powder	2 tbsp	2 tbsp	2 tbsp
Salt	to taste	to taste	to taste
Garnish			
Curry leaves, deep-fried	25 g	1 oz	1 oz
Papad, julienned and roasted	1 pc	1 pc	1 pc
Mung beans sprouts	10 g	⅜ oz	⅜ oz
Red chilli flakes			

PREPARATION

Laccha Paratha

- Combine all the ingredients and knead the mixture until it becomes dough. Let the dough rest for 20 min then divide it into 4 portions. Dust each portion with flour, apply ½ tsp of sunflower oil and then roll it out. Fold each portion of dough to form triangles then roll again. Fry the triangles of dough on a *tawa* (flat frying pan) until they turn golden brown on both sides. Remove and lay on kitchen tissue to remove excess oil.

Pahadi Kebab

- Cut the chicken breast into 1.25 cm/½ inch-cubes. Set aside.
- Heat the oil in a saucepan and sauté the garlic and ginger. Add the chicken, sauté for a while, then add the coriander leaves, mint leaves, yogurt, pepper and salt.
- Serve hot with the *paratha* and garnish with deep-fried curry leaves, *papad* strips, mung bean sprouts and red chilli flakes.

JHANGORA PUDDING

Serves 4 • 142 Calories per serving • Protein 5 g • Carbohydrate 28 g • Fat 2 g

INGREDIENTS	Metric	Imperial	American
Fruit Salsa			
Cape gooseberries, diced	3 pcs	3 pcs	3 pcs
Papaya, diced	20 g	¾ oz	¾ oz
Pineapple, diced	20 g	¾ oz	¾ oz
Mint leaf, julienned	1 tsp	1 tsp	1 tsp
Orange rind, chopped	a pinch	a pinch	a pinch
Banana, diced	20 g	¾ oz	¾ oz
Pomegranate	20 g	¾ oz	¾ oz
Apple	40 g	1½ oz	1½ oz
Jhangora Pudding			
Jhangora, soaked	80 g	3 oz	¾ cup
Non-fat milk	200 ml	7 fl oz	1 cup
Palm sugar	80 g	3 oz	⅓ cup
Green cardamon, crushed	1 pc	1 pc	1 pc
Saffron, dissolved in water	a pinch	a pinch	a pinch
Dry roasted cashew nuts	½ tbsp	½ tbsp	½ tbsp
Garnish			
Sugar	50 g	2¾ oz	¼ cup
Water	1 tsp	1 tsp	1 tsp

PREPARATION

Fruit Salsa

• Combine all the ingredients, mix well and set aside.

Jhangora Pudding

• Wash the *jhangora* thoroughly, then soak it in water for 30 min. Drain well. Roast the *jhangora* for 5 min over a low flame. Add milk and let the mixture simmer. When the *jhangora* is almost done, add the palm sugar, cardamon, saffron and cashew nuts. Leave the pudding to simmer until the *jhangora* is fully cooked.

• Divide the *jhangora* into 4 portions and serve chilled. Garnish with tropical fruit salsa on the side.

Garnish

• Dissolve the sugar in water and heat it over a low flame until the mixture turns light brown. Using a spoon, pour the caramel on a greased surface to create an abstract pattern. Leave it to cool, then use as garnish.

CHAANCH

Serves 4 • 54 Calories per serving • Protein 4 g • Carbohydrate 9 g • Fat 1 g

INGREDIENTS	Metric	Imperial	American
Yogurt	150 ml	5 fl oz	½ cup
Water	400 ml	13½ fl oz	1⅔ cups
Green chilli, seeded and chopped	½ tsp	½ tsp	½ tsp
Coriander leaves, chopped	1½ tsp	1½ tsp	1½ tsp
Mint leaves, chopped	1 tsp	1 tsp	1 tsp
Ginger, chopped	1 tsp	1 tsp	1 tsp
Rock salt	½ tsp	½ tsp	½ tsp
Salt	to taste	to taste	to taste
Cumin, toasted and ground	1 tsp	1 tsp	1 tsp

PREPARATION

• Blend all the ingredients together and serve chilled garnished with cumin powder.

The Indonesian Kitchen

SELAMAT MAKAN

S pices such as nutmeg, clove and pepper were the main reason traders from China, India and Arabia were drawn to Indonesia in the early days. These spices also attracted Europeans traders in the 1500s, who by then had begun to use them for their medicinal properties and as food preservatives.

The Indonesians were influenced not only by these traders' religious beliefs and traditions, but also by their cuisine. *Satay* is most likely a reinterpretation of the *kebab,* a dish introduced by Arab traders. The Arabs' religious beliefs also led to the importance of goat and lamb as meats in Indonesia—pork being forbidden and served only where the community is predominantly either Chinese or Hindu. Stir-fried dishes, and the use of the wok as a kitchen utensil, are no doubt the result of Chinese influence. Like Indian cuisine, Indonesian cuisine also involves the use of the pestle and mortar (pictured above) to grind spices into a fine paste which is then fried to release their aroma and flavour.

Many of the spices used in Indonesian cooking are also common to other cuisines. For instance, shrimp paste is also used in Thailand, Vietnam and the Philippines. Turmeric, root ginger and cumin are important spices in Indian cuisine, while lemon grass and coriander are commonly used in Thai dishes. All can be found in Indonesian dishes.

Despite the amalgam of influences, Indonesian cuisine is immediately recognisable. Rice is a staple, as in other Southeast Asian countries. Meat, fish and vegetables are condiments meant to flavour the staple. Hot chillies, coconut milk and spices are a must, although they are used in differing amounts in different parts of Indonesia. All these ingredients can be found in the following recipes from the Javana Spa in West Java, Indonesia.

CHICKEN SATAY

Serves 4 • 186 Calories per serving • Protein 34 g • Carbohydrate 2 g • Fat 4 g

INGREDIENTS	Metric	Imperial	American
Chicken breast, halved	4 pcs	4 pcs	4 pcs
Marinade			
Soya sauce	1 tbsp	1 tbsp	1 tbsp
Water	60 ml	2 fl oz	¼ cup
Sugar	1 tsp	1 tsp	1 tsp
Lime juice	1 tbsp	1 tbsp	1 tbsp
Garlic, minced	½ clove	½ clove	½ clove
Curry powder	½ tsp	½ tsp	½ tsp
Red pepper flakes	a pinch	a pinch	a pinch
Peanut Sauce			
Peanut butter	1 tbsp	1 tbsp	1 tbsp
Lemon juice	1 tbsp	1 tbsp	1 tbsp
Coconut extract	¼ tsp	¼ tsp	¼ tsp
Garlic	¼ tsp	¼ tsp	¼ tsp
Soya milk	6 tbsp	6 tbsp	6 tbsp
Red pepper flakes	1 tsp	1 tsp	1 tsp
Cornstarch	1 tbsp	1 tbsp	1 tbsp
Garnish			
Lemon zest, grated	2 tsp	2 tsp	2 tsp

PREPARATION

- Combine all the ingredients for the marinade and blend until smooth.
- Debone the chicken and remove the skin. Cut each piece into 3 strips lengthwise and thread each strip on a skewer. Place the skewer in a shallow baking dish and pour the marinade over. Cover and refrigerate for 8 hr or overnight.
- Except for the red pepper flakes, blend all the ingredients for the peanut sauce. Stir in the red pepper flakes and set aside.
- Prepare the grill (or preheat the broiler if you are using one). Place the skewers of marinated chicken on the hot grill (or under the preheated broiler). Turn the skewers once in a while to ensure the chicken is evenly cooked.
- To serve, place 3 skewers on each plate. Spoon 2 tbsp of peanut sauce on the side and garnish with lemon zest.

EAST JAVANESE CHICKEN SOUP

Serves 4 • 138 Calories per serving • Protein 11.5 g • Carbohydrate 8.7 g • Fat 6.5 g

INGREDIENTS	Metric	Imperial	American
Soup			
Garlic	10 g	⅜ oz	⅜ oz
Ginger	5 g	⅛ oz	⅛ oz
Turmeric root, peeled	5 g	⅛ oz	⅛ oz
Chicken meat	120 g	4 oz	4 oz
Vegetable oil	3 tsp	3 tsp	3 tsp
Shrimp paste	a pinch		
Chicken stock	320 ml	11 fl oz	1⅓ cups
Non-fat milk	375 ml	12½ fl oz	1½ cups
Salt	to taste	to taste	to taste
Ground white pepper	to taste	to taste	to taste
Garnish			
Dried glass noodle, soaked in warm water for 20 min	40 g	1½ oz	1½ oz
Sour finger carambolas, sliced thinly	10 g	⅜ oz	⅜ oz
Shallots, peeled, sliced thinly, deep-fried	3 tsp	3 tsp	3 tsp

PREPARATION

Soup

- Dice the garlic, ginger, turmeric root and chicken meat.
- Heat the vegetable oil in a shallow stockpot. Add the diced garlic, ginger and turmeric root and sauté for 2 min. Stir in the shrimp paste and continue to sauté for approximately 2 min or until the paste has been thoroughly mixed in.
- Add chicken stock and non-fat milk gradually, stirring frequently. Season sparingly with salt and pepper.
- Bring the soup to the boil, then lower the heat. Let the soup simmer for 20 min and continue to stir to prevent the milk from settling. Remove from heat.

Garnish

- Arrange the glass noodles, sour finger carambola slices and fried shallots in individual soup plates. To serve, ladle in the soup.

GRILLED MACKEREL ON BALINESE SAUCE

Serves 4 • 522 Calories per serving • Protein 24.6 g • Carbohydrate 68 g • Fat 17.7 g

INGREDIENTS

	Metric	Imperial	American
Balinese Sauce			
Red chillies, seeded	80 g	3 oz	2½ cups
Green chillies, seeded	10 g	⅜ oz	⅓ cup
Lemon grass stalk	20 g	¾ oz	¾ oz
Garlic	5 g	⅛ oz	⅛ oz
Tomatoes, peeled, seeded	40 g	1½ oz	1½ oz
Olive oil	1 tsp	1 tsp	1 tsp
Coconut milk	60 ml	2 fl oz	¼ cup
Coriander powder	2 tbsp	2 tbsp	2 tbsp
Shrimp paste	10 g	⅜ oz	⅜ oz
Brown sugar	2 tsp	2 tsp	2 tsp
Grilled Mackerel			
Mackerel fillets, halved	320 g	11 oz	11 oz
Olive oil	1 tsp	1 tsp	1 tsp
Garlic, minced	1½ tsp	1½ tsp	1½ tsp
Soya sauce	1 tbsp	1 tbsp	1 tbsp
Lemon juice	60 ml	2 fl oz	¼ cup
Salt	to taste	to taste	to taste
Pepper	to taste	to taste	to taste
Cooked rice	600 g	1 lb 5 oz	7 cups
Mixed vegetables	300 g	10½ oz	3 cups

PREPARATION

Balinese Sauce

- Dice the red chillies, green chillies, lemon grass stalk, garlic and tomatoes. Then sauté them until they turn golden brown. Add the coconut milk, coriander, shrimp paste and brown sugar, and boil for 8 to 10 min. Stir slowly until the sauce thickens.
- Remove from the heat and transfer the contents into a blender. Purée until smooth and set aside.

Grilled Mackerel

- Place the fillets in a shallow dish, skin side down. Mix the remaining ingredients and sprinkle over the fillets. Leave the fillets to marinate in the refrigerator for 1 hr.
- Prepare the grill by coating it with olive oil—this prevents the fillets from sticking to the grill. Brush the marinated fillets with the Balinese sauce and place them on a baking tray. Grill the fillets until both sides are cooked.
- Place the fillets on individual plates and spoon the sauce over. Serve with rice and stir-fried mixed vegetables.

RICE CUSTARD

Serves 4 (3 bundles per serving) • 534 Calories per serving • Protein 0.9 g • Carbohydrate 19.8 g • Fat 2.7 g

INGREDIENTS	Metric	Imperial	American
Rice flour	400 g	13½ oz	2 cups
Tapioca flour	2 tbsp	2 tbsp	2 tbsp
Non-fat milk	240 ml	8 fl oz	1 cup
Coconut milk	4 tbsp	4 tbsp	4 tbsp
Salt	½ tsp	½ tsp	½ tsp
Fragrant screwpine leaf	1	1	1
Palm sugar, in cylindrical blocks	1	1	1
Banana leaves, 25 by 15 cm (10 by 6 inches)	12	12	12

PREPARATION

* Combine the rice flour, tapioca flour, non-fat milk, coconut milk and salt. Mix them well then add the screwpine leaf. Cook the mixture over low heat and stir continuously. When the mixture becomes fairly thick, remove it from the heat and leave it to cool.

* To make the rice bundle, put 2 tbsp of the rice mixture on a banana leaf. Top it with 1 tsp of palm sugar in the centre, then add another 1 tbsp of the rice mixture. Bring the 2 lengths of the leaf towards the centre so that they overlap, covering the mixture. Then tuck the 2 ends underneath.

* Prepare the steamer by boiling the water beforehand. Steam the rice bundles for 20 min. Serve cold.

WARM GINGER MILK

Serves 4 • 104 Calories per serving • Protein 1.4 g • Carbohydrate 25 g • Fat 0.4 g

INGREDIENTS	Metric	Imperial	American
Water	1.2 litres	2 pts 8 fl oz	5 cups
Ginger roots, sliced	200g	7 oz	7 oz
Cinnamon powder	1 tsp	1 tsp	1 tsp
Non-fat milk	60 ml	2 fl oz	¼ cup
Brown sugar	60 g	2 oz	¼ cup

PREPARATION

* Bring the water and ginger to the boil. Add the cinnamon powder and reduce the heat. Leave the mixture to simmer uncovered for 1 hr.

* Line a strainer or colander with a double thickness of cheese cloth and set it over a bowl. Strain the ginger juice and discard the residue. Add the milk and sugar to the strained mixture and let it simmer over very low heat, stirring frequently.

* Transfer the contents into a glass and serve.

The Japanese Kitchen

A DASH OF DAIKON AND DESIGN

Japanese cuisine, besides being unique, is also famed for its careful attention to the detail, form and balance of every dish served. Even the humblest of ingredients is presented in an elaborate fashion. Having a Japanese meal is akin to being presented a work of art; the shapes, colours and textures found in the dish are all part of a masterful design.

The traditional Japanese diet has a healthy reputation—it is one of the world's lowest in fat. When Buddhism was declared Japan's official religion in the 6th century, the Japanese were forbidden from consuming meat. Then in 1600, a ban on foreigners entering the country forced the Japanese to consume only local produce. This lasted until the ban was lifted in 1868.

Japan being a predominantly coastal country, it is no wonder that fish is such an important ingredient in the Japanese diet. The Japanese eat fish at least once a day and they typically consume 'fatty fish' such as salmon, sardines and mackerel. These 'fatty fish' contain omega-3, a type of 'fat' believed to make our arteries less likely to clog, hence lowering the risk of heart disease. It is also believed to improve brain function and provide iron and zinc.

As an alternative to meat, the Japanese consume tofu, which is virtually fat-free, for their protein requirements. Most Japanese meals are prepared with very little or no oil and hence are very light compared to other Asian and Western cuisines. Perhaps it is out of necessity that the Japanese pay such attention to how a dish looks. The perceived blandness of low-calorie low-fat food is compensated by the visual appeal of the dish.

Chef Jimmy Chok from Salt in Singapore presents some of Japan's favourite recipes such as *sashimi, sushi* and *miso* soup with tofu. The seaweed used to wrap the *sushi* is rich in iodine while *miso* is thought to aid digestion, regulate metabolism, increase vitality and promote youthful skin.

SEARED MAGURO LOIN AND DAIKON SALAD

Serves 4 • 250 Calories per serving • Protein 28 g • Carbohydrate 18 g • Fat 15 g

INGREDIENTS

INGREDIENTS	Metric	Imperial	American
Sashimi maguro	500 g	1 lb 1½ oz	1 lb 1½ oz
Low-sodium soya sauce	50 ml	2 fl oz	¼ cup
Togarashi	2 tbsp	2 tbsp	2 tbsp
Black pepper	1 tbsp	1 tbsp	1 tbsp
Daikon	200 g	7 oz	1 cup
Daikon cress	1 tbsp	1 tbsp	1 tbsp
Olive oil	100 ml	3½ fl oz	½ cup

PREPARATION

- Marinate the *maguro* with soya sauce, *togarashi* and black pepper. Then pan-sear the marinated *maguro* over high heat and set it aside to cool. Slice thinly when it is cooled.
- Grate the *daikon* into noodle-like strips. Arrange the *daikon* strips with the *daikon* cress on one side of the plate and the sliced *maguro* on the other end.
- Before serving, heat the olive oil and pour it over the *maguro*.

CHILLED TOFU AND LIGHT MISO SOUP

Serves 4 • 100 Calories per serving • Protein 15 g • Carbohydrate 10 g • Fat 8 g

INGREDIENTS

INGREDIENTS	Metric	Imperial	American
Water	400 ml	13½ fl oz	1½ cups
White *miso* paste	100 g	3½ oz	½ cup
Konbu	2 tbsp	2 tbsp	2 tbsp
Tofu	4 pcs	4 pcs	4 pcs
Wakame (marinated seaweed)	2 tbsp	2 tbsp	2 tbsp
Spring onion, julienned	1 tbsp	1 tbsp	1 tbsp

PREPARATION

- Bring the water to the boil then add the *miso* paste and *konbu*. Let the mixture simmer for 10 min before removing the *konbu*. Slice it for use as garnish.
- Place 1 piece of tofu in a soup bowl and spoon the soup over. Garnish with *wakame*, sliced *konbu* and spring onion.

BUCKWHEAT SOBA WITH DASHI BROTH

Serves 4 • 200 Calories per serving • Protein 30 g • Carbohydrate 25 g • Fat 19 g

INGREDIENTS	Metric	Imperial	American
Dried *konbu*	1 tbsp	1 tbsp	1 tbsp
Water	1 litre	2 pts 2 fl oz	4 cups
Dried *bonito* flakes	2 tbsp	2 tbsp	2 tbsp
Enoki mushroom	200 g	7 oz	1 cup
Honshimeiji	200 g	7 oz	1 cup
Coriander	250 g	9 oz	1 cup
Soba (buckwheat noodles)	500 g	1 lb	2½ cups
Cherry tomatoes	8	8	8

PREPARATION

- Boil the *konbu* in water. Just before it comes to the boil, remove the *konbu* and add the *bonito* flakes. Then remove from fire and allow the *bonito* flakes to sink to the bottom. Strain the broth, then add the mushrooms and coriander.
- To serve, pour the broth over the *soba* and garnish with tomatoes.

FRUIT SUSHI ROLL

Serves 4 • 180 Calories per serving • Protein 38 g • Carbohydrate 80 g • Fat 28 g

INGREDIENTS	Metric	Imperial	American
Sushi rice	500 g	1 lb 1½ oz	2½ cups
Water	7.5 litres	15 pts 14 fl oz	32 cups
Coconut milk	50 ml	2 fl oz	¼ cup
Pineapple	200 g	7 oz	7 oz
Mango	200 g	7 oz	7 oz
Papaya	200 g	7 oz	7 oz
Nori sheets	2 pcs	2 pcs	2 pcs

PREPARATION

- Rinse the *sushi* rice and add water and coconut milk to it. Bring it to the boil, then lower the heat and let it simmer for 15 min.
- Cut the fruit into long strips.
- To make the *sushi* roll, place a *nori* sheet on a *sushi* mat. Spread a quarter of the rice evenly over two-thirds of the *nori* sheet. Arrange the fruit strips neatly across the centre of the rice. Roll the *sushi* mat so that the fruit strips are firmly packed in the rice. When the roll is secure, unroll the *sushi* mat. Repeat the process for the remaining *nori* sheets.
- Cut each roll into bite-sized pieces. Place 3 pieces of *sushi* roll on a plate and serve with warm green tea.

ICED GREEN MINT TEA

Serves 4 • 60 Calories per serving • Protein 2 g • Carbohydrate 2 g • Fat 0 g

INGREDIENTS	Metric	Imperial	American
Japanese green tea bags	4 bags	4 bags	4 bags
Hot water	600 ml	1 pt 4 fl oz	2½ cups
Mint leaves, chopped	2 tbsp	2 tbsp	2 tbsp
Mint	4 sprigs	4 sprigs	4 sprigs
Ice	as required	as required	as required

PREPARATION

- Infuse the tea bags in hot water for 3 min then remove them.
- Add the mint leaves into the tea.
- Pour the tea into 4 glasses and add ice if preferred. Garnish with mint and serve.

The Thai Kitchen

SIAMESE SENSATIONS

Thai cuisine is piquant—a mixture of hot, sour, salty, sweet and bitter. Chinese and Indian influences are evident, as most Thai dishes are either stir-fried or steamed in a wok, and spices such as lemon grass, ginger and coriander are ground using a pestle and mortar.

Thai cuisine is distinctively hot. Portuguese traders from as early as the 16th century brought chilli to Thailand and it has been a central ingredient in Thai cooking ever since. Chilli is used dried, whole, chopped, crushed, or sliced into rings.

The Thais believe that eating chillies is good for health: chillies help get rid of flatulence, aid digestion and relieve stomach cramps. The Thais also believe that those who perspire profusely after eating chilli are in fact ridding their bodies of toxic substances.

An invitation to a meal, 'rappattan arhan', literally means 'come and eat rice'. The Thais seldom dine without their staple of rice or noodles, served with a few dishes of vegetables, fish and spices. Raw vegetables are preferred for their natural crunchiness and flavour. Salad dressing rarely contains oil or vinegar, and is instead mostly made up of lime juice, shallots and chillies.

Chiva-Som (Haven of Life) in Hua Hin, Thailand, strives to dispel the myth that nutritious food always tastes bland. The following recipes combine organic fruit and vegetables with characteristically Thai ingredients such as nam pla (fish sauce) and kapi (shrimp paste). Nam pla is rich in Vitamin B and protein and makes an excellent salt substitute. The dishes are also cooked with very little or no oil, making the meal tasty and healthy all at once.

GLASS NOODLE SALAD

Serves 4 • 274 Calories per serving • Protein 4.3 g • Carbohydrate 63.7 g • Fat 0.5 g

INGREDIENTS	Metric	Imperial	American
Glass noodles, soaked in water	200 g	7 oz	2 cups
Carrot, julienned	1	1	1
Chinese mushrooms, soaked and finely shredded	3 pcs	3 pcs	3 pcs
Bird chillies	4	4	4
Garlic, crushed	1 clove	1 clove	1 clove
Shallots, sliced	2	2	2
Spring onions, chopped	2	2	2
Honey	1½ tsp	1½ tsp	1½ tsp
Lemon juice	2 tbsp	2 tbsp	2 tbsp
Soya sauce	1 tbsp	1 tbsp	1 tbsp
Coriander leaves	1 sprig	1 sprig	1 sprig

PREPARATION

- Place the soaked glass noodles in a fine-mesh sieve and blanch them for 8 to 10 sec. Stir the noodles to prevent them from sticking together. Remove the noodles and rinse them under cold running water. Shake off any excess water.

- Combine the glass noodles, carrot, Chinese mushrooms, bird chillies, garlic, shallots, spring onions, honey, lemon juice and soya sauce in a bowl. Mix gently but thoroughly until all the ingredients are well-coated. Transfer to a plate and garnish with Chinese parsley and coriander leaves.

HOT AND SOUR CHICKEN SOUP (TOM KHA GAI)

Serves 4 • 192 Calories per serving • Protein 15.6 g • Carbohydrate 32.3 g • Fat 1.9 g

INGREDIENTS	Metric	Imperial	American
Chicken breast, skinned	140 g	5 oz	5 oz
Vegetable stock	1 litre	2 pts 2 fl oz	4 cups
Fresh mushrooms (preferably straw mushrooms)	120 g	4 oz	4 oz
Bird chillies	3	3	3
Kaffir lime leaves	4	4	4
Lemon grass	25 g	1 oz	1 oz
Apple concentrate	1½ tsp	1½ tsp	1½ tsp
Lime juice	2½ tbsp	2½ tbsp	2½ tbsp
Soya sauce	3 tbsp	3 tbsp	3 tbsp
Cherry tomatoes, halved	65 g	2½ oz	2½ oz
Coconut water	120 ml	4 fl oz	½ cup
Non-fat milk	120 ml	4 fl oz	½ cup
Coriander leaves	1½ tsp	1½ tsp	1½ tsp

PREPARATION

- Cut the chicken breast into pieces approximately the same size as the halved tomatoes. Bring the vegetable stock to the boil. Add the mushrooms, bird chillies, kaffir lime leaves, lemon grass, apple concentrate, lime juice and soya sauce. Simmer for 5 min.

- Add the chicken and tomatoes and simmer for another 5 min, or until the chicken is fully-cooked.

- Finally, add the coconut water and milk and simmer for another 2 to 3 min. Garnish with the coriander leaves and serve.

GREEN CHICKEN CURRY (GAENG KHEW WHAN GAI)

Serves 4 • 167 Calories per serving • Protein 26.7 g • Carbohydrate 10 g • Fat 2.2 g

INGREDIENTS	Metric	Imperial	American
Green curry paste	3 tsp	3 tsp	3 tsp
Chicken or vegetable stock	120 ml	4 fl oz	½ cup
Chicken breast, skinned and sliced	400 g	14 oz	14 oz
Thai eggplant, halved	100 g	3½ oz	3½ oz
White eggplant, halved	100 g	3½ oz	3½ oz
Lime leaves, chopped	4	4	4
Nam pla (fish sauce)	1 tbsp	1 tbsp	1 tbsp
Red chillies, shredded	5	5	5
Thai basil leaves	150 g	5 oz	5 oz
Non-fat milk	120 ml	4 fl oz	½ cup

PREPARATION

- Gently fry the curry paste with 30 ml/1 fl oz /2 tbsp of chicken or vegetable stock until almost dry.
- Add the chicken to the pan and stir well, making sure the chicken slices are well-coated with the paste. Continue to add the stock, a little at a time, to prevent the chicken slices from sticking to the pan. Put the remaining stock, eggplants, lime leaves, fish sauce and a desired amount of chillies into the pan. Simmer for 3 to 5 min, or until the eggplants are cooked.
- Add the Thai basil leaves and milk. Use the remaining shredded chilli and basil leaves as garnish.

STEAMED CUSTARD IN PUMPKIN (SANGKHAYA FAK THONG)

Serves 4 • 112 Calories per serving • Protein 10.1 g • Carbohydrate 16.8 g • Fat 1.1 g

INGREDIENTS	Metric	Imperial	American
Pumpkin, small	1	1	1
Egg whites	7	7	7
Non-fat milk	250 ml	8½ fl oz	1 cup
Apple concentrate	75 ml	2½ fl oz	⅓ cup
Shredded coconut	2 tbsp	2 tbsp	2 tbsp
Salt	a pinch	a pinch	a pinch

PREPARATION

• Wash the pumpkin carefully. Using a large, sharp kitchen knife, slice open the top of the pumpkin and save it for the lid. If necessary, cut the base of the pumpkin so the pumpkin sits upright. Be careful not to cut a hole in the base. Remove and discard the seeds.

• Blend the remaining ingredients together and fill the pumpkin shell with the resulting custard. Place the lid back on the pumpkin, and steam the pumpkin for 30 to 60 min, depending on its thickness and type. For a traditional finish, carve flowers or other decorative patterns on to the pumpkin before steaming it.

• Cut the pumpkin into wedges and serve hot or cold.

HERBAL LEMON GRASS TEA

Serves 4 • 1 Calorie per serving • Protein 0 g • Carbohydrate 0.3 g • Fat 0 g

INGREDIENTS	Metric	Imperial	American
Lemon grass	2 tsp	2 tsp	2 tsp
Hot water	300 ml	10 fl oz	1¼ cup

PREPARATION

Preheat the oven at 75°C/167°F.

Place the lemon grass on a tray and bake it for 12 to 15 hr on very low heat. Remove and allow it to cool, then store it in a cool dry place. Infuse the dry lemon grass in hot water. Serve warm.

The Vietnamese Kitchen

DELECTABLE INDO-CHINESE

Vietnamese cuisine, like others in Indo-China, has been deeply influenced by the Chinese, the Indians, and to a significant extent the French.

Like the Chinese, the Vietnamese use chopsticks and eat from bowls rather than plates. They stir-fry their food and regard rice and noodles as their staples. Within Vietnam itself, North Vietnamese cuisine bears the most resemblance to Chinese cuisine. This could be due to the area's proximity to the Chinese border. Soya sauce is preferred over fish sauce, and black peppers rather than chillies are used to spice up a dish.

In contrast, South Vietnamese cuisine features *nuoc mam* (fish sauce), chillies, coconut and spices, ingredients more commonly found in Thai or Indian cuisines. *Nuoc mam* accompanies practically every dish just as *nam pla* (as fish sauce is known in Thailand) accompanies most Thai dishes.

As to the French, their presence in Vietnam from the 16th to the mid-20th centuries saw them introducing their philosophy of food and eating to the Vietnamese. Ingredients such as asparagus and avocados, and techniques of cooking such as sautéing, were introduced into Vietnamese cuisine. For instance, a Vietnamese sandwich can be made from a baguette and pâté.

Today, the distinct flavours we associate with Vietnamese cuisine come primarily from mint leaves, coriander, lemon grass, shrimp, *nuoc mam*, ginger and other herbs. A typical Vietnamese meal comprises rice or noodles, fresh vegetables and herbs. Vietnamese dishes are also usually cooked in water rather than oil. Desserts are not common, although sweets and cakes are offered to guests at the end of a meal.

Sample a few Vietnamese dishes with the following recipes from the Ana Mandara Resort in Nha Trang, Vietnam.

CHICKEN AND ONION SALAD (GOI GA)

Serves 4 • 620 Calories per serving • Protein 64 g • Carbohydrate 32 g • Fat 3.6 g

INGREDIENTS	Metric	Imperial	American
Chicken	1	1	1
Rau ram (Vietnamese mint leaves)	30	30	30
White onion	1	1	1
Lime	2	2	2
Salt	a pinch	a pinch	a pinch
Pepper	a pinch	a pinch	a pinch
Sugar	a pinch	a pinch	a pinch

PREPARATION

- Rub the chicken with a little salt, pepper and chopped *rau ram*. (If *rau ram* leaves are not available, use basil leaves as an alternative.)
- Steam the chicken until it is fully cooked, then debone it. Shred the chicken into thin strips and mix it with onion, lime juice, sugar and the remaining *rau ram*. Add salt and pepper to taste.
- Arrange the salad into a conical shape and serve. Alternatively, you may serve the salad with roasted Vietnamese rice crackers.

STAR FRUIT AND CLAM SOUP (CANH NGHEU)

Serves 4 • 650 Calories per serving • Protein 73 g • Carbohydrate 42 g • Fat 1.3 g

INGREDIENTS	Metric	Imperial	American
Chicken stock	1.5 litres	3 pts 3 fl oz	6⅓ cups
White clams	24	24	24
Vegetable oil	1 tbsp	1 tbsp	1 tbsp
Garlic, finely chopped	2 cloves	2 cloves	2 cloves
Baby leeks, finely chopped	2 tsp	2 tsp	2 tsp
Nuoc mam	2 tbsp	2 tbsp	2 tbsp
Shrimp paste	1 tsp	1 tsp	1 tsp
Star fruit, sliced	2	2	2
Garnish			
Coriander	a pinch	a pinch	a pinch
Rau ram (Vietnamese mint leaves)	a pinch	a pinch	a pinch

PREPARATION

- Bring the chicken stock to the boil, then add the clams and cook until the shells open. Remove the clam flesh and set aside.
- Heat the oil in a pan and sauté the garlic and baby leeks until they are soft. Add the cooked clams and season with *nuoc mam* and shrimp paste. Bring to the boil. Add the chicken stock and star fruit, then immediately turn off the heat. Garnish with coriander and *rau ram* to serve.

SAUTÉED DUCK WITH GARLIC AND OYSTER SAUCE (UC VIT)

Serves 4 • 1,060 Calories per serving • Protein 69 g • Carbohydrate 35 g • Fat 4.2 g

INGREDIENTS	Metric	Imperial	American
Duck breasts	4 pcs	4 pcs	4 pcs
Salt	a pinch	a pinch	a pinch
Pepper	a pinch	a pinch	a pinch
Vegetable oil	2 tbsp	2 tbsp	2 tbsp
Garlic	4 cloves	4 cloves	4 cloves
Sugar	1 tsp	1 tsp	1 tsp
Oyster sauce	2 tsp	2 tsp	2 tsp
Green mustard leaves	10	10	10
Steamed rice	400 g	14 oz	4½ cups

PREPARATION

- Rub the duck with salt and pepper and leave it for 30 min.

- Heat the oil in a pan and sauté the duck until it is slightly crispy. The duck should still be quite rare or no more than medium-cooked. Slice the duck into thick strips.

- In the same pan, add a little more oil and sauté the garlic, sugar, oyster sauce and pepper. Add the green mustard leaves and lightly toss them for 10 sec or until they are well-coated with the sauce. Remove the leaves and set aside.

- To serve, arrange the green mustard leaves on the plate and place the warm duck breast strips on top. Then pour the remaining sautéed sauce over. Serve with the steamed rice on the side.

SWEET STICKY RICE WITH MANGO, MANDARIN AND GINGER

Serves 4 • 640 Calories per serving • Protein 36 g • Carbohydrate 82 g • Fat 4.3 g

INGREDIENTS	Metric	Imperial	American
Sweet Sticky Rice			
Vanilla pod	1	1	1
Non-fat milk	1.2 litres	2 pts 9 fl oz	5 cups
Fructose	80 g	3 oz	3 oz
Dried star anise	2	2	2
Desiccated coconut (toasted)	2 tbsp	2 tbsp	2 tbsp
Short grain cooking rice	200 g	7 oz	1 cup
Fresh mango purée	350 ml	12 fl oz	1½ cups
Garnish			
Fresh mango	1	1	1
Pickled red ginger stem	1	1	1
Mandarin	2	2	2
Fructose	90 ml	3 fl oz	⅜ cup
Water	4 tbsp	4 tbsp	4 tbsp
Low-fat butter, melted	½ tsp	½ tsp	½ tsp
Fresh mint	4 sprigs	4 sprigs	4 sprigs

PREPARATION

Sweet Sticky Rice

- Preheat the oven to 160°C/325°F.
- Split the vanilla pod in half lengthwise and scrape out the seeds into a large casserole dish. Add the milk, fructose, star anise and half the dessicated coconut. Leave it to simmer for 5 min then remove the star anise and vanilla pod.
- Wash the rice and add it to the simmering milk. Let it simmer for 5 min before mixing in the mango purée. Cover the mixture with tin foil and put it in the preheated oven for 20 min. Remove and leave it to cool until the rice is just warm, not hot.

Garnish

- Peel and dice the mango and ginger stem. Segment the mandarins and combine half with the mango and ginger.
- Boil the fructose and water for about 4 min to get fructose syrup.
- In a large saucepan, warm the fructose syrup, then add the diced fruit, ginger and mandarins. Remove from heat, cover the pan and leave the mixture to marinate for 1 hr in the refrigerator.
- To serve, line 4 small open ring moulds (about 5 cm/2 inches in diameter) with melted butter. Fill the rings with the warm rice, place them on a serving dish and carefully remove the rings.
- Arrange the marinated fruit on top of the rice. and the remaining mandarin segments and dessicated coconut as shown. Lightly drizzle the fructose syrup and top with the mint.

VIETNAMESE SINH TO

Serves 4 • 580 Calories per serving • Protein 28 g • Carbohydrate 16 g • Fat 0.9 g

INGREDIENTS	Metric	Imperial	American
Fructose	1 tbsp	1 tbsp	1 tbsp
Water	2 tsp	2 tsp	2 tsp
Avocado	50 g	2 oz	2 oz
Star fruit	50 g	2 oz	2 oz
Apple	50 g	2 oz	2 oz
Dried banana	50 g	2 oz	2 oz
Papaya	50 g	2 oz	2 oz
Jack fruit	50 g	2 oz	2 oz
Dried raisins	50 g	2 oz	¼ cup
Sapodilla	50 g	2 oz	2 oz
Grilled peanuts	½ tbsp	½ tbsp	½ tbsp
Crushed ice cubes	50 g	2 oz	½ cup
Coconut milk	30 ml	1 fl oz	⅛ cup

PREPARATION

- Boil the fructose and water for about 4 min to get fructose syrup. Blend all the ingredients, except for the ice and coconut milk, until smooth, then pass the mixture through a fine-mesh sieve.
- To serve, pour the drink into chilled tall glasses, add the ice cubes and top with coconut milk. This beverage is also usually served with a shot glass of iced water to remove any aftertaste.

The New Asian Kitchen

ASIAN FUSION WITH A TWIST

A familiar greeting often heard in Asia, 'Have you eaten yet?' is used in the same manner as 'How are you today?'. This charming tradition reflects the importance that is placed on a good meal, broadly defined as a meal that contributes to your physical and mental well-being. The nutritional value of a meal is considered as important as the experience of having it—the Vietnamese, for instance, view mealtimes as a time of bonding with family or friends.

In the culinary world, Asia is broadly divided into three areas: Northeast (India, Pakistan, Sri Lanka and Burma), Southeast (Thailand, Laos, Cambodia, Vietnam, Indonesia, Malaysia, Singapore and Brunei) and Southwest (China, Korea and Japan). Some ingredients and dishes are common to all—spices are invariably used, curries are served, and rice and noodles are generally regarded as staples. Yet the cuisine in each area remains distinct in that its use of ingredients and preparation methods differ. For instance, curries in Northeast and Southeast Asia are generally coconut-milk-based while those from Southwest are yogurt-based.

In New Asian cuisine, Asian ingredients and dishes are used and prepared in ways commonly regarded as Western. Ingredients from different cuisines are prepared alongside each other and the influence of different countries' cuisines can be found within a meal.

The following recipes, prepared by The Beaufort Singapore, show evidence of Japanese, Indian and Thai influences. The tuna tartare with *wasabi* dressing reflects Japanese-style cooking; mint chutney is a common accompaniment to Indian meals; and the main course, with its use of lemon grass, galangal and coriander, is clearly Thai-influenced.

ASIAN TUNA TARTARE ON CUCUMBER CARPACCIO WITH HERB SALAD

Serves 4 • 684.3 Calories per serving • Protein 20.8 g • Carbohydrate 10.2 g • Fat 64.3 g

INGREDIENTS	Metric	Imperial	American
Asian Tuna Tartare			
Tuna	320 g	11 oz	11 oz
Cucumber	140 g	5 oz	5 oz
Spring onions	40 g	1½ oz	1½ oz
Tuna Dressing			
Balsamic vinegar	120 ml	4 fl oz	½ cup
Olive oil	4 tsp	4 tsp	4 tsp
Sesame oil	4 tsp	4 tsp	4 tsp
Wasabi dressing	100 ml	3½ fl oz	⅜ cup
Wasabi	a pinch		
Asian Vinaigrette			
Olive oil	180 ml	6 fl oz	¾ cup
Sesame oil	4 tsp	4 tsp	4 tsp
Soya sauce	4 tsp	4 tsp	4 tsp
Rice wine vinegar	8 tbsp	8 tbsp	8 tbsp
Ginger	12 g	⅜ oz	⅜ oz
Fresh Herb Salad			
Coriander	8 g	¼ oz	¼ oz
Chervil	8 g	¼ oz	¼ oz
Sprouts	8 g	¼ oz	¼ oz
Parsley	8 g	¼ oz	¼ oz
Watercress	8 g	¼ oz	¼ oz
Red leaf lettuce, sliced	8 g	¼ oz	¼ oz
Enoki mushrooms	10 g	⅜ oz	⅜ oz

PREPARATION

- Dice the tuna and 40 g of the cucumber. Slice the spring onions very finely and combine it with the diced tuna and cucumber. Mix the ingredients for the tuna dressing and use half over the tuna tartare.
- Combine the ingredients for the Asian vinaigrette. Combine the herbs for the herb salad, then add the Asian vinaigrette, lettuce and *enoki* mushrooms. Mix well.
- Slice the remaining cucumber thinly and place it on a plate. Arrange the tuna tartare on top of the cucumber, followed by the herb salad. Drizzle the remainder tuna dressing over the salad and serve.

CHILLED YOGURT SOUP WITH MINT CHUTNEY

Serves 4 • 15.4 Calories per serving • Protein 0.5 g • Carbohydrate 3.5 g • Fat 0.2 g

INGREDIENTS	Metric	Imperial	American
Mint Chutney			
Chilli powder	¼ tsp	¼ tsp	¼ tsp
Ginger	¼ tsp	¼ tsp	¼ tsp
Garlic	¼ tsp	¼ tsp	¼ tsp
Green chilli	¼ tsp	¼ tsp	¼ tsp
Sugar	½ tsp	½ tsp	½ tsp
Yogurt, plain	2 tbsp	2 tbsp	2 tbsp
Lemon juice	1 tsp	1 tsp	1 tsp
Mint leaves	8 g	¼ oz	¼ oz
Yogurt Soup			
Cucumber, peeled	480 g	1 lb	1 lb
Yogurt	500 ml	1 pt	2 cups
Garlic	4	4	4
Salt	to taste	to taste	to taste

PREPARATION

- Blend all the ingredients for the mint chutney until it becomes a smooth paste. Blend all the ingredients for the yogurt soup and keep it chilled in a refrigerator.
- To serve, transfer the yogurt soup into a chilled soup bowl. Garnish with mint chutney and fresh mint leaves.

THAI-SPICED CHICKEN BREAST, AND VEGETABLE COUSCOUS WITH TAMARIND AND GINGER CHUTNEY

Makes 1 serving • 825.8 Calories per serving • Protein 27.1 g • Carbohydrate 31.2 g • Fat 66.5 g

INGREDIENTS	Metric	Imperial	American
Thai-spiced Chicken Breast			
Lemon grass, chopped	a pinch	a pinch	a pinch
Galangal, chopped	a pinch	a pinch	a pinch
Garlic, chopped	¼ tsp	¼ tsp	¼ tsp
Coriander leaves, chopped	¼ tsp	¼ tsp	¼ tsp
Coconut milk	500 ml	1 pt	2 cups
Chicken breast	480 g	1 lb	1 lb
Vegetable Couscous			
Celeriac	40 g	1½ oz	1½ oz
Zucchini	40 g	1½ oz	1½ oz
Eggplant	40 g	1½ oz	1½ oz
Asparagus	40 g	1½ oz	1½ oz
Olive oil	40 ml	1½ fl oz	⅛ cup
Salt	to taste	to taste	to taste
Pepper	to taste	to taste	to taste
Couscous	3 tsp	3 tsp	3 tsp
Chicken stock	150 ml	5 fl oz	½ cup
Tamarind and Ginger Chutney			
Tamarind pulp	40 g	1½ oz	1½ oz
Chilli powder	a pinch	a pinch	a pinch
Ginger powder	a pinch	a pinch	a pinch
Fennel seed, ground	a pinch	a pinch	a pinch
Cumin seed, ground	a pinch	a pinch	a pinch
Palm sugar	a pinch	a pinch	a pinch
Sugar	a pinch	a pinch	a pinch

PREPARATION

Thai-spiced Chicken Breast

• Combine the lemon grass, galangal, garlic, coriander leaves and coconut milk. Marinate the chicken breast in the mixture for 30 min and grill it. Set it aside.

Vegetable Couscous

• Oven-roast the celeriac, zucchini, eggplant and asparagus in olive oil. Add salt and pepper to taste. Cook the couscous in chicken stock, then put it aside.

Tamarind and Ginger Chutney

• Cook all the ingredients for the tamarind and ginger chutney.

• To serve, place the couscous on a plate with the vegetables on top. Then slice the chicken breast, arrange the slices over the couscous, and spoon the chutney over the slices.

FRESH MANGO SOUP WITH BERRIES AND YOGURT ICE-CREAM

Serves 4 • 132.6 Calories per serving • Protein 0.2 g • Carbohydrate 36.2 g • Fat 0 g

INGREDIENTS	Metric	Imperial	American
Fresh mango, in cubes	320 g	11 oz	11 oz
Water	200 ml	7 fl oz	¾ cup
Honey	40 ml	1½ fl oz	⅛ cup
Lemon juice	4 tsp	4 tsp	4 tsp
Strawberry	60 g	2 oz	2 oz
Blueberry	60 g	2 oz	2 oz
Raspberry	60 g	2 oz	2 oz
Yogurt ice-cream	120 ml	4 fl oz	½ cup
Mint leaves	4	4	4

PREPARATION

- Cook the mango, water, honey and lemon juice for about 12 min on low heat, then chill the mango soup.
- Transfer the mango soup to a soup plate and add the fresh berries. Scoop the yogurt ice-cream and place it in the middle of the soup plate. Garnish with mint leaves to serve.

FRESH GUAVA AND LIME CRUSH

Serves 4 • 237.2 Calories per serving • Protein 3.9 g • Carbohydrate 57.2 g • Fat 2.7 g

INGREDIENTS	Metric	Imperial	American
Ripe guavas	6	6	6
Lime	1	1	1
Sugar syrup	to taste	to taste	to taste
Water			
Ice cubes			

PREPARATION

- Peel the guavas and squeeze the lime over the guava flesh. Lightly sweeten with sugar syrup if desired, then add a little water and some ice cubes. Blend until smooth.
- To serve, pour the mixture into a glass.

The Continental Kitchen

A GLOBAL EPICUREAN ADVENTURE

his last chapter of Spa Cuisine presents continental cuisine—a term loosely used to encompass all non-Asian cuisines—at its healthiest. In continental spa cuisine, emphasis is placed not so much on where the recipe originates, but on its nutritional value. Generally, your diet should include a variety of different foods. Plenty of grain products, vegetables and fruit are also a must. Where possible, healthier substitutes for foods high in fat and salt should be used. For instance, tofu is a good alternative source of protein as it has a much lower fat content compared to meat.

The Amrita Spa in Singapore aims to dispel the myth that good-tasting food must necessarily be bad for you. Its continental spa cuisine promises an enjoyable dining experience with nutritious dishes that are relatively high in protein but low in fat, saturated fat and cholesterol. The cuisine is also designed to provide adequate amounts of nutrients such as iron, zinc and calcium, and fibre content from vegetables, cereals and pulses. For instance, ingredients such as tofu and fresh-from-the-garden vegetables—namely, avocados, spinach and broccolis—are used in the following recipes. Avocados are said to contain the most protein of all fruit, while broccolis are believed to contain high levels of antioxidants.

Clearly, a nutritious meal from Amrita Spa is more than just low calorie-counts. Given that it is difficult, if not impossible, to create a single dish that fulfils all your nutritional needs, Amrita Spa advocates that at least two dishes—for example, an appetiser and a main course—be consumed and fresh fruit taken as dessert.

SPINACH, AVOCADO, SUN-DRIED BLUEBERRIES AND CITRUS FRUIT WITH CORIANDER MINT VINAIGRETTE

Serves 4 • 266 Calories per serving • Protein 0 g • Carbohydrate 40 g • Fat 9 g

INGREDIENTS	Metric	Imperial	American
Coriander Mint Vinaigrette			
White wine vinegar	120 ml	4 fl oz	½ cup
Coriander	40 g	1½ oz	1½ oz
Mint leaves	30 g	1 oz	1 oz
Dijon mustard	60 ml	2 fl oz	¼ cup
Sugar	50 g	2 oz	¼ cup
Sea salt	¼ tsp	¼ tsp	¼ tsp
Black pepper	1½ tsp	1½ tsp	1½ tsp
Olive oil	700 ml	1 pt 8 fl oz	3 cups
Salad			
Avocado, sliced	320 g	11 oz	11 oz
Baby spinach	200 g	7 oz	7 oz
Dried blueberries	120 g	4 oz	½ cup
Fennel bulb, finely sliced	160 g	5½ oz	5½ oz
Fresh mild chilli, very finely sliced	40 g	1½ oz	1½ oz
Oranges, peeled and segmented	240 g	8½ oz	8½ oz
Pink grapefruit, peeled and segmented	240 g	8½ oz	8½ oz
Radicchio lettuce	240 g	8½ oz	8½ oz
Coriander mint vinaigrette	4 tsp	4 tsp	4 tsp
French bread	4	4	4

PREPARATION

- Infuse the white wine vinegar with the mint and coriander leaves. Combine the rest of the ingredients for the coriander mint vinaigrette. Combine all the salad ingredients in a salad bowl and add the coriander mint vinaigrette. Toss well. Arrange the French bread as shown and serve.

CARROT, BROCCOLI, TOMATO AND TOFU SOUP

Serves 4 • 75 Calories per serving • Protein 6 g • Carbohydrate 13 g • Fat 14 g

INGREDIENTS	Metric	Imperial	American
Vegetable Broth			
Leeks, chopped	100 g	3½ oz	3½ oz
Medium-sized onions, chopped	250 g	9 oz	9 oz
Carrots, chopped	200 g	7 oz	7 oz
Celery stems, chopped	250 g	9 oz	9 oz
Parsley stems, chopped	50 g	2 oz	2 oz
Bay leaves, halved	2	2	2
Dried marjoram, crushed	a pinch	a pinch	a pinch
Dried thyme, crushed	a pinch	a pinch	a pinch
Cold water	1.2 litres	2 pts 9 fl oz	5 cups
Carrot, Broccoli, Tomato and Tofu Soup			
Carrots, peeled and chopped	225 g	8 oz	8 oz
Broccoli florets	80 g	3 oz	3 oz
Tomatoes, peeled and seeded	150 g	5 oz	5 oz
Vegetable broth	400 ml	13½ fl oz	1⅔ cups
Tomato purée	5 g	⅛ oz	1 tsp
Soya milk	100 ml	3½ fl oz	½ cup
Tofu, diced	100 g	3½ oz	3½ oz
Garnish			
Basil leaves	20 g	¾ oz	¾ oz

PREPARATION

Vegetable Broth

- Combine all the ingredients in a large pot and bring to the boil over high heat. Lower the heat and let the mixture simmer for 1 hr. Line a strainer or colander with a double thickness of cheesecloth and set it over a very large bowl or pot. Strain the stock, discard the residue, and let the stock cool. To store, cover tightly and leave in the refrigerator.

Carrot, Broccoli, Tomato and Tofu Soup

- Blend the carrots, broccoli florets, tomatoes, vegetable broth and tomato purée. Add soya milk until you get a desired consistency.
- Before serving, add the diced tofu and garnish with basil leaves. Serve cold.

STEAMED SEA BASS FILLET AND
SAUTÉED SPINACH LEAVES WITH HORSERADISH SAUCE

Serves 4 • 185 Calories per serving • Protein 27 g • Carbohydrate 7 g • Fat 3 g

INGREDIENTS

	Metric	Imperial	American
Non-fat plain yogurt	200 ml	7 fl oz	1 cup
Prepared horseradish	5½ tbsp	5½ tbsp	5½ tbsp
Olive oil	120 ml	4 fl oz	½ cup
Red onions, thinly sliced	90 g	3 oz	3 oz
Sea bass fillets, halved	500 g	1 lb	1 lb
Balsamic vinegar	4 tsp	4 tsp	4 tsp
Freshly ground black pepper	1 tsp	1 tsp	1 tsp
Lemon juice	4 tbsp	4 tbsp	4 tbsp
Lemon thyme	1 tsp	1 tsp	1 tsp
Large spinach leaves	400 g	14 oz	14 oz
Vine tomatoes, sliced	280 g	10 oz	10 oz
New baby potatoes, boiled and peeled	400 g	14 oz	14 oz
Parsley, chopped	80 g	3 oz	1 cup
Herb Salad			
Red capsicum, julienned	30 g	1 oz	½ cup
Fennel	15 g	½ oz	½ oz
Basil leaves	15 g	½ oz	½ oz
Coriander	15 g	½ oz	½ oz
Chives, snipped	15 g	½ oz	½ oz

PREPARATION

- Mix the yogurt with the horseradish in a small bowl. Set aside.

- Heat the olive oil over medium heat in a nonstick pan. Sauté the onions for 4 to 5 min, or until they turn translucent. Lay the fish over the onions, add the vinegar, and season with pepper, lemon juice and thyme. Cover tightly and bake for about 10 min, or until the fish is opaque and fully-cooked.

- Sauté the spinach leaves for a few seconds, then set aside. Combine all the ingredients for the herb salad and toss well.

- To serve, centre the spinach with the tomatoes and onions on the side. Arrange the fillets on top and and ladle some horseradish sauce over. Garnish the potatoes with parsley and place them next to the herb salad.

ORANGE-POACHED PEACHES WITH LIME SHERBET

Serves 4 • 129 Calories per serving • Protein 2 g • Carbohydrate 30 g • Fat 0 g

INGREDIENTS	Metric	Imperial	American
Lime Sherbet			
Non-fat milk	400 ml	13½ fl oz	1⅔ cups
Sugar	400 g	14 oz	2 cups
Water	400 ml	13½ fl oz	1⅔ cups
Lime juice	400 ml	13½ fl oz	1⅔ cups
Fresh lime zest	40 g	1½ oz	1½ oz
Orange-poached Peaches			
Fresh orange zest	1 tbsp	1 tbsp	1 tbsp
Peaches	4	4	4
Orange juice	600 ml	1 pt 4 fl oz	2½ cups
Apple juice	120 ml	4 fl oz	½ cup
Cornflour	10 g	⅜ oz	1 tsp
Lime sherbet	280 g	10 oz	10 oz
Raspberries	50 g	2 oz	2 oz
Blueberries	50 g	2 oz	2 oz

PREPARATION

Lime Sherbet

- Bring the milk, sugar and water to the boil in a small saucepan. Then place the saucepan in an ice-bath for 2 hr or overnight, in a chiller. Add the lime juice and lime zest, and process the mixture in an ice-cream machine for 8 to 10 min or until frozen.

Orange-poached Peaches

- Bring half a saucepan full of water to the boil over high heat then add the orange zest. Let it simmer for about 3 min or until softened. Drain, refresh under cool running water and set aside.
- Blanch the peaches for 40 to 50 sec. Then, using a slotted spoon, gently lift them from the water. Transfer to a colander and refresh under cool running water.

- Peel and halve the peaches. Combine the peaches with the orange and apple juices. Simmer the mixture over medium heat for about 10 min or until the peaches begin to soften. Carefully remove the peaches using a slotted spoon and set aside. Dissolve the cornflour in water and add the cornflour mixture into the juices. Let it simmer, stirring occasionally, until the sauce is thickened. Remove from the heat and chill before serving.
- To serve, arrange 2 peach halves on each plate and spoon the sauce over. Then add a scoop of lime sherbert and garnish with the lime zest and berries.

STRAWBERRY SMOOTHIE

Serves 4 • 160 Calories per serving • Protein 6 g • Carbohydrate 30 g • Fat 1 g

INGREDIENTS	Metric	Imperial	American
Fresh strawberries	4	4	4
Strawberry sorbet	120 ml	4 fl oz	½ cup
Strawberry yogurt	445 ml	15 fl oz	2 cups
Fresh lime juice	3 tsp	3 tsp	3 tsp
Ice cubes	8	8	8
Salt	to taste	to taste	to taste
Strawberries, sliced	4	4	4

PREPARATION

- Blend all the ingredients until smooth. Serve in chilled mocktail glasses garnished with strawberries.

Spa Digest

Asia provides a variety of backdrops for a spa experience to suit every taste—beaches, rainforests, mountains, even urban centres. In these sensuous and luxurious surroundings, retreat from the daily grind and be feted by therapies from the East and West.

Many Asian spas offer high-touch therapies inspired by the healing cultures from the region, and the latest high-tech treatments from the rest of the world. You may also enrich your overall spa experience with complementary therapies from acupuncture to visualisation, physical activities from aikido to yoga, and cultural experiences such as getting acquainted with a new cuisine or folding a lotus flower. Or rejuvenate your body, mind and spirit in solitude.

The following pages introduce you to Asia's top spas.

Amrita Spa at Raffles Grand Hotel d'Angkor

SIEM REAP, CAMBODIA

ABOVE: The cool blue-and-white tiled jacuzzi area.

BELOW RIGHT: The spa is decorated with fresh lotus flowers. Every morning, nimble-fingered staff 'fold the lotus flower' by coaxing the outer petals inwards while retaining the original shape of the inner petals.

Since 1932, travellers paying homage to the ruins of Angkor's temples have enhanced their visits by staying at the elegant Raffles Grand Hotel d'Angkor, eight kilometres away on the edge of Siem Reap. The hotel still retains much of her colonial charm—from her original cage elevator to visual elements from the temple complex and Art Deco motifs—albeit with latter-day luxuries. Tributes to her recent restoration, employing environmentally friendly materials and local craftwork, include mention in the Condé Nast Gold List for World's Best Places to Stay 2001.

Most suites and villas have balconies with a view of the 60,000-square metre (645,834-square foot) Royal Crusade for Independence formal gardens which lie between the hotel and the royal Summer Residence. The hotel's two luxurious villas, inspired by Cambodian folk architecture, are equipped with private wine cellars. Longer-staying guests typically ask for the self-contained studio suites which are equipped with work stations and pantry facilities.

The Cabana Rooms have direct access to a 35-metre (115-foot) lap pool

inspired by the ancient royal bathing ponds of Angkor, and a family fun pool.

The Amrita Spa, overlooking the swimming pool and garden, is decorated with pink lotus flowers which give a touch of the exotic. The spa offers an assortment of Ayurvedic techniques, European mud and seaweed wraps, and skin care treatments.

Skin care treats include the Multi Vitamin Power Treatment which is said to combat ageing by improving skin elasticity, tone and texture through the use of fruit enzymes and hydroxy acids.

Couples typically favour packages such as the Aroma Retreat (hydrobath with essential oils and mineral salts, full-body aromatherapy massage, skin care treatment, warm oil scalp massage and reflexology) and the Ultimate Amrita Spa Sanctuary (exfoliating Mineral Salt Body Glow, de-stressing aromatherapy hydrobath, full-body therapeutic massage, skin care treatment, reflexology, and manicure and pedicure). Lunch is included in both packages.

The three-and-a-half-hour Total Body Wellness package is bundled with a mineral-rich Sea Salt Scrub, Sea Mud Wrap, a warm Sea Mud Hair Treatment with a relaxing scalp massage and facial acupressure point massage, a full body massage and an aromatherapy facial.

ABOVE RIGHT: Honeymooners or couples celebrating an anniversary typically opt to spend at least half a day in the VIP Treatment Room.

BELOW RIGHT: Some of the suites are named after famous visitors to the hotel such as Charles de Gaulle and Andre Malraux.

SPA STATISTICS

SPA AREA
400 sq m (4,306 sq ft)

FACILITIES
1 double VIP room, 4 single treatment rooms, 1 hydrotherapy room, 1 mud wrap room; 1 sauna, 1 steam room each in the locker rooms, 3 jacuzzis (1 each for men, women and unisex); 1 gymnasium, 2 swimming pools; 1 hair salon; spa boutique

SIGNATURE TREATMENTS
Ayurvedic Panch Karma, Multi Vitamin Power Treatment, Tranquility Hydro and Body Wrap

OTHER TREATMENTS AND THERAPIES
Ayurvedic Shiro Dhara, body bronzing, body masks, body scrubs, body wraps, foot massage, massage therapies, skin care treatments, reflexology; spa packages

PROVISIONS FOR COUPLES
VIP Raffles Siana Room

SPA CUISINE
Available at all times

ACTIVITIES
Cooking classes, folding of the lotus flower (guests will be taught how to fold the outer petals inwards while keeping the shape of the inner petals); jogging, tennis; meditation, yoga

SERVICES
Personal training; fortune-telling; 24-hour valet service

ADMISSION
Exclusively for members and hotel guests

CONTACT
1 Vithei Charles De Gaulle
Khum Svay Dang Kum
Siem Reap
Cambodia
Tel: (855-63) 963 888
Fax: (855-63) 963 168
Email: raffles.grand@bigpond.com.kh
Website: www.raffles.com or www.amritaspas.com

Amrita Spa at Raffles Hotel Le Royal

PHNOM PENH, CAMBODIA

affles Hotel Le Royal, established in 1929, exudes old-world charm with its Khmer, Art Deco and French Colonial architecture. Set in a fragrant tropical garden in the heart of Phnom Penh's social scene, it's within easy reach of the Royal Palace, Central Market and National Museum. Guest rooms and suites, spread over three low-rise wings overlooking the garden courtyard and swimming pool, feature Art Deco furnishings and traditional Cambodian folk *objets d'art*. Stay in one of the Personality Suites named after luminaries who've stayed over in the past or drink to their memory at the Elephant Bar with cocktails such as Femme Fatale (inspired by Jacqueline Kennedy) and Million Dollar Cocktail (immortalised in Somerset Maugham's *The Letter*).

Amrita Spa, on the second floor, faces the hotel's entrance and garden. It is decorated in warm earthy colours, with jasmine and lotus flowers in each treatment room. Like her sister spa in Raffles Grand Hotel d'Angkor, this spa offers Ayurvedic techniques, European mud and seaweed wraps, massage therapies and skin care treatments. Ayurvedic treatments include Ayurvedic Panch Karma, Abhyang & Mardan or Malish, Shiro Dhara, Shiro Abhyang, and Padabhyang and Padaghat (a 15-minute session foot massage with oils).

The spa has a good selection of wraps such as the Enzymatic Sea Mud Wrap (which includes an acupressure point facial massage and a scalp

ABOVE: Leave some time after your treatment to relax in the jacuzzi.

ABOVE RIGHT: One of the spa's single treatment rooms.

OPPOSITE TOP: The hotel, established in 1929, still exudes the old-world charm of Khmer, Art Deco and French Colonial architecture.

OPPOSITE BELOW LEFT: Cocktails at the Elephant Bar are named for luminaries who once stayed at the hotel.

OPPOSITE BELOW RIGHT: The well-equipped gymnasium overlooks the lovely garden courtyard.

massage), a Herbal Detox Wrap (where steaming herbal-soaked linen wrapped around your body helps eliminate toxins and reduces muscle tension) and a Tranquility Hydro and Body Wrap (which is prefaced by a relaxing hydrobath and massage). The two latter treatments include a face and head massage using Ayurvedic *marma* point techniques.

Signature skin care treats include the Multi Vitamin Power Treatment which combats signs of ageing through the use of fruit enzymes and hydroxy acids.

Should you have at least two-and-a-half hours, opt for a packaged treat such as Beyond Heaven which begins with a back massage to release tension in stressed muscles and soft tissue, followed by a Classic Skin Care Treatment customised to enhance your skin, a Nourishing Eye Treatment and a reflexology-style foot massage.

SPA STATISTICS

SPA AREA
404 sq m (4,349 sq ft)

FACILITIES
4 single treatment rooms; 1 mud wrap room; 1 jacuzzi, 2 saunas, 2 steam rooms; 1 gymnasium, 2 swimming pools; 1 hair salon; spa boutique

SIGNATURE TREATMENTS
Ayurvedic Panch Karma, Multi Vitamin Power Treatment, Tranquility Hydro and Body Wrap

OTHER TREATMENTS AND THERAPIES
Aqua wellness, Ayurvedic Shiro Dhara, body bronzing, body masks, body scrubs, body wraps, foot massage, massage therapies, skin care treatments, reflexology; spa packages

PROVISIONS FOR COUPLES
No facilities for couples, but couples get discounts if they have their treatments in 2 separate rooms simultaneously

SPA CUISINE
Available at all times at the Monivong Café. You can enjoy your meal at the café, in the garden or at the poolside. Special dietary needs can be catered to on request

ACTIVITIES
Aerobics, Conscious Movement, Neuromuscular Integrative Action, strength/stretch, water aerobics; yoga/stretch

SERVICES
Baby-sitting; personal training

ADMISSION
Exclusively for hotel guests and members

CONTACT
92 Rukhak Vithei Daun Penh (off Monivong Boulevard)
Sangkat Wat Phnom
Phnom Penh, Cambodia
Tel: (855-23) 981 888
Fax: (855-23) 981 168
Email: raffles.hlr.ghda@bigpond.com.kh
Website: www.raffles.com or www.amritaspas.com

Club Oasis at Grand Hyatt Shanghai

SHANGHAI, CHINA

ABOVE: The hotel occupies the 53rd to 87th levels of Jin Mao Tower which has 88 levels.

Listed in the *Guinness Book of Records 2000* as the highest hotel in the world, the Grand Hyatt Shanghai occupies the 53rd to 87th levels of the 88-storey Jin Mao Tower.

The award-winning 5-star hotel is located in the heart of Pudong, Shanghai's financial district. The hotel's architecture is a modern take on the pagoda, said to be the first Chinese skyscraper. The interior décor features contemporary Art Deco and traditional Chinese motifs. The furniture and artwork is Chinese-made, right down to the ceramic ice buckets fired in local kilns.

All the ultra-luxurious guest rooms and the 12 restaurants and bars have commanding views over Shanghai.

High-tech features throughout the hotel include a shower tower with three shower heads in the in-room shower cubicles and wireless broadband connection even from the poolside on the 57th level in this highest spa in the world.

The 16-metre (52-foot) long 'sky pool' is maintained at a comfortable 26 to 28 degrees Celsius.

Like the pool, Club Oasis has a breathtaking view of the entire city, giving a new meaning to feeling on-top-of-the-world after working out at the well-equipped gym or indulging in one of the spa's Western or Chinese therapies.

Celebrity spa visitors include actors Dennis Hopper and Jude Law who've had the energy flow to their body, mind and spirit restored and balanced with the Deep Tissue Massage, a traditional Chinese therapeutic treatment which relieves muscular cramps and soreness. Supermodel Kate Moss had the Oasis Stone Massage, where heated or cooled smooth stones and warm essential oils offer a type of relaxation not achievable by hand. A popular treatment with Asian ladies who treasure fair skin is the Whitening Body Wrap which helps lighten and repair skin after it's been exposed to the sun. Your feet will benefit from a

ABOVE LEFT: It's a surreal sensation, swimming in the 'sky pool' built 57 levels above the ground.

ABOVE RIGHT: A pampering treatment such as the Oasis Stone Massage on the spa on Level 57 gives new meaning to being in seventh heaven.

BELOW: The Grand Room with stunning views of the city.

OPPOSITE BELOW LEFT: Contemplating the Shanghai skyline from the relaxation area is repose in itself.

OPPOSITE BELOW CENTRE: Like the rest of the hotel, treatment rooms echo what is chic about both East and West.

OPPOSITE BELOW RIGHT: Products available from the spa boutique include elegant burners and exotic candles calligraphed with Tang poems.

Shanghai Pedicure where the nails and cuticles are trimmed, and dead skin and callouses removed.

The spa's silver-and-white colour scheme contributes to the airiness and lightness expected of a heavenly retreat for the body and mind. The spacious mosaic- and marble-lined spa has separate areas for men and women. Chinese spa products may be purchased from the spa boutique.

SPA STATISTICS

SPA AREA
300 sq m (3,229 sq ft)

FACILITIES
7 single treatment rooms; 6 spa pools with 3 temperatures, 2 saunas and steam rooms; 1 gymnasium, 1 indoor swimming pool; spa boutique

SIGNATURE TREATMENTS
Deep Tissue Massage, Oasis Stone Massage, Shanghai Pedicure

OTHER TREATMENTS AND THERAPIES
Body scrubs, body wraps, eyebrow shaping, eyelash perm, facial treatments, hand and foot treatments, manicures/pedicures, massage therapies, oxygen therapies, waxing; spa packages for men and women

SPA CUISINE
Not available, but tailored menus can be catered to on request

ACTIVITIES
Gong fu and *tai ji* classes

SERVICES
Baby-sitting; personal training

ADMISSION
Exclusively for hotel guests and invited members

CONTACT
Jin Mao Tower
88 Century Boulevard
Pudong, Shanghai 200121
China
Tel: (86-21) 5049 1234
Fax: (86-21) 5049 1111
Email: info@hyattshanghai.com
Website: www.shanghai.hyatt.com

The Spa at Hilton Shanghai

SHANGHAI, CHINA

The grand Hilton Shanghai stands 43 levels above the city's commercial district, and is positioned perfectly between two shopping streets. The hotel is a short walk to the subway station and exhibition centre, and a 15-minute ride to the famous Bund and the Shanghai Grand Theatre.

The Spa, which is managed by the Sportathlon Group, is located on the fourth level of the luxury hotel, and was completely renovated in October 2000. The Spa's smart, sophisticated design complements the staff's friendly and professional attitude.

The unique Ozone Enriched Bio-Climatised Air system extracts harmful gases, leaving behind clean and crisp oxygenated air that will help boost circulation and eliminate toxins.

The Spa artfully combines traditional Asian therapies and modern techniques, with the use of natural and organic products to create the Shanghainese Tui Na and Javanese Lulur.

The Spa's signature treatment, the Orange & Coconut Body Polish Delight, is made from half a cup of coconut milk, half a cup of dessicated coconut and grated orange rind. The body is exfoliated with a soft body brush before the gently warmed mixture is applied along the body. Many guests are captivated by the delicious scent which remains long after the polish is rinsed off.

ABOVE: Guests relax with a refreshing glass of healthy fruit juice at the Spa Bar while sharing spa experiences.

RIGHT: Guests can rest on the comfortable leather chairs in the relaxation rooms before and after their treatments.

Hydrotherapy treatments include a Hydrobath, Vichy Shower and an Aromatic Oil Steam Capsule. The female and male changing area features therapeutic waterworks such as Hot and Cold Plunge pools, Japanese Twin Showers and a traditional shower room with a therapeutic jet massage shower.

Special facilities include the Kneipp Bath Hydromassage rooms. The treatments work along the same lines as reflexology. You walk on a bed of smooth rounded stones soaked in lukewarm water while numerous water jets gently massage your body. At the same time, a waterfall stream stimulates the circulation with a hydro head massage.

Each changing area features a traditional Finnish Sauna Bath and a Turkish Herbal Steam Room. The latter has a herbal steam infusion unit decorated with colour therapy lights.

ABOVE LEFT: The backdrop to the jacuzzis in both the male and female areas is a gentle waterfall that spills over a glass feature—a soothing sight and sound.

ABOVE RIGHT: The octagonal 15-metre by 15-metre (49-foot by 49-foot) swimming pool.

BELOW LEFT: The Orange & Coconut Body Polish Delight is an all-over body treatment that leaves the skin feeling stimulated and refreshed.

SPA STATISTICS

SPA AREA
3,000 sq m (32,292 sq ft)

FACILITIES
1 double treatment room, 6 single massage and treatment rooms, 1 Cellu M6 and G5 equipment room, 1 hydrotherapy bath room, 2 Kneipp Bath Hydromassage rooms; 2 Finnish Sauna Baths, 2 cold plunge pools, 2 hot plunge pools, 2 hydromassage rooms, 2 Japanese twin showers, 8 Therapeutic Jet Showers, 2 Turkish Herbal Steam rooms with Colour Therapy; 1 indoor heated swimming pool, 1 group exercise room, 1 gymnasium, 1 squash court, 1 tennis court with floodlights

SIGNATURE TREATMENT
Orange & Coconut Body Polish Delight

OTHER TREATMENTS AND THERAPIES
Body masks, body scrubs, body wraps, facial treatments, anti-ageing treatments, endermologie, firming and toning treatments, hand and foot treatments, hydrotherapy, lymphatic drainage, massage therapies; half-day and full-day packages

PROVISIONS FOR COUPLES
1 private double treatment room

SPA CUISINE
Available in the Spa Bar & Restaurant and the Outdoor Sun Terrace. Special dietary needs can be catered to on request at all F&B outlets

ACTIVITIES
Squash, swimming and tennis classes; aerobics (step and high-low impact), boxing, Spa Bo, spinning, *tai ji*; yoga, Pilates; fitness assessments, programming and personal training

SERVICES
Medical centre, baby-sitting services

ADMISSION
The Spa Health Club is exclusively for hotel guests and members, although spa treatments are available to walk-in guests

CONTACT
250 Hua Shan Road
Shanghai 200040
China
Tel: (86-21) 6248 0000 ext 2600
Fax: (86-21) 6248 3848
Email: spa_shanghai@hilton.com
Website: www.hilton.com or
www.thespahealthclubs.com

The St. Regis Spa & Club

BEIJING, CHINA

L ocated in the heart of the city's diplomatic, business and shopping precinct, The St. Regis Beijing is just a few minutes away from popular tourist attractions such as Tiananmen Square. The hotel has received various accolades from *Condé Nast Traveller* including being on its 2002 Gold List, 2001 Hot List and 2001 Readers' Choice.

The St. Regis Spa & Club is a complete retreat centre with amenities such as a state-of-the-art gymnasium, squash and badminton courts, golf driving area and putting green.

The indoor swimming pool on the first level is partially encased by glass and receives lots of natural light. In addition, the ceiling is fitted with special lights that change colours during the night—giving

the effect of being under a velvet sky of stars. You can literally 'take the waters' at the spa which is tucked away in the basement. Natural hot mineral spring water—from 1,500 metres (4,921 feet) below ground—is piped into the spa facilities, its VIP rooms and the hotel's apartments. Imported Jurlique products are used in spa treatments and can be purchased from the spa boutique. The

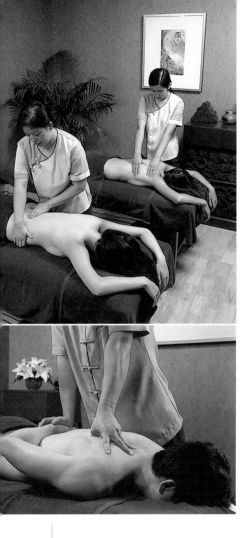

SPA STATISTICS

SPA AREA
1,500 sq m (16,146 sq ft)

FACILITIES
2 VIP treatment suites, 1 triple treatment room, 1 double treatment room, 4 single treatment rooms; 3 jacuzzis (1 outdoor), 2 saunas, 2 steam rooms; 1 gymnasium, 1 indoor swimming pool; spa boutique

SIGNATURE TREATMENT
St. Regis Spa Signature Treatment

OTHER TREATMENTS AND THERAPIES
Anti-cellulite treatments, bath treatments, body masks, body scrubs, body wraps, eye treatments, facial treatments, hand and foot treatments, hair care and services, manicures/pedicures, massage therapies, professional makeup, reflexology, waxing; spa packages

PROVISIONS FOR COUPLES
VIP Suites

SPA CUISINE
Available at the Pool Bar, Astor Grill Restaurant, The Garden Court and in-room dining. Special dietary needs can be catered to on request

ACTIVITIES
Dance classes, aerobics, badminton, billiards and snooker, bowling, golf driving area and putting green, *gong fu*, *tai ji*, rhythmic body stretch, squash, tennis, yoga

SERVICES
Crèche; Chinese medicine consultations, customised fitness programmes, fitness assessment, personal training

ADMISSION
Non-hotel guests and non-members pay an entry fee to use spa, pool and gymnasium (use restricted during peak hours) if not having treatments

CONTACT
21 Jian Guo Men Wai Da Jie
Beijing 100020
China
Tel: (86-10) 6460 6688
Fax: (86-10) 6460 3299
Email: beijing.stregis@stregis.com
Website: www.stregis.com/beijing

TOP: The Aromatherapy Full Body Massage relaxes your body and mind.

ABOVE: The Express Aromatherapy Back Massage helps ease muscular tension.

ABOVE RIGHT: The spa offers a nutritious menu.

OPPOSITE TOP: The spa's jacuzzis are next to the swimming pool.

OPPOSITE BELOW LEFT: By day, the indoor swimming pool receives natural light.

OPPOSITE BELOW RIGHT: The Aromabath with Rose Petals is a soothing, cleansing and hydrating treatment.

spa also works with doctors trained in Chinese traditional medicine. These practitioners can prescribe herbal tonics, which a local dispensary then delivers to the hotel. Customised massages for specific needs can also be requested.

The spa's most popular treatments are the Ritual Packages. A must-try is the two-hour Signature Treatment. It involves a full-body deep tissue Chinese aromatherapy massage, followed by a facial, and ends with a two-course nutritious Western lunch.

Should you have multiple days to indulge in, three-day and five-day spa adventures are also available. But if you have only 15 to 30 minutes for a pick-me-up, the spa offers express treatments ranging from Express Scalp Massage to Express Aromatherapy Back Massage.

The VIP Treatment Suites—available on an hourly basis—are particularly popular with guests desiring more privacy, longer packages or to celebrate special occasions. Treatments include a Deluxe Aromatique Bath and Massage, Austrian Moor Bath and Aromabath with Rose Petals. In-suite facilities include a hot mineral spring bath and aroma steam. For an extra fee, you can enjoy the spa treatments in your hotel room or outside the spa's regular operating hours.

The St. Regis Spa Shanghai

SHANGHAI, CHINA

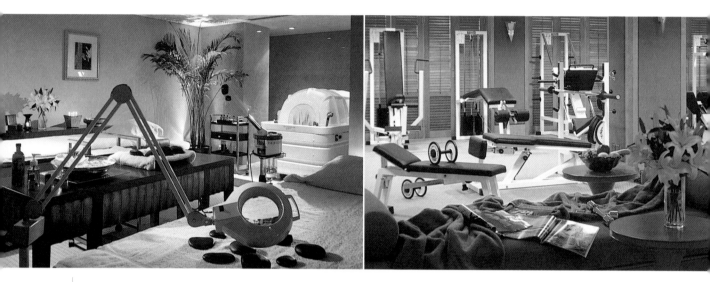

ABOVE: Guests opting for the Herbal Mud Wrap will be given a facial and neck massage as they lie in the Thermo Derm capsule (in the background).

ABOVE RIGHT: Guests can have a comprehensive workout in the well-equipped fitness centre.

BELOW: The Bellenera essential oils and incense used in treatments are also on sale at the spa boutique.

The tall, sleek St. Regis Shanghai, in the heart of Pudong's central business district, hints of new-world chic and old-world luxury. Furnished with rich fabric and artwork, guest rooms and suites boast designer furniture including a Herman Miller 'Aeron' chair and Bose audio system (CDs can be borrowed at no charge). Personal touches derive from the discreet and detailed guest records (right down to the preferred types of pillows) and round-the-clock English-style butler service. A butler acts as personal assistant for guests on each floor; his duties include seeing that complimentary beverages are delivered as soon as guests awaken.

The hotel group's flexible Starwood Preferred Guest loyalty programme has won repeat guests for the property. The hotel has also won awards such as the Best New Business Hotels of 2001 award by *Forbes* magazine.

The St. Regis Spa on the sixth level is chic yet serene. Treatment areas are segregated, with two to three beds—easily separated with partitions—per room. Male therapists provide treatment on male guests, female therapists on female guests. Each treatment room features a rainforest shower for an invigorating rinse and a Thermo Derm capsule for guests opting for a Herbal Mud Wrap. As steam from the capsule helps pores absorb minerals from the volcanic mud, a therapist performs a non-oil facial and neck massage. The spa's signature La Stone Massage uses smooth volcanic stones warmed to about

ABOVE: The glass-encased hotel is outlined with a red LED light at night.

LEFT: The floor-to-ceiling windows around the indoor swimming pool let in plenty of natural sunlight.

40 degrees Celsius. These are applied to the body with warm oils and long strokes. A Back Stone Massage is also available. Other popular treatments include Holistic Aromatherapy (deep tissue massage and full-body treatment using essential oils), Essential Oil Wrap (massage with essential oils followed by a blanket wrap), Herbal Body Glow (a herbal steam and full-body massage using salts and oils) and Purifying Back Treatment (with salts and oils, followed by a mud blanket treatment).

Spa packages such as the five-hour Half Day Purity (comprising Herbal Body Glow, Herbal Mud Wrap, Deep Tissue Massage, Facial Aromatherapy and Scalp Massage) are also available. Other treatments include the Jet Lag Treatment (a non-oil-based traditional Oriental massage) and the Foot Massage (traditional foot reflexology).

SPA STATISTICS

SPA AREA
620 sq m (6,674 sq ft)

FACILITIES
1 female treatment room with 3 beds,
1 male treatment room with 3 beds;
2 cold plunge pools, 2 hot plunge pools,
2 saunas, 2 steam rooms; 1 gymnasium,
1 indoor lap pool with jacuzzi; 1 hair
and beauty salon

SIGNATURE TREATMENT
La Stone Massage

OTHER TREATMENTS AND THERAPIES
Body scrubs, body wraps, facial
treatments, foot massage, hair services,
manicures/pedicures, massage therapies,
purifying back treatment, waxing; spa
packages

PROVISIONS FOR COUPLES
Couples can enjoy their treatments
together in one of the treatment rooms

SPA CUISINE
Available at the International Restaurant.
Special dietary needs can be catered
to on request

ACTIVITY
Tennis classes

SERVICES
24-hour personal butler service;
personal training

ADMISSION
Open to in-house and walk-in guests.
Membership not required for the spa, but
required for the gymnasium and pool

CONTACT
889 Dong Fang Road
Pudong
Shanghai 200122
China
Tel: (86-21) 5050 4567
Fax: (86-21) 6875 6789
Email: stregis.shanghai
@starwoodhotels.com
Website: www.stregis.com

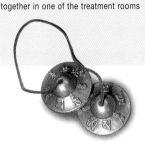

Ananda-In the Himalayas Destination Spa

UTTARANCHAL, INDIA

ABOVE: The Music Pavilion, an open-air marble-floor shelter, is embraced by a still pool at the south end of the Palace Lawn.

BELOW: The Royal Crest, a heritage that has been carried through the ages.

Ananda-In the Himalayas Destination Spa sits on the foothills of the majestic Himalayas, overlooking the river Ganges and the holy Rishikesh town and valley. Located 260 kilometres (162 miles) north of New Delhi, the spa is easily accessible by rail, road and air.

The retreat is built on 40 hectares (100 acres) of virgin forest on the Maharaja of Tehri-Garhwal's palace estate. The facilities include the Viceregal Palace, built in 1910 to honour the British Viceroy. The palace houses a glass pavilion boardroom with the Maharaja's old library, India's oldest billiards table and a tea lounge where guests can sample fine teas. The latter is adorned with photographs of visiting luminaries who have offered their *salaams* (a salutation or ceremonial greeting) to the Maharaja.

The 75 rooms and suites are subtle statements of style and luxury. Built on the mountain ridge, the rooms offer breathtaking views of the valley and the city of Rishikesh or the palace. One of the main features of the rooms is the independent patio balcony with views of the Himalayas, where you can relax or even practise yoga.

ABOVE: The regal façade of the Viceregal Palace.

ABOVE RIGHT: Dinner shows are often scheduled at the Ananda Hill Theatre in pleasant weather.

RIGHT: A relaxing soak in a bath with fresh rose petals is part of a traditional Indian wedding treatment the spa has dubbed The Royal Bath.

A walk through the woods and manicured lawns brings you to the three-storeyed Ananda Spa, where staff greet guests with *Namshkar* (I bow to the god in you). The airy atrium is cooled by breezes scented by ancient pines and wildflowers. Pure Himalayan spring water is used as much as possible for therapies. It also flows into the spa's hydrotherapy areas and pools.

The spa's holistic approach to body, mind and soul is derived from its proximity to the Himalayas—the birthplace of yoga, meditation and Ayurveda. The spa is dedicated to providing guests with a total

immersion experience while discovering a lifestyle oriented towards well-being, and based on holistic therapy.

By focusing on wellness according to yogic and Ayurvedic philosophies, the personalised therapy and activity programmes are designed to meet individual needs and health goals along with guidance in the areas of deep relaxation, stress management, nutrition, exercise, detoxification and anti-ageing.

The spa features 20 luxurious therapy rooms with dramatic views of the Himalayan landscape, along with a state-of-the-art Fitness Centre, an Olympic-sized swimming pool, modern hydrotherapy facilities and a boutique, each complementing the spa's philosophy of holistic wellness.

Ayurvedic therapies, yoga and meditation are at the core of the spa's treatments. The Ayurvedic treatments include the seven-day Santvanam (calming) therapy, 14-day Sodhanam (liberation) therapy and 21-day Rasayanam (rejuvenation) therapy.

Inclusive of diagnosis, prescription, medication, diet, yoga and meditation, these programmes are designed to be completed in multiples of seven days in accordance with the Ayurvedic belief that the human body operates in such cycles.

Experience the deep meditative calm of the Himalayan outdoors through individual sessions at the five yoga venues. Whether you are a beginner or an advanced participant, you are encouraged to experience a higher level of personal contentment by incorporating devotion, dedication and discipline into your lifestyle. Activities are also recommended to help you explore the physiological, philosophical and theoretical goals of yoga.

Couples can opt for packages such as the Ananda Couple's Bliss performed in the Kama Suite decorated with candles and flowers. The ritual includes an hour-long massage (either aromatherapy or Swedish), a jacuzzi bath, foot cleansing and massage, and a private steam bath.

All the traditional treatments and accessories have been enhanced by constant research and practise at Ananda. Two signature experiences at the spa are the Ananda Sanjeevni (combining Eastern and Western body, beauty and self-care practices) and the Himalayan Experience (a combination of an ancient Indian Honey and Sandalwood rub, Indian body mask and a body massage using century-old recipes).

The cuisine at Ananda is a delectable mix of spa and gourmet culled from Ayurvedic, Asian and European cuisines which can be enjoyed in unique dining venues such as The Tree Top Deck, The Hill Side Theatre and The Winter Garden. The Show Kitchen is a place of discovery as one journeys into macrobiotic, Ayurvedic and spa cuisine under the expert guidance of the Ananda chefs.

ABOVE: The 75 rooms and suites are subtle statements of style and luxury.

TOP LEFT: The glass-domed roof and open portals let in light and breeze to The Restaurant.

OPPOSITE TOP RIGHT: The traditional Ayurvedic table is made of medicated wood.

OPPOSITE BELOW RIGHT: Bath time with a stunning view of the Ganges Valley.

OPPOSITE BELOW LEFT: Gold leaf panels inspired by Buddhist temples decorate the ceiling of the spa's lobby.

The Ananda experience envelops your every sense—be it through the magic of the Himalayan landscape and forest; the salubrious climate throughout the year; the luxury spa oriented towards the personal goals of each guest; the elegant and well-appointed rooms with majestic views; the old Viceregal Palace exuding the charm of a bygone royal era; the mystical Hill Theatre for cultural evenings or the explorative adventure opportunities of river rafting in the Ganges, trekking and visiting the Rajaji wildlife sanctuary.

SPA STATISTICS

SPA AREA
1,951 sq m (21,000 sq ft)

FACILITIES
1 couple's suite, 11 single therapy rooms,
4 relaxation rooms, 4 consultation rooms,
5 indoor and outdoor yoga and meditation
venues; 2 cold plunge pools, 2 Finnish
saunas, 2 indoor and outdoor jacuzzis,
2 Kneipp footbaths, 2 Turkish steam
rooms; 1 16-station life fitness gymnasium
with cardio, strength training and aerobics
facility; 1 hair and nail salon; spa boutique

SIGNATURE TREATMENTS
Ananda Sanjeevni Experience, Ayurvedic
therapies, Pranayama, meditation and
yoga (all with nutritional advice), Aveda
signature treatments

OTHER TREATMENTS AND THERAPIES
Traditional Indian body and beauty
treatments, body wraps, body scrubs,
hydrotherapy, massage therapies such
as Thai and Swedish, aromatherapy
treatments, Aveda skin, body and hair
therapies, nail, hair and makeup services;
spa packages

PROVISIONS FOR COUPLES
Ananda couple's massage, romance
packages; Kama Suite with massage area
and jacuzzi

SPA CUISINE
Mix of spa and gourmet culled from
Ayurvedic, Asian and European cuisines.
Various dietary requirements, in
particular Ayurvedic cuisine, vegetarian
meals and low-fat diets, can be catered
to on request

ACTIVITIES
Adventure and nature walks, mountain
trekking to the Himalayan foothills, white-
water rafting on the Ganges, visits to the
Rajaji National Park wildlife reserve,
spiritual excursions for the evening *Ganga
Arti* ceremony, visits to *ashrams* in
Rishikesh; spa cuisine demonstrations;
aerobics, billiards, body conditioning
programmes, tennis, squash

SERVICES
Lifestyle consultations, Ayurvedic
consultations, nutrition advice, personal
fitness consultations, body assessment
analysis and training, personalised yoga
and meditation classes

CONTACT
The Palace Estate
Narendra Nagar
District Tehri-Garhwal
Uttaranchal 249175
India
Tel: (91-1378) 27 500
Fax: (91-1378) 27 550
Sales & Reservation Office
Tel: (91-11) 689 9999
Fax: (91-11) 613 1066
Email: administrator@anandaspa.com
Website: www.anandaspa.com

Somatheeram Ayurvedic Beach Resort

KERALA, INDIA

he six-hectare (15-acre) hilltop Somatheeram Ayurvedic Beach Resort slopes gently down to the sea. Intimate and beautifully detailed traditional Kerala guest houses provide a perfect refuge for holidaymakers wanting sun, sand and sea.

Many visitors come specifically to seek treatment for ailments or health concerns; others come to relax and rejuvenate by seeking the preventive benefits of the ancient Ayurvedic system of medicine. Treatment packages that include accommodation and meals are available. An Ayurvedic physician at Somatheeram Ayurvedic Hospital and Yoga Centre will analyse a guest's physical and psychological makeup before prescribing treatment and diet.

Some treatments run in seven-day cycles in accordance with Ayurvedic beliefs. These include the various forms of Dhara, where a steady stream of herbal oils and medicated milk is dripped on to the forehead. Njavarakizhi uses applications of medicated herbs and milk in muslin bags to the body. The resulting perspiration is known to ease joint and limb ailments. Shirovasti funnels lukewarm herbal oil into a leather cap worn for 15 to 60 minutes a day. The treatment is recommended for those with nasal ailments.

The Rejuvenation Massage therapy improves circulation of the blood and lymphatic systems. It is also believed to stimulate the body's 107 vital points. A therapist uses the soles of his feet to

SPA STATISTICS

SPA AREA
557 sq m (6,000 sq ft)

FACILITIES
24 single treatment rooms

SIGNATURE TREATMENTS
Dhara, Njavarakizhi, Pizhichil,
Rejuvenation Massage, Shirovasti

OTHER TREATMENTS AND THERAPIES
Beauty care, body immunisation/longevity
treatment, body purification therapy,
ear treatment, eye treatment, facial
treatments, massage therapies, medicated
steam bath, psoriasis treatment
programme, slimming programme;
spa packages

SPA CUISINE
Guests are prescribed a diet
according to their needs after a
consultation with the physician

ACTIVITIES
Indian dance, literature, music and
philosophy classes; houseboat cruises,
beach games, boating, cultural
performances, indoor games; meditation,
yoga

SERVICES
Consultations with nutritionists

CONTACT
Chowara
South of Kovalam
Via Balarampuram
Trivandrum 695501
Kerala
South India
Tel: (91-471) 268 101
Fax: (91-471) 267 600
Email: somatheeram@vsnl.com
Website: www.somatheeram.com

massage the guest who lies on the floor.
Meanwhile, he hangs on to a rope
suspended from the ceiling to keep his
balance and to exert the right pressure.

Hatha yoga sessions, under the
guidance of a guru, in the morning or
evening, complement the Ayurvedic
therapies. Guests can enrich their stay
by taking Indian dance, literature, music
and philosophy classes. Those taking a
break from their treatments may want to
admire Kerala's network of lakes,
lagoons, canals and rivers from a
luxurious two-hour or overnight cruise.

For four years running (since 1997/
1998), the resort has won Best Ayurvedic
Centre in the Tourism Awards given out
by the government of Kerala. It has also
won the Heritage Ayurvedic Resort
award. Famous guests include European
royalty, social activist Bianca Jagger, and
Indian musicians and movie stars.

TOP RIGHT: A wide-mouthed
earthern vessel steadily drips
a liquid of herbal oils and
medicated milk butter on to
the forehead of the patient.

BELOW RIGHT: In Pizhichil,
the guest lies on a wooden
treatment table while two
to four therapists rhythmically
pour oil over his body.

OPPOSITE TOP: The top-of-the-
line Deluxe Palace Suite is
a granite palace with an
octagon-shaped living room
and an open courtyard with a
bath looking to the sky.

OPPOSITE BELOW LEFT: Njavarakizhi
manages rheumatism, joint
pain, high blood pressure and
skin diseases through medical
puddings tied up in muslin
bags applied to the body.

OPPOSITE BELOW RIGHT: Ninety-
minute yoga sessions are
conducted every morning
and evening.

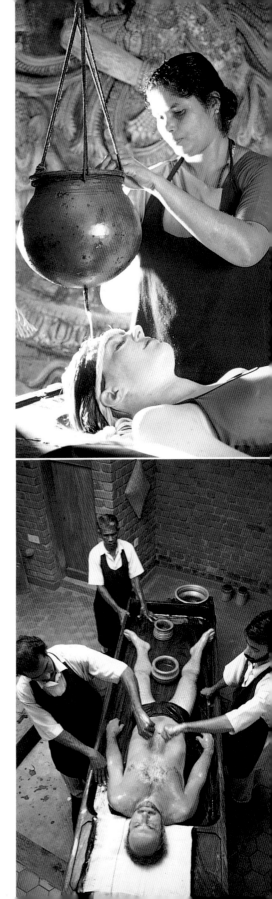

Apsara Residence & Spa at Hotel Tugu Malang

EAST JAVA, INDONESIA

ABOVE: Guests in the Apsara Residence enjoy their spa treatments in this Cambodian-flavoured Hall of Dancer.

ABOVE RIGHT: This low bed with colourful drapes and antique sculptures depicting classical dances create a passionate ambience for couples.

OPPOSITE TOP: An antique headboard helps add to the Apsara Residence's romantic atmosphere.

OPPOSITE CENTRE: Feel tension slip away in this floral-scented bath.

OPPOSITE BELOW: This long orange corridor leads to the Apsara Spa.

otel Tugu Malang, the first in a series of museum boutique hotels built to house the overflowing antique collection of its owner, is nostalgic of colonial life enjoyed by Dutch planters and civil servants in the highland town of Malang in East Java. This is evident throughout the three-storey mansion from the Raja Gula Room (featuring the personal effects of the late Sugar Baron Oei Tiong Ham) to the Raden Saleh Suite (themed and named after the 19th-century painter).

The property has won various accolades—including a ranking in the 101 Best Hotels in the World by UK Tatler, 1995, as well as an award by the Indonesian Institute of Architects.

The centre of pampering, Apsara Spa, is inspired by an ancient love story involving a Javanese prince who ruled a Cambodian kingdom and a beautiful Apsara dancer sent from heaven.

The Javanese-Cambodian influence is manifested in the romantic rhythm of classical Cambodian music that lulls the mind into a dream-like state, as the therapist's hands move across your back in a tender touch massage reminiscent of the graceful movements of an Apsara dancer. This special technique is incorporated with a traditional Javanese deep tissue massage in the Apsara Beauty Floral.

The top-selling treatment, Apsara Herbal Relaxation, combines a Javanese massage with a rub using a heated pack of local spices—an aromatic experience that warms the body and skin, and stimulates blood circulation.

Day Dream at Angkor is a four-hour package for couples. Employing ingredients of local herbs, spices and flowers, the treatments that pamper the hair, face, nails, body and feet hark back to the beauty rituals enjoyed by Javanese kings and queens of yore. The Day

Dream concludes with a lunch or dinner of a healthy, gourmet selection of classic Balinese and Southeast Asian favourites at Tirta Gangga Fine Dining, located in a newer extension of the hotel. For a stay that includes spa treatments, check into the elaborately furnished Apsara Residence. While few are able to afford the daily rack rate, the hotel is adamant that this suite is only open to those who respect the romantic histories of both Indonesia and Cambodia.

SPA STATISTICS

SPA AREA
175 sq m (1,884 sq ft)

FACILITIES
1 double room, 1 single room with small silver bathtub; 1 manicure/pedicure area, 1 beauty parlour; 1 giant bathtub made by local artisans; spa boutique

SIGNATURE TREATMENTS
Apsara Beauty Floral, Apsara Herbal Relaxation, Day Dream at Angkor

OTHER TREATMENTS AND THERAPIES
Bath treatments, body masks, body scrubs, facials, hair treatments, manicures/pedicures, massage therapies, reflexology; spa packages

PROVISIONS FOR COUPLES
Day Dream at Angkor; double treatment room

SPA CUISINE
Healthy gourmet Indonesian, Southeast Asian and Western meals. Special dietary needs can be catered to on request

ACTIVITIES
Antique appreciation, cooking, *jamu* herbal drinks and tropical floral arrangement classes

SERVICES
Baby-sitting; consultations with nutritionists; transfers from hotels in the vicinity

CONTACT
Jalan Tugu Number 3
Malang 65119
East Java, Indonesia
Tel: (62-341) 363 891
Fax: (62-341) 362 747
Email: malang@tuguhotels.com
Website: www.tuguhotels.com

Asmara Tropical Spas
at Mayang Sari Beach Resort

BINTAN ISLAND, INDONESIA

ABOVE: Asmara Tropical Spas, on the western end of the resort, is surrounded by a grove of coconut trees and a lush tropical garden; its entrance is marked by a grass and Palimanan limestone chequered path.

RIGHT: Treatments use various herbs and spices such as cloves, cinnamon and ginger.

Mayang Sari Beach Resort on Bintan Island is a 45-minute ferry ride from Singapore. The resort attracts holidaymakers who want to get away from the bustle of city life.

The tangerine-walled Asmara Tropical Spas encircles a lush garden, echoing Mayang Sari's laidback appeal. Decorated with Javanese teak furniture and rich sari fabric, the spa has the casualness of a friend's home.

With a chilled ginger, lemon grass and honey drink in hand, you can choose to browse through a book in the living room or wander into the adjoining shaded garden courtyard—both known as the Green Room—to laze in a hammock. You can also request to have a pedicure or ask for a head, neck and shoulder massage in the massage chair. The bright doors around the living room open on to single or double treatment rooms.

If you're a couple or a group of three, ask to be upgraded to the Asmara Pavilion for a nominal fee. Pick a spa package that includes a flower bath in the coppery-blue tub where your body will be dappled by sunlight. Light Asian or classical music and the sound of waves on the nearby shore will enhance your spa experience. Like the treatment rooms, the pavilion is so airy that the ceiling fan almost seems unnecessary.

SPA STATISTICS

SPA AREA

1,672 sq m (18,000 sq ft)

FACILITIES

2 double treatment rooms with outdoor shower each, 3 Asmara Pavilions (can accommodate up to 3 people each) with outdoor shower and bath tub, 3 single treatment rooms, 1 manicure/pedicure room; 1 relaxation lounge; 1 spa boutique

SIGNATURE TREATMENTS

Mandi Lulur, Traditional Riau Massage

OTHER TREATMENTS AND THERAPIES

Body masks, body scrubs, facial treatments, foot massage, foot scrub, manicures/pedicures, massage therapies; spa packages

PROVISIONS FOR COUPLES

Special rates for spa packages in the Pavilion

SPA CUISINE

Fruit juices and tonics are served at the Green Room; spa cuisine available at Spice Restaurant in conjunction with some spa programmes; special dietary needs can be catered to on request

ACTIVITIES

Guests at Mayang Sari can take part in games and activities organised by Nirwana Resort Hotel (free-form swimming pool with jacuzzi; gymnasium, jogging track; sea sports) and Mana Mana Beach Club (banana boat, catamaraning, jet skiing, kayaking, laser sailing, parasailing, pedal boating, scuba diving, snorkelling, surf and body boarding, wakeboarding, water-skiing, windsurfing). Some activities cost extra

SERVICES

Baby-sitting; free transfers between resorts on Bintan and any Asmara-managed spa on the island

CONTACT

Bintan Utara, Riau
29152 Indonesia
Tel: (62-770) 692 565
Fax: (62-770) 692 602
Email: asmaras@indosat.net.id
Website: www.asmaraspas.com

Singapore Booking Office
Tel: (65) 6227 6334
Fax: (65) 6227 2225

TOP: Each treatment room features full-length louvered windows that open to a pond and garden. Double treatment rooms have their own outdoor shower and grotto-like jacuzzi.

ABOVE: The relaxation lounge, dubbed the Green Room, resembles a hippie's abode draped with rich sari fabric. The vividly coloured doors lead to the treatment rooms.

Asmara, which means 'the beloved' in old Malay, relies mainly on ancient recipes from Oriental and Asian folk traditions. Signature treatments include the Traditional Riau Massage which uses focused pressure and a traditional Malay mix of spice oils to release muscle tension. The spa's biggest hit is the Mandi Lulur (a combination of herbal turmeric scrub, yogurt rub, full body traditional massage and a floral bath).

Apart from treatments which use all-natural herbs and spices, the spa offers two others using Shiseido's Ayura range: Shiseido Ayura Spa Treatment (a choice of a Relaxing Massage, Clarifying Body Scrub or Thermal Lift Body Mask, followed by a floral bath with Bath Essence or Vita Spa Bath Pack) and Shiseido Ayura Tropical Face Spa (which includes a chest and foot massage). Asmara is constantly expanding its treatment range and will launch Asmara Oriental Spa in the second half of 2002.

You can enjoy a fruit juice or tonic (such as the energy-boosting Pineapple and Ginger Zinger, which relieves menstrual bloating) in the Green Room or take it home in a traditional glass bottle. A range of products is on sale at the spa boutique, from Asmara Tropical Lifestyles essential oils to locally crafted goods.

Jamu Traditional Spa at AlamKulKul Resort

BALI, INDONESIA

ABOVE: At the Jamu Body Shop, guests can buy aromatic lotions to relive the spa experience back home.

The intimate AlamKulKul Resort—decorated with antique Indonesian furniture, local crafts and natural materials of bamboo, rattan and teakwood—is a five-minute stroll from the bustle of Kuta-Legian. Couples in search of romance should opt for villas comprising four-poster beds (the most exclusive villas have private gardens and outdoor bathrooms). The resort caters for families too, with a choice of rooms that sleep four and a supervised play area for children. Early-arriving and late-departing guests are given a suite equipped with conveniences such as a shower, internet access and newspapers.

Jamu Traditional Spa, set within a tropical garden courtyard, echoes the homely feel of this 4-star, environmentally friendly resort. It's no coincidence that the spa's founder, South-American born Jeannine Marie Carroll, was inspired by age-old Balinese and Javanese treatments, which in the past were only practised in local homes. Together with her Indonesian husband, they designed and set up AlamKulKul in 1988.

Following recipes for beauty and health, which for generations have

passed down from mother to daughter, many of the spa's elixirs are composed of ingredients so fresh (no chemicals or preservatives are used), they're mixed by hand just moments before the treatment starts. Electronic devices are not used.

Three newer and more novel treatments add a fresh twist to centuries-old beauty rituals. In the Papaya, Kemiri (Candlenut), Mint Body Wrap, the body, fresh from a traditional massage, is slathered with a lotion of freshly blended ingredients and left to absorb the nutrients under a blanket of banana leaves. In the Earth & Flower Body Mask, a mask made from freshly cut flowers is applied over your body to draw out the toxins after a traditional massage; this is followed by an application of fresh honey yogurt to hydrate the skin.

The Aloe Lavender treatment involves the application of a balm of fresh aloe vera and lavender essential oil to soothe sunburnt skin.

Other popular treatments include the Tropical Nuts Facial, Hibiscus Lime Hair Hydration Creambath and Javanese Lulur. The latter two are especially popular with Japanese guests.

The cup of tonic you sip as you relax at the conclusion of your treatment doesn't have to spell the end of your spa experience. You can take part in a three-hour course to take with you the techniques and knowledge of preparing and applying ingredients used in the Javanese Lulur and traditional massage.

Or buy handmade and ready-packaged gifts such as a Javanese Lulur Home Kit—containing a *lulur* powder sachet, jasmine massage oil and a how-to brochure—from the Jamu Body Shop.

ABOVE LEFT: *Jamu* tonic, said to improve the blood's circulation, is given to guests at the end of their treatments.

ABOVE CENTRE: Ingredients are so fresh, they are mixed just minutes before the treatment.

ABOVE RIGHT: The body is slathered with papaya, kemiri and mint, then left to braise under banana leaves in one of the spa's New Age treatments.

SPA STATISTICS

SPA AREA
250 sq m (2,691 sq ft)

FACILITIES
1 facial room, 1 foot and arm treatment room, 4 wet treatment rooms with bath, open air garden pavilion for creambath; whirlpool; Jamu Body Shop

SIGNATURE TREATMENTS
Aloe Lavender Treatment, Earth & Flower Body Mask, Javanese Lulur, Papaya, Kemiri, Mint Body Wrap

OTHER TREATMENTS AND THERAPIES
Body scrubs, facials, foot and arm treatments, hair hydration, sugar waxing, traditional massage

PROVISIONS FOR COUPLES
Treatment rooms with 2 massage beds

SPA CUISINE
Fresh, local and tropical; all ingredients are selected for their health and healing benefits. Meals are available at the Bunga Kelapa Restaurant overlooking Legian Beach. Spa cuisine is included in some packages or can be catered to on request

ACTIVITIES
Massage classes, *lulur* training course

SERVICES
Car transfers for guests with a minimum treatment time of 2 hours

CONTACT
Jalan Pantai Kuta
Legian
Bali 80361, Indonesia
Tel: (62-361) 752 750
Fax: (62-361) 752 519
Email: jamubali@jamutraditionalspa.com
Website: www.jamutraditionalspa.com

Javana Spa

WEST JAVA, INDONESIA

Founded by an Indonesian aficionado of Californian spas, the Japanese-inspired grounds of Javana Spa is cradled by the rainforest slopes of Mount Salak. Encompassing 123 hectares (304 acres) including undeveloped land and hiking trails, the property is a two-hour drive south from Jakarta. You can virtually show up with the clothes on your back as sweatsuits, anoraks, bathrobes and kimonos are supplied. Accommodation comprises 20 modest rooms with another 10 more luxurious ones overlooking the *onsen*— with waters piped in from the mountain's heated springs—and the Japanese gardens. With no newspapers or televisions, you're cocooned from the distractions of the outside world. There are no telephone lines in or out due to the resort's remoteness; only cellphones for operational purposes.

Your day's schedule, presented at breakfast, can be filled with physical activities or pampering body treatments, a combination of both or neither—it depends on how you're inclined.

Prescribed activities can range from low-impact callisthenics to overnight adventure trips which include white water rafting. Walks to any of seven waterfalls in the area are pleasant in the perennially cool weather. Alternatively, hike to the volcano where you can soak your body in the sulphur mud and water springs as

ABOVE: Located in the highlands one kilometre above sea level, Javana Spa is almost cut off from the outside world.

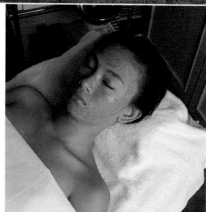

RIGHT: Lie back and enjoy pampering treatments such as this Aromatheraphy Facial where pure essential oils coupled with concentrated plant, flower and fruit extracts soothe, hydrate and detoxify your skin.

SPA STATISTICS

SPA AREA
170,000 sq m (1,829,864 sq ft)

FACILITIES
9 private dry treatment areas, 4 private wet treatment rooms,
2 hydrotherapy treatment rooms, 3 herbal wrap rooms;
6 hair treatment stations, 2 beauty rooms, 4 nail/reflexology
studios; 1 *onsen*; 1 dance/aerobis studio, 3 gymnasiums,
1 jogging track; spa boutique

SIGNATURE TREATMENT
Ginger Compress

OTHER TREATMENTS AND THERAPIES
Body masks, body scrubs, body wraps, facial treatments, hair
and scalp treatments, hydrotherapy, manicures/pedicures,
reflexology

PROVISIONS FOR COUPLES
Romantic Spa Getaway

SPA CUISINE
Available at all times

ACTIVITIES
Cooking classes; hikes to volcano and waterfalls; aerobics,
aqua stretch and tone, circuit training workout, dance
exercises, fitness and strength workouts, rock climbing, tennis,
white water rafting; meditation, yoga

SERVICES
Customisation for groups, personal training, private exercise
classes (book when making reservations)

CONTACT
Cangkuang-Cidahu
Sukabumi
West Java
Indonesia
Tel: (62-21) 719 8327/8
Fax: (62-21) 719 5555
Email: javana@indo.net.id
Website: www.javanaspa.com

ABOVE: Enjoy a hydrotherapy session courtesy of Mother Nature at one of seven waterfalls in the area. Along the way, your guides will point out local flora which have traditionally been used for their healing properties.

Sudanese pilgrims did in the past. Within the spa property are two swimming pools: one with cool water for laps and a heated one for aerobics classes.

While massages are favoured by most guests, it's the warming properties of the Ginger Compress—where you are swaddled in linen soaked in water and freshly grated ginger, which stimulates blood circulation and soothes away aches and pains—that is especially delightful in the cool highland climate.

Warm ginger milk is typically served in the morning at breakfast which, like all meals, is served in the Dining Terrace overlooking the manicured gardens. Low in sugar, fat and salt, the meals are balanced, though portions depend on your goals for your weight. The organic vegetables, plucked fresh from the

garden, aid detoxification. Alcohol is not available, but meat is. Before dinner, you can enjoy a cup of blackcurrant tea by the log fire, read or play board games.

Packages include accommodation, meals, the use of fitness facilites and the *onsen*, and certain treatments. There are no more than 40 guests at the resort at any given time. Programmes, however,

can be customised for families or groups on business or team-building retreats.

For couples, a three-day/two-night Romantic Spa Getaway package includes four choices of spa treatments per person, the private use of facilities such as the sauna and other romantic accoutrements such as candlelit dinners and a midnight bath in their rooms.

Parwathi Spa at Matahari Beach Resort & Spa

BALI, INDONESIA

The luxurious Matahari Beach Resort & Spa is situated between the volcanic mountain range of the Bali Barat National Park and the black lava sand edged by the Java Sea on Bali's northwest. This hideaway is three hours by road or about 40 minutes by air from the international airport at Denpasar.

Elaborately carved Balinese bungalows blend in with gardens lush with bougainvillaeas, frangipanis, hibiscus, lilies and jasmines.

The double doors to each of the resort's 32 rooms open up to a four-poster bed under a golden raffia-plaited ceiling of temple-like proportions.

The bathing area comprises an oversized indoor marble tub and a tropical backyard shower under a water-spouting stone dragon.

Besides enjoying the various watersports available, or being feted day and night, a stay at the Matahari can involve an awakening on various levels.

Attend a lesson in Balinese carving, cuisine, dance and massage if you're looking to stir your artistic side.

Or you can choose to rejuvenate your body and soul with traditional Balinese body treatments at the Parwathi Spa which recalls an ancient water palace.

The spa's signature relaxing Sukha and revitalising Sthira massages mirror each other like *yin* and *yang*.

You and your partner can enjoy a massage under a Balinese pavilion to the constant chant of the wave—or a four-

SPA STATISTICS

SPA AREA
1,000 sq m (10,764 sq ft)

FACILITIES
2 double treatment rooms, 1 single
treatment room; 1 gymnasium; 1 beauty
salon; spa boutique

SIGNATURE TREATMENTS
Royal Parwathi Package, Sthira
and Sukha massages

OTHER TREATMENTS AND THERAPIES
Balinese massage, Solo massage;
body and face scrubs

PROVISIONS FOR COUPLES
Double treatment rooms

SPA CUISINE
Daily vegetarian menu available at the
Dewu Ramona restaurant

ACTIVITIES
Balinese dance, cooking, craft, massage
and painting classes; dolphin-watching and
sunset cruises; badminton, golf driving
range and putting green, mountain biking,
snorkelling, scuba diving, tennis, trekking,
volleyball; yoga

SERVICES
Baby-sitting; personalised sightseeing
trips; professional gym instruction;
transfers from the airport at Denpasar
(by car, helicoptor, plane or seaplane)

CONTACT
Pemuteran Village
Singaraja, Bali 81155
Indonesia
Tel: (62-362) 92 312
Fax: (62-362) 92 313
Email: mbr-bali@indo.net.id
Website: www.matahari-beach-resort.com

handed variation in a treatment room,
performed simultaneously by two
therapists per guest.

These massages are also available
as part of a supporting sequence of bath
treatments, body masks and body
scrubs infused with essential oils.

For couples, a litany of Sthira or
Sukha treatments—with a bottle of
champagne—in the Royal Parwathi
Package replicates the rituals practised
by pre-nuptials from the Brahmana caste.

These rituals culminate in a 10-
course gala dinner served in the spa
pavilion. You and your partner are then
left to spend the rest of your romantic
night in the privacy of the spa's Bali Sari—
a bed open on all sides—lulled to sleep
by the soothing sound of splashing
fountains and the gentle caresses of
breezes laced with the floral scent of
lotuses and frangipanis.

TOP RIGHT: Bath time in
your villa's king-sized tub
and garden shower is a
sensual delight.

ABOVE RIGHT: Two therapists
work in harmony in a four-
handed version of the
Sthira or Sukha massage.

BELOW: The spa area is
reminiscent of a water palace
complete with fountains in a
garden courtyard.

OPPOSITE TOP AND BELOW:
The resort is an oasis set
against the rugged Bali
Barat National Park.

Pita Maha Spa

BALI, INDONESIA

 Recreated Balinese palaces barely get more authentic than when its architect's credentials include being the son of the Prince of Ubud. At the boutique resorts of Pita Maha A Tjampuhan Resort & Spa, the 24 villas are styled like a series of *bale* (traditional Balinese pavilions) and laid out like a classical Balinese village perched on the slopes of Tjampuhan Valley. Stepping into the resort's lobby lounge, the guest is greeted by the verdant surroundings, a sensation heightened by sipping a glass of *brem barong* (Balinese rice wine). The villas, while equipped with modern conveniences such as air-conditioning, satellite television and 24-hour villa service, are also luxuriously decorated with hand-hewn Balinese furniture and crafts. Most have private swimming pools.

The resort's intimacy and hideaway factor has attracted celebrities such as supermodel Cindy Crawford.

LEFT: Guests can enjoy a glass of Balinese rice wine in the lobby lounge.

BELOW RIGHT: The open-air dining room provides a splendid view of the lush greenery surrounding the resort.

BELOW CENTRE: In addition to the indoor treatment room, the one-villa spa has an open-air treatment area for a back-to-nature experience.

OPPOSITE: The Private Spa Villa, located in a secluded spot, is framed by a cluster of pools.

The Private Villa Spa—concealed in a remote corner of the resort—is virtually in a world of its own. You and your partner can literally have the whole spa to yourselves—for it's only available to a couple at a time—with a minimum two-hour session. Treatments at this solo spa villa are enjoyed in the indoor treatment room which resembles a bedroom with wraparound windows, or in the outdoor treatment pavilion.

Two classic choices from the menu of six traditional treatments (excluding the manicure/pedicure) are the Balinese massage (a full-body massage using your choice of aromatic oils) and Traditional Lulur (a herbal skin scrub which is followed by a yogurt massage).

The cluster of pools—the infinity-edge swimming pool, sauna, hot and cold jacuzzis, and pool overflowing with flowers—the spa's most striking feature, appears to be hanging off the tropical Eden hillside. Other guests don't have to miss out on the spa experience should the Private Villa Spa be booked, for they can enjoy their choice of treatments without leaving their own villas.

SPA STATISTICS

SPA AREA
350 sq m (3,767 sq ft)

FACILITIES
1 Private Villa Spa with 1 indoor treatment room and 1 outdoor treatment room, 1 flower pool, 1 hot jacuzzi and 1 cold jacuzzi, 1 sauna, 1 steam room and 1 swimming pool,

SIGNATURE TREATMENTS
Balinese Massage, Traditional Lulur

OTHER TREATMENTS AND THERAPIES
Acupressure Massage, Herbal Back Massage, Facial Massage, manicures/pedicures, Traditional *Boreh*

PROVISIONS FOR COUPLES
Private Spa Villa

SERVICES
Baby-sitting; free shuttle services for guests around Ubud

CONTACT
Jalan Sanggingan
P O Box 198
Ubud
Bali 80571
Indonesia
Tel: (62-361) 974 330
Fax: (62-361) 974 329
Email: pitamaha@dps.mega.net.id
Website: www.pitamaha-bali.com

Spa at Maya

BALI, INDONESIA

LEFT: The spa pavilions and reception (left) and the pool by the River Café (right) is nestled some 30 metres (98 feet) down the cliff side.

BELOW: The lush surrounds of the River Café and pool at the spa area is especially alluring at sundown.

Resplendent in 10 hectares (25 acres) of hillside gardens and tropical parklands, Maya Ubud Resort & Spa is conveniently located close by the village of Ubud—Bali's legendary artist community.

East-facing rooms and villas greet the sunrise over the Petanu River Valley, while those with a Western aspect delight in the sunsets over the rice terraces of Peliatan. The most beautiful view of the valley can be enjoyed from Bar Bedulu with a *goyang-goyang* (a drink made from Balinese rice wine with mango, green lime and coconut cream) in hand.

All villas and suites feature classically weathered furnishings juxtaposed against vibrantly coloured contemporary materials creating eclectic luxury. In contrast, the guestrooms are furnished in contemporary, minimalist style.

To discover the unique Spa at Maya, you descend by elevator 30 metres (98 feet) down the cliff face to a cluster of thatched pavilions. Each pavilion has its own private facilities discreetly hidden by lush foliage and cooled by ceiling fans and tropical breezes. An integral part of the overwhelming peaceful ambience is the soothing sound of the Petanu River.

Three single pavilions sit at the water's edge. If you are with a partner, luxuriate, post-treatment, in the handcrafted stainless steel bathtub or on the daybed in the two double treatment pavilions that overlook the river.

The comprehensive menu of pampering treatments includes the Gentle Four Hands Massage—where two therapists work on your body in tandem; the Soothing Maya Massage—an invigorating treatment of long strokes and aromatherapy; and the traditional Balinese Massage. For total indulgence, the most popular option is the body scrub with fresh natural coconut, cinnamon and tangerine or Balinese pandan leaves, or the Javanese *lulur*—followed by the Massage Bliss and culminating in an aromatic flower bath.

ABOVE LEFT: The Deluxe Pool Villa's bathroom overlooks a plunge pool. The bathtub and wash basin are made from beaten stainless steel, the countertop recycled from teak railway sleepers, the mirror frame was once a cartwheel and the lampshades are fashioned from traditional fish traps and baskets.

ABOVE: The *bale* (traditional Balinese pavilion) and bathtub in the double treatment pavilion are draped with sheer fabric for privacy.

BELOW LEFT: Fresh ingredients for a mask—orange, avocado, cucumber, yogurt, egg, honey, mint leaf, apple cider vinegar and ground corn—displayed in the treatment area.

SPA STATISTICS

SPA AREA
1,000 sq m (10,764 sq ft)

FACILITIES
2 double treatment pavilions, 3 single treatment pavilions; 2 outdoor jacuzzis; 2 swimming pools; spa boutique

SIGNATURE TREATMENTS
Gentle Four Hands Massage, Maya Facial, Soothing Maya Massage, Relaxing Balinese Massage

OTHER TREATMENTS AND THERAPIES
Activities combined with spa treatments, facials, hand/foot massages, *lulur*, manicures/pedicures and nail art, scrubs

PROVISIONS FOR COUPLES
2 double treatment pavilions complete with 2 massage tables, a bathtub for 2 and 2 showers (1 indoor, 1 outdoor)

SPA CUISINE
Available at the River Café; guests are provided with healthy snacks and beverages post-treatment

ACTIVITIES
Balinese cooking, Balinese dance, bamboo percussion, basketry, flute, mask painting and offering making classes; elephant safari rides, nature walks, sky tours; aquaerobics, cycling, golf pitch and putt, meditation, rafting, tennis, trekking, yoga

SERVICES
Free shuttle services to/from Ubud Central Market; internet and email facilities; complimentary afternoon tea served daily in the lobby; spa retail; library

CONTACT
Jalan Gunung Sari
Banjar Ambengan
Ubud
Bali 80571
Indonesia
Tel: (62-361) 977 888
Fax: (62-361) 977 555
Email: spa@mayaubud.com
Website: www.mayaubud.com

The Spa at The Chedi by Mandara

BALI, INDONESIA

he Chedi sits on the brink of the lush Ayung River Valley in Bali's central foothills, surrounded by rice- and palm-covered slopes, just a short drive from the artistic colony of Ubud. On cool mornings, a delicate mist wraps the hills surrounding this intimate yet luxurious Balinese 'village'.

All 54 deluxe rooms, housed in two-storey blocks, offer a panoramic view of the Ayung Valley.

The rooms on the ground floor each have a garden terrace and outdoor backyard bathroom. The four suites have outdoor sunken baths and wraparound terraces. But the view, best admired as you swim in the infinite-edged ebony swimming pool, is not the only facet that inspires the spirit and quiets the soul.

The Spa at The Chedi, which opened in 1996, was the first in the Mandara spa empire that now operates therapeutic getaways in hotels and resorts in

ABOVE: This path over the lotus pond leads to the double deluxe spa pavilion (far end) and single spa suites (right).

RIGHT: The sanctuary is tucked against a peaceful backdrop of lush green hills.

ABOVE: Couples can be pampered together in this double deluxe spa villa.

SPA STATISTICS

SPA AREA
2,100 sq m (22,604 sq ft)

FACILITIES
1 double deluxe spa pavilion, 1 double deluxe spa suite, 1 double deluxe spa villa, 1 double deluxe Thai massage suite, 2 single spa suites; 1 manicure/pedicure pavilion; spa boutique

SIGNATURE TREATMENTS
Balinese Massage, Chedi Massage, Chedi Indulgence

OTHER TREATMENTS AND THERAPIES
Ayurvedic therapies, body treatments, facial treatments, manicures/pedicures, massage therapies

PROVISIONS FOR COUPLES
The Deluxe Spa Villa, Spa Pavilion and double Spa Suite have ensuite bathroom, outdoor tub, waterfall showers and relaxation lounge

SPA CUISINE
Light and healthy fusion cuisine. Make special dietary requests when booking accommodation

ACTIVITIES
Balinese dancing classes; art gallery tours, guided nature walks, village treks; cycling, yoga, *tai ji*

CONTACT
Desa Melinggih Kelod
Payangan, Gianyar
Bali 80572, Indonesia
Tel: (62-361) 975 963
Fax: (62-361) 975 968
Email: chediubd@ghmhotels.com
Website: www.ghmhotels.com or www.mandaraspa-asia.com

Indonesia, Malaysia, the Maldives and beyond (including out at sea, aboard luxury cruise liners).

Its moniker comes from an ancient Sanskrit legend which tells of a river of eternal youth. While they do not promise you immortality, the spa's treatments and therapies are designed to relax and rejuvenate, and to celebrate the youth and beauty that come from within.

The spa's most important ingredient is the Balinese way of giving from the heart. There's a saying in Bali: 'Giving without feeling is like food with no salt.' And most Balinese would not eat food without adding salt. Before each treatment, the spa's therapists take a few moments to attune themselves with your needs, so they are able to give something of their inner selves.

The spa menu, strong on Balinese flavour, incorporates treatments from other Asian cultures (such as Ayurvedic Shiro Dhara, Indian Head Massage, Traditional Thai Massage and Warm Stone Massage), as well as facials and body treatments using products handmade from fresh ingredients.

The signature treatment is the Chedi Massage developed by Mandara Spa, a synchronised choreography consisting of five different massage styles (Japanese Shiatsu, Thai, Balinese, Swedish and Hawaiian Lomi Lomi) performed in tandem by two therapists.

An extension of the Chedi Massage is the Chedi Indulgence, with an aromatherapy footbath, a lavender body wash and a scrub prefacing the famous massage. The session is capped with a facial and reflexology session.

Perhaps the most hedonistic treat is luxuriating outdoors in a petal-filled bath sunk in a lotus pond. Enjoy the solitude, or better yet, share it with a partner.

The Spa at The Legian

BALI, INDONESIA

ABOVE: A stone pathway and lotus garden leads from the spa boutique to the treatment suites.

LEFT: The aromatherapy floral bath is fragranced with a few drops of essential oil and the caress of fresh frangipani flowers.

Situated between *padi* fields and Seminyak Beach, The Legian is conveniently near the shops and nightlife of Kuta yet distant enough from its bustle. The resort's minimal décor, fused with subtle Balinese elements, acts as a backdrop to an unhurried vacation of luxury—and also a changing exhibition of paintings, jewellery and artwork from various parts of the Indonesian archipelago.

The most striking place to catch some rays and gaze out at the sea is on the deck by the two terraced swimming pools which lead down to the beach. The most intimate spot to relax with a loved one would be under the thatched pavilion by the edge of the sand. This seascape, particularly dramatic when at sunset, can also be admired from your suite balcony.

Beyond the 67 suites, there are 11 villas clustered in a separate area known as The Club at The Legian. Occupants at this resort within the resort can dine at an exclusive lounge overlooking a 35-metre (115-foot) lap pool. Alternatively, your private butler can lay it out at your dining *bale* (traditional Balinese pavilion) overlooking your private 10-metre (33-

LEFT: Spa suites overlook a private garden as well as the Indian Ocean.

BELOW: The spa boutique provides spa amenities such as the specially blended Legian Spa oils for those who wish to bring home a part of the spa experience.

foot) pool. Facilities such as the spa and gymnasium, located in the south gardens of the main resort, are a buggy ride away.

Surrounded by stone walkways and a private garden with lotus ponds, the treatment suites in the spa have a view of the sandy beach and the blue ocean.

Both single and double spa suites are equipped with a huge bathtub and shower room with steam.

The Asian-flavoured therapies include Balinese, traditional Thai and Warm Stone Massages; a traditional Asian Facial; Ayurveda Shiro Dara; Reflexology, and Manicure and Pedicure.

One of the most popular packages is the Legian Indulgence, which includes an eponymous five-style massage—Balinese, Hawaiian Lomi Lomi, Shiatsu, Swedish and Thai—performed by two therapists. Spa packages are also available for those who prefer to spread the pampering over two, three or five days. The Bulan Madu package for two, which is performed only at sundown, comes with candlelight, canapés and

sparkling wine. After the session that comprises a floral foot bath, lavender body wash, body scrub, floral bath and Balinese massage, you and your partner adjourn to the privacy of your suite to partake in a four-course set dinner.

SPA STATISTICS

SPA AREA
2,100 sq m (22,604 sq ft)

FACILITIES
2 Double Spa Suites, 2 Single Spa Suites, 1 Thai massage Spa Suite; 1 Manicure/Pedicure Lounge; 1 gymnasium with sauna, 1 two-tiered swimming pool; spa boutique

SIGNATURE TREATMENT
Legian Indulgence

OTHER TREATMENTS AND THERAPIES
Ayurveda Shiro Dara, facial treatments, manicures/pedicures, massages, reflexology

PROVISIONS FOR COUPLES
Couples get a special rate on treatments (except manicures/pedicures). Double treatment suites are available. Bulan Madu is a romantic sundown package designed for 2

SPA CUISINE
Seafood and vegetarian set menus are available at The Restaurant. Specially created light meals are available with the Bulan Madu and Legian Indulgence packages

ACTIVITY
Yoga

SERVICES
Baby-sitting; gourmet food hampers for day outings; tours and excursions

CONTACT
Jalan Laksmana
Seminyak Beach
Bali 80361, Indonesia
Tel: (62-361) 730 622
Fax: (62-361) 730 623
Email: legian@ghmhotels.com
Website: www.ghmhotels.com

Taman Sari Royal Heritage Spa

JAKARTA, INDONESIA

Upon entering the three-storey building, you trade the bustle of Indonesia's capital for the serenity of what appears to be a Javanese palace. Walk past the tall atrium anchored by a big brass chandelier, and you'll see an indoor swimming pool flanked by two whirlpools under a wooden structure reminiscent of royal Javanese baths.

The spa menu replicates what the spa's founder enjoyed as a princess growing up in the Javanese Royal Palace. Besides manual treatments such as the Therapeutic Massage that treats specific problem areas, it also includes high-tech therapies from the West such as the Paradiso Capsule that relaxes the body through heat, vibration, aroma and music. Packages, ranging from three to 40 days, include some specific ones that see women from marriage through to childbirth. These include the Beautiful Bride Package (which pampers and prepares the bride for her husband about six days before the wedding, with beauty

ABOVE: The Lulur is a traditional body treatment using indigenous herbs and spices.

RIGHT: The therapists reflect the warmth and hospitable nature of the Javanese people.

SPA STATISTICS

SPA AREA
1,500 sq m (16,146 sq ft)

FACILITIES
1 Executive Room (2 beds), 10 single treatment rooms, 1 Villa Spa (2 beds), 2 hydrotherapy rooms; 1 Alpha 33 Paradiso Capsule; 2 saunas, 2 steam rooms, 2 whirlpools; 1 gymnasium, 1 meditation room, 1 multi-purpose room, 1 indoor swimming pool; 1 beauty salon; 1 *jamu* bar; spa boutique

SIGNATURE TREATMENTS
Physical Conditioning Programme, Royal Javanese Pampering, Total Foot Spa, Total Relaxation Get Away

OTHER TREATMENTS AND THERAPIES
Breast care, bridal packages, facial treatments, hair and makeup services, intimacy care, manicures/pedicures, massages for babies, massage therapies, post-natal massages, waxing; spa packages

PROVISIONS FOR COUPLES
Executive Physical Conditioning; 1 Executive Room, 1 Villa Spa

SPA CUISINE
Snacks such as chicken wings and french fries are served at the Wedang Café along with fruit desserts, juices and *jamu* drinks

ACTIVITIES
Aerobics, stretch, *tae bo*; meditation, yoga

SERVICES
Health, hygiene, beauty and fitness consultancy, therapies and treatment

ADMISSION
A day pass to use the facilities is required if no treatments or packages are taken up

CONTACT
Jalan K.H. Wahid Hasyim No. 133
Jakarta Pusat 10240
Indonesia
Tel: (62-21) 314 3585
Fax: (62-21) 330 100
Email: spa@mustika-ratu.co.id
Website: www.mustika-ratu.co.id

TOP: A treatment with the mineral-rich Merapi Volcano Mud may help detoxify and relax the body.

ABOVE: Hydrotherapy treatments include baths of milk, herbs or sea salts.

BELOW: The spa offers a range of herbal drinks.

treatments as well as exercises and care for her intimate areas), post-natal packages and massages for babies.

Signature packages include the Royal Javanese Pampering (Javanese Massage, Herbal Body Scrub, Herbal Body Mask, Royal Facial Treatment and Javanese Herbal Bath) and Total Relaxation Get Away (Sea Salt Body Glow, French Massage, Seaweed Body Wrap, Merapi Volcano Mud, Facial Treatment and Thalasso or Seaweed Bath). Both packages are three-and-a-half hours long. The two-hour Physical Conditioning Programme (a Lulur or Papaya Enzyme scrub, massage and Milk or Herbal Hydrobath) can also be taken as a package for two. Called Executive Physical Conditioning, it includes the use of the Executive Room that would otherwise cost extra.

Another treatment room for couples, available at a surcharge, is the ornately decorated Villa Spa that comes with a day bed and attached jacuzzi.

The spa's single treatment rooms bring the outdoors inside. Shower areas resemble grottos with rushing water and twittering birds. Gamelan music can also be heard. The spa boutique offers various products—including the best-selling Papaya Enzyme Body Polish and Lulur—retailed under the Mustika Ratu and Taman Sari labels. Travellers to Yogyakarta can visit the sister Taman Sari Royal Heritage Spa at Sheraton Mustika.

Thalasso Bali at Grand Mirage Resort

BALI, INDONESIA

Water lovers will take pleasure in the several peaceful pockets within the Grand Mirage Resort. There's a lagoon-like swimming pool where you can relax with a cocktail in hand. Or a number of watering holes from which you can contemplate the sky and sea. To do so from your room, you should opt for one with a water view in the sprawling low-rise complex or a top-of-the-line Sultan Suite with a *bale* (traditional Balinese pavilion).

At Thalasso Bali, French-trained hydrotherapists and masseurs employ sophisticated water equipment together with ingredients harvested from Neptune's medical chest to provide a physical and spiritual rebirth to those seeking wellness, beautification or relaxation. Apart from being cocooned within an exotic garden by the beach, there is no illusion that this thalassotherapy centre is another tropical spa. Such centres may dot the coast of France but are currently a rarity in Bali, not to mention Southeast Asia.

The *pièce de résistance* is the aquamedic pool in a Balinese pavilion with stone deities (representing beauty,

FAR LEFT: Seasoned with a seaweed paste, your body is rolled under a warm blanket to allow it to absorb minerals.

CENTRE: The Manuluve involves a scrub and seaweed massage which cleanses, softens and moisturises hands and arms.

LEFT: The bain d'algues keeps muscles toned and skin cleansed.

OPPOSITE: The aquamedic pool, with freshly pumped warm seawater, is set in a Balinese pavilion and contains waterfalls and underwater jets.

RIGHT: The thalassotherapy centre also offers traditional Indonesian treatments using fresh local ingredients and herbs.

health and relaxation) constantly filling it with seawater from their granite pitchers.

The pool comprises a circuit of underwater jets and geysers; the water piped in fresh from the nearby Indian Ocean. Activities range from reclining on an in-water massage bed to having a gentle workout of aquaerobics guided by a physiotherapist.

Programmes can be tailor-made from the 11 thalasso treatments on the à la carte menu. Or you may consider pre-packaged proposals prescribed for pain, slimming or smoking.

There's even a selection designed for males. Male guests have a preference for the Creambath (a treatment which reconditions the hair, and comprises a scalp, neck and shoulder massage) at the unisex beauty salon.

A thalassotherapy classic is the Seaweed Deluxe Application in which your freshly exfoliated body is painted with warm seaweed. Next you are rolled in a plastic wrap and coddled under a heated blanket. The nerve-soothing Affusion Shower Massage involves a masseur kneading aromatic oils into your body while a falling rain of warm seawater moistens your skin.

Large groups are welcome at Thalasso Bali. The centre can treat 200 guests daily and the 5-star hotel has conference facilities and 310 rooms.

SPA STATISTICS

SPA AREA
5,203 sq m (56,000 sq ft)

FACILITIES
1 aerosol marine room, 2 affusion shower rooms, 27 air-conditioned private treatment rooms, 2 *douche au jet* rooms, 1 manuluve room, 6 massage rooms, 2 pressotherapy rooms, 5 seaweed deluxe application rooms; 1 aquamedic pool, 2 balneotherapy tubs, 2 pediluve tubs, 2 saunas, 3 seaweed deluxe hydrobaths, 2 steam rooms; 1 gymnasium, 1 fitness centre, 1 swimming pool; 1 beauty salon; spa boutique

SIGNATURE TREATMENTS
An à la carte menu of 11 thalassotherapy treatments which are also available in packaged suggestions

OTHER TREATMENTS AND THERAPIES
Traditional Indonesian treatments at the thalasso centre, French Phytomer facial treatments; hair treatments, manicures/pedicures; spa packages

SPA CUISINE
Light spa lunches are included in treatment packages, though they can be sold separately

ACTIVITIES
Balinese flower arrangement, cooking, dancing and palm leaf weaving classes; aquaerobics, boat-gliding, canoeing, jet skiing, para-sailing, scuba diving, snorkelling, table tennis, tennis, water polo, windsurfing

SERVICES
Native Western and Japanese staff available for in-depth consultations; private one-on-one consultations with trained professionals such as doctors, physiotherapists and nurses available at all times; arrangements for Balinese or Western-style wedding ceremonies; baby-sitting; business and internet centre; complimentary transfers from hotels in the vicinity; Japanese-speaking staff; tailor-made teambuilding events and social activities for groups

CONTACT
Jalan Pratama 72–4
Tanjung Benoa, Nusa Dua
Bali 80363
Indonesia
Tel: (62-361) 773 883
Fax: (62-361) 772 247
Email: thalasso@denpasar.wasantara.net.id
Website: www.thalassobali.com

Tjampuhan Spa

BALI, INDONESIA

Erected in 1928 for guests of the Prince of Ubud, Hotel Tjampuhan & Spa is also celebrated as the birthplace of Pita Maha (Great Shining), an artist's association—founded by Tjokorda Gde Agung Sukawati and Western artists such as Walter Spies and Rudolf Bonnet—which nurtured and promoted the talents of local artists.

Located high on the banks of the holy river after which the property is named,

the hotel's 67 cottages, some ventilated by fan, others air-conditioned, are surrounded by tropical flora—a sanctuary for exotic birds and butterflies.

Within this natural haven are two swimming pools, one of which is filled with natural spring water, and has walls and a floor created in 1934 from stone from the river. The cool spring water emerges naturally from the ground and its chemical-free overflow spills into the Oos River Valley.

The air is scented with distilled oils and herbal essences at the spa's outdoor private treatment pavilions overlooking the Oos and Tjampuhan rivers.

Traditional favourites include the Balinese massage and Mandi Lulur. A variety of massages (such as acupressure, Balinese and Swedish) and a range of invigorating body and facial scrubs are also on the spa menu.

The spa's focal point, a grotto decorated with Balinese carvings and

LEFT: Some of the 67 cottages are ventilated by fan.

BELOW RIGHT: The Spa Café offers healthy snacks and a view of the swimming pool and Oos River Valley.

BELOW CENTRE: Take a cool dip in one of two swimming pools—a regular one (pictured) and another of natural spring water.

BELOW LEFT: Ground spices, roots, flowers and leaves are just some of the fresh local ingredients used in traditional treatments such as the Mandi Lulur.

OPPOSITE: The grotto provides a near-primal experience for spa-goers.

stonework, is set near the edge of Tjampuhan River. This intimate setting comprises cold and hot jacuzzis which can hold up to eight and 10 people respectively. Should you only want to select a treatment from the à la carte spa menu or use the spa facilities, a day fee will cover your use of the grotto, jacuzzi, and sauna and steam rooms.

Alternatively, the spa packages— such as Spa Adventure where a trek to a traditional village prefaces a treatment—come bundled with the use of these facilities.

Another package, Spa Harmony, is made up of a treatment with a healthy meal and non-alcoholic beverage from the Spa Café.

SPA STATISTICS

SPA AREA
800 sq m (8,611 sq ft)

FACILITIES
2 open-air double treatment rooms, 3 open-air single treatment rooms; 1 hot jacuzzi, 1 cold jacuzzi, 2 sauna and steam rooms; 3 open-air hot private jacuzzis; 2 swimming pools (1 with natural spring water)

SIGNATURE TREATMENTS
Traditional Balinese Massage, Traditional Mandi Lulur

OTHER TREATMENTS AND THERAPIES
Traditional Balinese Boreh, Swedish Massage, Acupressure Massage, Facial Massage; spa packages

PROVISIONS FOR COUPLES
Double treatment rooms

SPA CUISINE
Available

SERVICES
Baby-sitting; complimentary shuttle services for guests around Ubud

CONTACT
Jalan Raya Campuhan
P O Box 198
Ubud
Bali 80571
Indonesia
Tel: (62-361) 975 368
Fax: (62-361) 975 137
Email: tjampuan@indo.net.id
Website: www.indo.com/hotels/tjampuhan

Waroeng Djamoe Spa at Hotel Tugu Bali

BALI, INDONESIA

ABOVE: A soak in a bath with spices and flowers perfumes the skin after a massage.

BELOW: Behind these ornate doors of the Kamar Solek, guests enjoy treatments such as a scalp massage.

he 22-suite Hotel Tugu Bali is sited between the *padi* fields near Batu Bolong temple and Canggu Beach. Listed in the 101 Best Hotels/ New Sensations section of Tatler Abercrombie & Kent –Travel Guide 1999, the boutique hotel is often described as a romantically charged antique storage hall and pays tribute to Indonesia's historical and artistic heritage. Highlights include a dining room transplanted piece by piece from a 300-year-old Chinese temple; and luxurious suites recreating the Balinese abodes of expatriate artists, Jean Le Mayeur and Walter Spies.

Waroeng Djamoe Spa ('Waroeng Djamoe' derives from an ancient Javanese word for 'traditional apothecary'), furnished with century-old massage beds, elaborately carved room dividers and an antiquated barber's chair, enhances the old-time feel of the therapies. Your first stop would be at a rustic Javanese apothecary, where you'll have a drink of *jamu* or juice, and with the help of your masseuse, select the ingredients for your treatments. You'll then be led to treatment areas such as the Kamar Solek (a hut dedicated to a Javanese lady's beauty regime). This small wooden room, fashioned from

RIGHT: These corked bottles containing oils made from the essence of local flowers inject a dose of old-world charm into a modern bathroom.

FAR RIGHT: The outdoor bathroom of the Walter Spies Pavilion features an old iron showerhead.

BELOW RIGHT: After a Mandi Lulur or scrub, enjoy a refreshing dip in the private pool without leaving the Kamar Seger Waras.

BELOW LEFT: Therapists can help guests select the best body scrub to match their skin type.

materials salvaged from an antique bed from the 19th century, is used for treatments such as scalp massages or beauty treatments once enjoyed by Central Javanese princesses. The spa uses the traditional 'ratus' hair treatment, where the hair and scalp is perfumed and steamed with water infused with local flowers. Other treatment rooms include an outdoor pavilion by the beach.

The aromatherapy, Balinese and Gemulai Penari massages are all-time favourites. The latter is popular for the dance-like movements of the therapist's hands as she follows the rhythm of the *gamelan*. For couples, the eight-hour Gemulai Penari package or the five-hour Keraton Leha-Leha, both involving body and beauty treatments, meditation and a light gourmet lunch, are recommended.

SPA STATISTICS

SPA AREA
250 sq m (2,691 sq ft)

FACILITIES
1 full-day treatment suite, 2 indoor rooms, 1 outdoor pavilion; 1 beauty salon; spa boutique

SIGNATURE TREATMENTS
Balinese massage, aromatherapy massage, Gemulai Penari massage

OTHER TREATMENTS AND THERAPIES
Body and scalp massages, facials, manicures/pedicures, scrubs; spa packages

PROVISIONS FOR COUPLES
Gemulai Penari, Keraton Leha-Leha; treatment rooms are designed for two

SPA CUISINE
Included in some packages or available on request; healthy options are available on the menu; special dietary needs can be catered to on request

ACTIVITIES
Mask dance, floral arrangement, *gamelan*, traditional Indonesian cooking and dance classes; meditation; horse riding on the beach; mountain biking, surf boarding, tennis

SERVICES
Baby-sitting; complimentary health drinks or *jamu*, complimentary traditional high tea; shuttle services to/from Kuta

CONTACT
Jalan Pantai Balu Bolong
Canggu
Bali 80351, Indonesia
Tel: (62-361) 731 701
Fax: (62-361) 731 704
Email: bali@tuguhotels.com
Website: www.tuguhotels.com

Jamu Nature Spa at The Andaman Datai Bay

LANGKAWI ISLAND, KEDAH, MALAYSIA

ABOVE: The day beds on the relaxation terrace in The Sari Villa overlook the blue Andaman Sea.

ABOVE RIGHT: Enjoy the view of Datai Bay, the world's seventh best beach, from your villa's relaxation terrace.

BELOW: Apart from traditional body treatments, Jamu Nature Spa also offers hair and scalp treatments using a blend of natural ingredients.

It's not uncommon for guests at The Andaman to see hornbills and flying squirrels around the 50-million-year-old rainforest on the edge of the sea or 40 of Langkawi's 351 species of butterflies flitting about the resort's ixora garden. For its special attention to the environment, The Andaman has garnered numerous accolades including the PATA (Pacific Asia Travel Association) Gold Award 2001.

Like the hotel, Jamu Nature Spa draws from the gifts of Mother Nature. Its therapies fuse Indonesia's traditional beauty rituals with the medicinal gifts from the surrounding rainforest, resulting in luxuriant treats such as the Tongkat Ali Scrub or the Gotu Kola Body Mask.

Fresh fruit, leaves, nuts, yogurt and honey are some ingredients used to prepare the treatments daily.

Your spa adventure can begin with a short walk through a canopied forest path from the hotel's north wing; otherwise, ask for a buggy transfer. As you walk from the spa's reception to the treatment villas perched on the hillside, you may see a perfectly postured Balinese therapist balancing a tray of ingredients on her head, while delicate white Chicha flowers gently float down from the treetops—a hint of your therapist's magical yet demure touch to come.

Luxuriating in your private treatment villa—exposed to the caress of the breeze, the songs of birds, the rhythm of the waves and sweeping view of Datai

Bay and the hills beyond, and yet protected from human view—is a decadent pleasure in itself. The expansive view is best enjoyed from your villa's relaxation terrace as your hair and scalp are conditioned with a Hair Hydrating Creambath, or while soaking in the bathtub of exotic flowers or rainforest leaves with your loved one.

The spa's signature packages include the four-hour Andaman Sunrise comprising aromatherapy or traditional massage, choice of body scrub, a body treatment, facial, creambath and a soak in the bath. The two-hour Rainforest includes a massage, facial and a bath; choose from a richly hydrating Tropical Nuts Facial or a Fresh Fruit Peel, which uses natural fruit acids to gently exfoliate and soften the skin. On a hot day, the Tropical Papaya & Kemiri Nut Wrap cools and refreshes. After the kemiri nut scrub, the body is covered with papaya and wrapped in banana leaves for the skin to absorb the nutrients.

A visit to the spa is a must for all couples. Special packages have been thoughtfully put together to give couples an intimate and romantic experience. Treatments for the gentleman and lady vary slightly to cater to their different needs. Look for Ultimate Nature and Intimate Nature, both of which showcase the Balinese therapists' magical yet subtle touch. With an extensive spa menu and breathtaking view, coupled with its location by the seventh best beach in the world as named by The Discovery Travel & Adventure Channel, Jamu Nature Spa is truly a wonderfully romantic experience for all to indulge.

ABOVE: The sun worshipper splashing about on the beach in Datai Bay would not be able to see what is going on in the villas. Four Rainforest Villas are housed in two duplexes perched on the side of a hill.

RIGHT: The resort's 188 rooms and suites, split into two four-level wings, overlook this lagoon-like swimming pool. Swimming in this sinuous pool—that features a slide and bubbling area—among the ancient trees is like taking a dip in a secret brook in the middle of the jungle.

SPA STATISTICS

SPA AREA
369 sq m (3,972 sq ft)

FACILITIES
4 Rainforest Villas (each with 2 treatment beds, bathtub, toilet and outdoor shower), 1 The Sari Villa with the same facilities plus rest area with floor mattresses and jacuzzi; 1 gymnasium, 1 swimming pool; spa retail corner

SIGNATURE TREATMENTS
Kemiri Nut Scrub, Andaman Sunrise, The Rainforest

OTHER TREATMENTS AND THERAPIES
Body wraps, body scrubs, facial treatments, hair crème bath, leg and arm treatment, leg and foot treatment, massage therapies, reflexology, waxing

PROVISIONS FOR COUPLES
Intimate Nature, Ultimate Nature; 4 Rainforest Villas, 1 The Sari Villa

SPA CUISINE
Not available, but low-cholesterol, low-fat and vegetarian dishes are available on the menu; special dietary needs can be catered to on request

ACTIVITIES
Traditional Malay cooking classes; batik painting; bird watching expeditions, coastal nature cruises, mangrove tours, jungle treks, nature walks; beach volleyball, billiard and games room, face painting, games, drawing, mountain biking, origami, paddle boarding, sandcastle building, snorkelling, traditional games, windsurfing

SERVICES
Baby-sitting and play area

ADMISSION
Priority is given to hotel guests and to guests of the neighbouring The Datai. The swimming pool and gymnasium are only open to in-house guests

CONTACT
P O Box 94, Jalan Teluk Datai
07000 Langkawi Island
Kedah
Malaysia
Tel: (60-4) 959 1088
Fax: (60-4) 959 1168
Email: anda@po.jaring.my or reservation@theandaman.com
Website: www.theandaman.com

Mandara Spa at The Datai

LANGKAWI ISLAND, KEDAH, MALAYSIA

 odie Foster and Chow Yun Fatt stayed at this luxury hideaway while filming *Anna and the King*. The Datai sits among century-old rainforests between the Macincang Range and the Andaman Sea. It took first place in *Condé Nast Traveller*'s Award 2001 for World's Top 100 resorts (October 2001 UK edition), and was given the Aga Khan Award 2001 for Architecture.

Rooms and suites are in two wings flanking the resort's main swimming pool, while the villas (some with private plunge pools) collectively resemble a Malay *kampung* or village. The Mandara Spa ('Mandara' derives from an ancient

Sanskrit quest for a longevity elixir) is about 100 metres (328 feet) from the beach. The spa is also a five- to 10-minute walk from the main building—down 170 steps carved out of the imposing structure—followed by a short walk along a wooden pathway cloaked by a bamboo thicket. Alternatively, you can request for a buggy ride.

At the reception villa, you'll unwind with a chilled face towel soaked in cucumber and peppermint. You may also sip ginger tea before your Balinese therapist leads you down the private path to one of four Spa Villas screened from each other by jungle foliage and sited along a mangrove stream.

The spa specialises in Balinese and local treatments. Bali coffee is used for a stimulating beauty treatment while Bali *boreh* is a scrub made up of fresh clove, cardamom, ginger and *galangal*, said to improve circulation.

The Rainforest Herbal Scrub uses *tongkat ali* leaves—reputed to contain nature's *Viagra* among other properties.

Longer treatments such as the Langkawi Luxury (which includes a Balinese massage) and The Ultimate Indulgence typically begin with your feet being scrubbed in an iron bowl of water afloat with flowers. A cool lavender wash follows. You'll spend some time in your in-suite steam room scented with lemon

grass, ginger, lime leaves, dry cloves, star anise and cinnamon sticks on a platter of woven coconut leaves, and luxuriate in the oversized bath—scented with jasmine buds and chrysanthemum blooms—overlooking the jungle. The Ultimate Indulgence doubles your pleasure with two therapists simultaneously coddling you with a body scrub—the spa's famous 'four-handed' Mandara Massage—and finishing up with a synchronised facial and reflexology.

Other popular packages include The Rainforest Harmony (foot bath, Balinese massage and foot reflexology) and Datai Dreams (foot bath, lavender wash, herbal steam infusion and Balinese massage).

Quick pick-me-ups and three- or five-day packages are also available.

ABOVE LEFT: From certain angles, the resort resembles a grand complex from a civilisation past.

ABOVE RIGHT: The swimming pool by the main building has a view of Thailand across the Andaman Sea.

BELOW: The relaxation deck of each Spa Villa sits above the mountain stream and faces a lush verdant wall of trees.

OPPOSITE LEFT: Soaking in the tub of sweet jasmines and colourful carnations is almost like bathing in a pool in the jungle.

OPPOSITE RIGHT: The hypnotic notes of the *gamelan* accompany a treatment in the Spa Villa.

SPA STATISTICS

SPA AREA
335 sq m (3,606 sq ft)

FACILITIES
4 double private Spa Villas with indoor steam shower and bathroom, double treatment area, outdoor oversized terrazzo bath, outdoor shower, private wooden balcony and relaxation area; 1 spa reception villa; 2 cold plunge pools, 2 saunas, 2 hot plunge pools; 1 gymnasium, 2 swimming pools; spa boutique in hotel

SIGNATURE TREATMENTS
Mandara Massage, Rainforest Herbal Scrub, Datai Dreams, Langkawi Luxury, Rainforest Harmony, The Ultimate Indulgence

OTHER TREATMENTS AND THERAPIES
Flower bath, foot treatments, massage therapies, spa packages

PROVISIONS FOR COUPLES
Discounts for couples having their treatments together; 4 double Spa Villas

SPA CUISINE
Not available but vegetarian, low-fat and gluten-free menus can be catered to on request

ACTIVITIES
Thai cooking classes; guided nature walks, jungle trekking and mangrove (kayaking) tours, picnics at waterfall; biking, boogie boarding, kayaking, sailing, snorkelling, windsurfing

SERVICES
Baby-sitting

ADMISSION
Priority is given to resort guests and guests of the neighbouring The Andaman. Other guests are permitted to use the spa during off-peak hours. The swimming pools and health club are only open to in-house guests

CONTACT
Jalan Teluk Datai
07000 Langkawi Island
Kedah
Malaysia
Tel: (60-4) 959 2500
Fax: (60-4) 959 2600
Email: datai@ghmhotels.com
Website: www.ghm.com or
www.mandaraspa-asia.com

Sembunyi Spa at Cyberview Lodge Resort & Spa

CYBERJAYA, SELANGOR, MALAYSIA

ABOVE LEFT: The hot jacuzzi in the male and female wet areas has a panoramic view of the great outdoors.

ABOVE RIGHT: The Garden Bath is a nourishing milk bath strewn with rose petals.

BELOW: Tropical Tango ends with your papaya-covered body wrapped in banana leaves.

The rustic low-rise chalets of Cyberview Lodge Resort & Spa, hidden among waterfalls and palm trees—that hint of the land's earlier existence as an oil palm plantation—are a refreshing anomaly in the futuristic landscape of Cyberjaya, considered to be Malaysia's Silicon Valley.

Still, guests remain wired as rooms come equipped with a computer and free internet access or wireless broadband connection. Alternatively you could become hooked on the chatter of squirrels playing in the tree tops or on swinging on hammocks by the pebbled swimming pool that tumbles over three levels. Initially designed to house tenants of its office block, the 5-star resort now includes Sembunyi Spa. Here, spa guests are welcomed with the traditional greeting, *Selamat Datang* (which means 'welcome' in Malay) with a slight bow and a hand over the greeter's heart.

The various indoor treatment areas, right down to the changing rooms, have an earthy Asian feel thanks to the sandstone walls and high *alang* (grass) roofs. You can gaze at guests fishing at the lagoon from the gymnasium or through a wide one-way glass pane from the hot jacuzzi or chilled pool in wet spa areas. The area reserved for women has the most dramatic view.

The Mayang Sari Suite is specially designed for couples. It is available at an

SPA STATISTICS

SPA AREA

929 sq m (10,000 sq ft)

FACILITIES

1 Mayang Sari Suite, 7 single treatment rooms (3 with private bath and 1 for hair treatment); 2 chilled plunge pools, 2 hot jacuzzis with waterfall, 2 saunas, 2 herbal steam rooms; lap pool with infinity edge; 1 gazebo; spa retail corner

SIGNATURE TREATMENTS

California Roll, Harmony Massage, Tropical Tango

OTHER TREATMENTS AND THERAPIES

Bath treatments, body scrubs, facial treatments, hair crème baths, hand and foot treatments, manicures/pedicures, massage therapies, sunburn treatments

PROVISIONS FOR COUPLES

Forever Yours treatment; Mayang Sari Suite with private bath, day bed, toilet and verandah

SPA CUISINE

Healthy Eastern and Western choices available at the Tasik Lounge on the spa's second floor. Special dietary needs can be catered to on request at other F&B outlets

ACTIVITIES

Fishing, karaoke, mini-basketball, mountain biking, telematch for groups or families, water volleyball

SERVICES

Baby-sitting and Jungle Jam Kids' Klub; shuttle services for in-house guests; computers with internet access in guest rooms and certain public areas such as the Tasik Lounge and Atap Lounge

ADMISSION

Local membership available but not required. In-house and walk-in guests using spa facilities without having a spa treatment are required to pay an entry fee. Entry fee to use the spa facilities is not included in some treatments

CONTACT

MSC Headquarters
63000 Cyberjaya
Selangor
Malaysia
Tel: (60-3) 8312 7000
Fax: (60-3) 8312 7001
Email: hotline@cyberview-lodge.com.my
Website: www.cyberview-lodge.com

ABOVE: Sembunyi Spa offers a comprehensive range of unique and exotic treatments.

BELOW: Spa cuisine such as this Soba Noodle Salad can be ordered from the Tasik Lounge.

hourly charge but is free with Lost in Paradise or Forever Yours.

Lost in Paradise is a five-hour feast of baths, massages, body and hair treatments and facials, inclusive of a one-hour lunch on the suite's Balinese day bed or on your private verandah.

Forever Yours starts with a floral and milk bath in a large slate tub contoured to fit the body, followed by a body scrub, yogurt dip, and earth and flower petal mask, and finishing up with a *melur* dream aromatherapy oil massage.

Forever Yours is designed for two, while Lost In Paradise can also be enjoyed by an individual.

A self-indulgent treat is the Harmony Massage with two therapists to one person using a pampering amalgamation of Shiatsu, Thai and aromatherapy techniques. Other quixotically named treatments on the Asian-flavoured spa menu include California Roll (a scrub of ground black rice and kaffir lime peel, and an algae body mask) and Tropical Tango (where you are wrapped in a banana leaf after a kemiri nut scrub and slathering of papaya pulp). A popular pick-me-up with convention-goers, or those who need to reset their body clocks, is a 30-minute dry rub in a massage chair. Enjoy this at the gazebo on the edge of the lake.

The Spa at
Berjaya Langkawi Beach & Spa Resort

LANGKAWI ISLAND, KEDAH, MALAYSIA

ABOVE: The resort is tucked in a cul-de-sac of Burau Bay.

BELOW: The range of body treatments offered by the spa includes back purifying therapies, body scrubs and body wraps.

 he stretch of beach in front of the 400-room Berjaya Langkawi Beach & Spa Resort is untouched by most casual sun seekers thanks to its location on the far end of Burau Bay.

The perspective from afar, of expansive Malay-style cottages perched on stilts above the water or peppered throughout the hilly 28-hectare (70-acre) property, changes dramatically on reaching the spa.

The spa resembles a serene Japanese-influenced landscaped garden. Most guests ride a tram to the western corner of the property as the spa is a longish walk from the main building.

To the left of the reception pavilion are two cosy Thai massage villas which offer treatments such as the Amazing Thai (a two-hour session that includes a loofah body scrub and Thai massage) and the Thai Double Delight (a one-hour Thai Body Massage performed simultaneously by two therapists).

Stairs from the reception area lead down to two Japanese-inspired single-storey blocks that separately house male and female guests. Besides modern showers, they have Japanese-style bathing areas with stools. Treatment rooms are able to accommodate a gamut of wraps, body polishes and massages. The most popular option is the one-hour

ABOVE: The resort's swimming pool is built around a rockery. A jacuzzi is located on an upper level.

ABOVE RIGHT: The spa's pool courtyard provides shady refuge even on a warm day.

full-body aromatherapy massage with a choice of lavender, orange or grapefruit essential oils. Before your treatment, you'll unwind with lemon grass tea in the lounge. Cool ginger tea and fresh fruit are served at the end of the treatment; you might want to enjoy these outdoors to the tune of the bubbling hot pool, the spa's star feature, on a sunny day.

The outdoor courtyard, an oasis of hot and chilled pools, is perched on an elevated deck surrounded by lush ferns and ancient trees concealing the beach below. Water from a large heated jacuzzi spills over into a smaller pool near a chilled one. The multi-level wooden sundeck provides shady nichés for relaxing to the chirp of cicadas, birds and monkeys in the surrounding treetops.

Many visitors to the spa are happy to skip treatments and pay a nominal fee which allows them to linger in this haven for a day. The area also provides refuge for hotel guests who've checked out early but need a place to hang around.

You can get light meals and drinks, or order in more sinful treats from the resort's room service, at the open-air Spa Bar Café, tucked into the lower deck of the spa grounds.

SPA STATISTICS

SPA AREA
1,200 sq m (12,917 sq ft)

FACILITIES
1 double treatment room with Hydrotherapy Circuit Bath, 2 Thai massage villas (1 double), 4 massage beds in one treatment room (male), 4 single treatment rooms (female), 2 facial rooms, 2 flotation tank rooms, 1 manicure/pedicure room; 2 saunas, 2 steam rooms, 1 outdoor bubbling hot pool, 1 outdoor chilled pool; spa retail corner

SIGNATURE TREATMENT
Aromatherapy Massage

OTHER TREATMENTS AND THERAPIES
Back purifying therapies, body scrubs, body wraps, facial treatments, flotation tank treatment, hydrotherapy circuit bath, manicures/pedicures, massage therapies, reflexology for hands and feet, waxing; spa packages

PROVISIONS FOR COUPLES
1 double treatment room, 1 Thai massage villa

SPA CUISINE
Light, healthy snacks, smoothies, fruit juices and herbal teas are available at the Spa Bar Café; special dietary needs can be catered to on request

ACTIVITIES
Fishing trips, boat joy rides, nature walks, jungle treks; banana boating, biking, canoeing, catamaraning, donkey rides, hobicat sailing, pool table, tennis, water-skiing, wind surfing

SERVICES
Baby-sitting (prior arrangement is required)

ADMISSION
Walk-in guests not having treatments are required to pay an entry fee to use the spa facilities

CONTACT
Karong Berkunci 200
Burau Bay
07000 Langkawi Island
Kedah
Malaysia
Tel: (60-4) 959 1888 ext 701
Fax: (60-4) 959 1886
Email: resvn@b-langkawi.com.my
Website: www.berjayaresorts.com

Spa Village at Pangkor Laut Resort

PANGKOR LAUT ISLAND, PERAK, MALAYSIA

oted second best island destination in the world by *Condé Nast Traveller* in October 1999, Pangkor Laut Resort's other accolades rave specifically about its swimming pool, oversized bathrooms or overall magic as the world's best honeymoon spot. In fact, when Italian tenor Luciano Pavarotti first saw the resort, he exclaimed, 'I almost cried when I saw how beautiful God had made this paradise.'

The luxury villas in the main resort are built on the lush two-million-year-old rainforested hillside or over water on stilts linked by wooden walkways. Eight 'estates', each with a dramatic swimming pool in its own landscaped garden, are clustered in a nearby secluded cove.

The spa's treatments are based on healing practices from Malaysia, China, India, Thailand and Japan. These are performed in Healing Huts at the Spa Village, which include a Chinese herbal shop, and Ayurvedic and Malay huts.

The spa recommends that guests see their Chinese and Ayurvedic professionals before treatment.

Treatment rooms include Thai Pavilions overlooking the sea where you can enjoy a Thai Herbal Massage.

Asian healing therapies range from the Qing-dynasty-based Herbal Hand and Foot Soak (with herbs such as cinnamon and angelica roots to promote circulation), Imperial Chinese Herbal

Facial (with aromatic herbs to wake up all senses, followed by acupressure face massage), Campur-Campur (Malay-Thai body massage) and Ayurvedic therapies.

Guests are invited to arrive one hour before their treatment so they can enjoy the tranquil surroundings as well as a complimentary Chinese Foot Pounding (a pre-conjugal treat once enjoyed by concubines and mistresses of powerful warlords in China's feudal societies).

Guests may choose one of the Bath Houses for a Shanghai Scrub, a vigorous body scrub and rinse in hot water, a free service for men and women. Other Asian bathing traditions include the Malay Bath (a circulation-enhancing treatment inspired by the old Balinese practice of walking to a lake wrapped in a sarong) and Japanese Bath (a body scrub with a *goshi-goshi* cloth before washing the body with a bucket of water and a dip in a heated pool). The spa menu at the Wrap House changes daily, with offerings that may include a Thai Herbal Wrap or Cucumber Aloe Wrap. All guests leave the spa with a batik sarong.

ABOVE LEFT: Some of the luxury villas are built over water on stilts and linked by wooden walkways.

ABOVE RIGHT: Pangkor Laut has been praised as the world's best honeymoon spot.

OPPOSITE: Over-sized bathtubs in some villas are located in private garden courtyards.

SPA STATISTICS

SPA AREA
16,187 sq m (174,240 sq ft)

FACILITIES
2 Bath Houses, 1 Belian Spa Treatment Pavilion, 3 Healing Huts, 3 Thai Pavilions, 8 Twin Spa Treatment Pavilions, 1 Wrap House (for 5 people); 3 Nap Gazebos, 1 Yoga Pavilion; 1 gymnasium, 3 swimming pools; 1 Jamu Bar; spa boutique

SIGNATURE TREATMENTS
Chinese Foot Pounding, Campur-Campur, Shanghai Scrub

OTHER TREATMENTS AND THERAPIES
Body wraps, facial treatments, hair care, manicures/pedicures, massage therapies; spa packages

PROVISIONS FOR COUPLES
1 Belian Spa Treatment Pavilion, 8 Twin Spa Treatment Pavilions

SPA CUISINE
Oriental cuisine with herbs from the Spa Village garden is available at Fisherman's Cove

ACTIVITIES
Batik painting classes; cruises, island hopping; nature walks, fishing, squash, stretching, tennis; meditation, yoga

SERVICES
Baby-sitting; complimentary consultations with Chinese herbalist and Ayurvedic physician at the beginning of your stay

CONTACT
Pangkor Laut Island
32200 Lumut
Perak
Malaysia
Tel: (60-5) 699 1100
Fax: (60-5) 699 1200
Email: plr@po.jaring.my
Reservation: travelcentre@ytlhotels.com.my
Website: www.pangkorlautresort.com

Taman Sari Royal Heritage Spa Awana Kijal

TERENGGANU DARUL IMAN, MALAYSIA

The active holidaymaker at the 368-room Awana Kijal Golf, Beach & Spa Resort can keep busy with a gamut of activities from teeing off at the 18-hole golf course to jogging along the beach. The laid-back can enjoy the charms around the fishing village of Kijal which is famous for its creamy, fleshy and small durian pods.

The resort's key area for rest, relaxation and rejuvenation is the 1,800-square metre (19,375-square foot) waterfall pool (covered with 67,000 blue tiles) which has two quaint little huts over outdoor jacuzzis that can seat up to 10 people at a time.

Another spot to unwind is in the resort's south wing, facing the tennis courts. In the Taman Sari Royal Heritage Spa Awana Kijal, Javanese therapists pamper guests with traditional treatments once enjoyed by Javanese royalty using all-natural ingredients as well as high-tech therapies from Europe.

The Javanese Massage, French Massage and Queen Massage are especially favoured by the spa's local and expatriate clientele. The gentle full body French Massage is recommended for the elderly, those with sensitive muscles and first-time spa-goers. In the Queen Massage, two therapists work simultaneously on each guest.

Of the body wraps available as part of a spa package, the Parem Body Wrap doesn't involve a heated blanket, thanks to the warming properties of its ginger ingredients. Other packages include the Taman Sari-Awana Spa Retreat (a five-to six-hour session that includes a Papaya Enzyme Body Polish, choice of massage, Floral Bath, Spa Lunch, Total Foot and Hand Aromatherapy Spa and

ABOVE: Hair is nourished with a concoction of green coconut shampoo and essential oils, and shoulders given a massage in a Creambath.

RIGHT: The traditional Javanese massage uses Taman Sari's Royal Heritage Essential Oils to relax you, reduce the toxic elements in your body, eliminate muscle tension, and improve blood and lymph circulation.

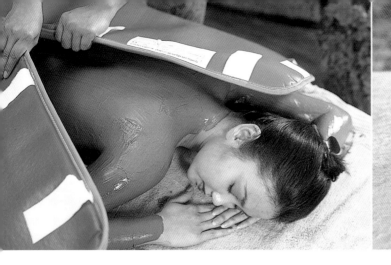

SPA STATISTICS

SPA AREA
1,876 sq m (20,193 sq ft)

FACILITIES
3 treatment rooms for females, 1 treatment room for males, 1 thalasso room; 2 jacuzzis, 1 sauna; 1 gymnasium, 1 swimming pool; 1 beauty salon; 1 *jamu* bar

SIGNATURE TREATMENTS
Royal Javanese Pampering, Taman Sari Awana Spa Retreat, Total Relaxation Get Away

OTHER TREATMENTS AND THERAPIES
Body scrubs, body wraps, bust care, facial treatments, hair treatments and services, hand and foot treatments, intimacy care, manicures/pedicures, massage therapies; spa packages

PROVISIONS FOR COUPLES
Royal Honeymoon Package

ACTIVITIES
Swimming and taekwondo classes; durian tours; creative art; banana boating, body and knee boarding, catamaraning, fishing, kayaking, jet-skiing, sailing, water-skiing, wind surfing; kite-flying and making, sand castle-building; aerobics, archery, beach football and volleyball, basketball, *beca* ride (trishaw ride), biking, bird watching, golf, horse riding, jogging, jungle trekking, *sepak takraw/ragabulat*, snooker and pool, table tennis, team building, tennis, water aerobics, water basketball, water polo, water volleyball; meditation, yoga

SERVICES
Child care; personal training

CONTACT
KM28, Jalan Kemaman-Dungun,
24100 Kijal
Kemaman
Terengganu Darul Iman
Malaysia
Tel: (60-9) 864 1188
Fax: (60-9) 864 1688
Email: awanakij@tm.net.my
Website: www.awana.com.my

ABOVE LEFT: The body relaxes under a heated blanket after it has been slathered with Merapi Volcano Mud or a Seaweed Mask.

ABOVE RIGHT: Hand Spa refers to a treatment that moisturises, tones and softens the skin on hands and arms.

BELOW: Papaya Enzyme, available as a body scrub or shower gel, helps cool, soften and soothe the skin.

BELOW LEFT: South Sea Mineral Bath Salts are available in three varieties: relaxing, refreshing and antiseptic.

Hair Nourishment), and three-and-a-half-hour sessions such as the Royal Javanese Pampering (which includes a Herbal Body Scrub or *Lulur*; Javanese Massage, Aromatherapy Hand or Foot Spa, Foot Aromatherapy Spa and Facial Treatment) and Total Relaxation Get Away (a Sea Salt Body Glow, choice of massage, Seaweed Body Wrap with Banana Leaf, Facial Treatment and Thalasso Bath or Seaweed Bath). Male and female therapists work on male and female guests respectively, but couples can have their treatments together in one of the massage rooms. The four-hour Royal Honeymoon Package, designed to improve sexual vitality between partners, includes a Pelvic Tilting Exercise and an Asmaragama Massage that concentrates on the stomach and back using oils with aphrodisiac qualities.

The Nautilus Spa at Coco Palm Resort & Spa

BAA ATOLL, THE MALDIVES

Sunrise breakfasts, sunset cocktails or barbecues for two. Such escapades to a deserted sandbank or island can be arranged by the couple-friendly Coco Palm Resort & Spa.

So too, can overnight stays under a tent—that is, if you can bear to tear yourselves away from your villa's four-poster bed or private garden bathroom.

Situated on its own island and surrounded by a ring of sugar-fine sand, the resort, a 30-minute seaplane flight from Malé, is composed of about 98 villas scattered among the foliage or built on stilts above the lagoon. Guests who want to tie the knot or renew their vows

may request for ceremonial weddings at sunset, with the bride arriving on a *dhoni* (traditional Maldivian boat) to greet her groom on the beach. Spa treatments for the couple are included as part of these celebrations. Two of the round, thatched-roof villas that make up the premises of Nautilus Spa have been dedicated to the use of couples. If you and your partner have the time for a lengthy treatment, opt for the 110-minute Harmony package that includes an Aromatherapy Footbath, Lavender Body Wash, body scrub of your choice and either a Balinese Massage or Traditional Asian Facial.

The 150-minute Ultimate Indulgence includes a few extras such as a foot

from the transparent turquoise lagoon at dawn. This is the same lagoon where you may find yourself in the company of graceful eagle rays and sting rays which regularly visit the shallows or turtles coming ashore to deposit their eggs at night. For its environmentally friendly practices—and for prompting its guests to do likewise—the property received the President of Maldives Green Resort Award 2001.

massage. One of the more exotic massages is the Royal Thai Massage.

You can sample The Nautilus Spa's smorgasbord of all-natural treatments—which are drawn from the ancient health and beauty traditions of Asia—by opting for the two-, three- or five-day spa packages which give you something to look forward to every day of your stay.

The manner in which water is used during the treatment process subliminally heightens the pleasure of the spa experience. For instance, therapists scoop water from an oriental jug and gently pour it over your body to wash away the scrub; and the water used in aromatherapy footbaths is drawn daily

SPA STATISTICS

SPA AREA
400 sq m (4,306 sq ft)

FACILITIES
2 double deluxe spa villas with private garden, 2 single spa villas with private garden and relaxation area; 1 aromatherapy floral bath and relaxation area, 1 jacuzzi; 1 gymnasium; spa boutique

SIGNATURE TREATMENTS
Harmony, Ultimate Indulgence

OTHER TREATMENTS AND THERAPIES
Body scrubs, manicures/pedicures, massage therapies, traditional facial treatments; spa packages

PROVISIONS FOR COUPLES
Special rates on most treatments; double deluxe spa villas

SPA CUISINE
Vegetarian food and light, healthy food choices available on the menu; special dietary needs can be catered to on request

ACTIVITIES
Excursions to nearby islands; aerobics, badminton, canoeing, catamaran sailing, dolphin watching, pool, sailing, scuba diving, snorkelling, surf-biking, table tennis, tennis, volleyball, water-skiing, windsurfing

SERVICES
Arrangements for ceremonial weddings and escapades to deserted islands

CONTACT
Dunikolu Island, Baa Atoll
The Maldives
Tel: (960) 230 011
Fax: (960) 230 022
Email: cocopalm@sunland.com.mv
Website: www.cocopalm.com.mv or www.mandaraspa-asia.com

Six Senses Spa at Soneva Fushi Resort & Spa

BAA ATOLL, THE MALDIVES

ABOVE LEFT: The main spa is located within this courtyard of a circular pond on which float stepping stones.

ABOVE RIGHT: Your fellow spa companion at Soneva Fushi could well be a celebrity as the property is favoured by the rich and famous for its seclusion.

International jet-setters and celebrities are among those who seek the seclusion of Soneva Fushi Resort & Spa, voted the World's Best Resort by *Condé Nast Traveller* in 2000 and 3rd Best Resort Spa in the World by Gallivanter's Guide 2000 Awards For Excellence. A 25-minute seaplane flight from Malé International Airport, the resort occupies the 1,400-metre (1,531-yard) long by 400-metre (437-yard) wide Kunfunadhoo Island in the Baa Atoll.

You're likely to encounter chickens and rabbits rather than other guests as you cycle along the raw trails in the jungle-like setting. Island life is akin to playing Robinson Crusoe—only with modern luxuries such as television sets hidden under woven baskets; or faxes delivered to your door in bamboo canisters. Some villas have private plunge pools, but each has a bathroom in a large walled garden and a private sandy lawn that leads into the warm sea.

Harmless baby black tip sharks patrol the shallows around the resort, while scuba divers frequently meet dolphins, manta rays and whale sharks in the waters around the Baa Atoll.

Like other Six Senses spas, this flagship spa of the Soneva and Evason properties appeals through the senses of sight, smell, touch, hearing, taste—

and intuition. Therapists, handpicked from around the globe, use this sixth sense to personalise treatments. The spa deliberately steers clear of faddish treatments, only offering tried and tested ones from both the East and West.

Treatment areas include bright and airy indoor treatment rooms with waterfalls trickling over the natural slate walls into indoor rivers.

Two newer spa suites, each with treatment areas, showers and jacuzzis under thatched roofs, offer the most privacy. The suites are equipped with steam and sauna facilities and day beds—and private relaxation lounges built among the treetops (one suite incorporates five large palm trees rather than uproot them).

Treatments in the outdoor treatment *champas* (thatched huts) by the sea, accessed through a shady grove of trees, seem to have an additional liberating quality. The spa's most back-to-nature treatment, the Maldivian Sand Massage, is performed at the water's edge on the beach. As your skin is scrubbed and rinsed with the surrounding sand and water, your body and mind unwinds to the ocean's chant and motion.

ABOVE: The masseurs and therapists are handpicked from around the globe.

BELOW LEFT: Each villa has a large bathroom complete with a bathtub and a separate shower.

BELOW CENTRE: Dust sand from your soles by running them over little hedgehog brushes stationed outside the villas and the spa.

OPPOSITE BELOW: The reception area in the spa is a shrine to the sublime.

SPA STATISTICS

SPA AREA
550 sq m (5,920 sq ft)

FACILITIES
2 spa suites with steam, jacuzzi and outdoor shower, 1 beauty treatment room, 1 double treatment room, 2 single treatment rooms, 1 wet treatment room with sauna and outdoor jacuzzi, 2 double-treatment *champas*; 1 meditation *champa*; gymnasium; spa boutique

SIGNATURE TREATMENTS
Indulge the Senses, Jet Lag Recovery, Maldivian Sand Massage

OTHER TREATMENTS AND THERAPIES
Beauty treatments, Decléor face and body treatments, massages, treatment baths (in guest room or spa); spa packages (detoxifying, destressing, rejuvenating)

PROVISIONS FOR COUPLES
Indulge the Senses; 5 double treatment areas; jacuzzis for 2

ACTIVITIES
Massage workshops, swimming classes; boat trips, cultural island excursion, fishing, island hopping, private picnics on uninhabited islands (champagne breakfast/sunset dining/GM's weekly sunset cocktail party); aikido, badminton, beach volleyball, boat trips, *boules*, canoeing, jogging, sailing, scuba diving, snorkelling, table tennis, tennis, windsurfing

SERVICES
Baby-sitting; general health consultations, personal training

SPA CUISINE
Available at all times; a health juice and tea menu is available in the spa and F&B outlets; grass-eater, hay, vegetarian, ovo lacto vegetarian, ovo vegetarian and pescetarian diets are available on request and following a consultation with the Executive Chef

CONTACT
Kunfunadhoo Island, Baa Atoll
The Maldives
Tel: (960) 230 304
Fax: (960) 230 374
Email: sonresa@soneva.com.mv
Website: www.six-senses.com

Six Senses Spa at Soneva Gili Resort & Spa

NORTH MALÉ ATOLL, THE MALDIVES

ABOVE: The upper deck of each villa is a vantage point for worshipping the sun and the sea's multiple shades of blue.

LEFT: Each villa's shower, encased by glass blocks and a thatched roof, is separated from the main bathroom by an open-air walkway over a private watergarden.

OPPOSITE TOP: It's easy to spend your stay in the comfort of your spacious wooden villa and enjoy the sumptuous spa cuisine.

OPPOSITE BELOW: The hand massage improves flexibility and stimulates circulation.

The luxurious Soneva Gili Resort & Spa on the island of Lankanfushi in the North Malé Atoll is a 15-minute speedboat ride from Malé International Airport. It is accessible enough for guests with limited time, though most would elect to maroon themselves here for an average of two weeks.

Water villa suites are perched above the lagoon on wooden stilts from jetties which fan out from the island. Soneva Gili Residences are at the very end of these jetties. The seven Crusoe Residences, which look out beyond the coral reef, offer the most seclusion; each can only be reached via a private rowboat from the jetty. Your entire stay can be spent in your spacious wooden villa sunbathing on the sun deck or dining on the upper deck under the midnight sky.

A variety of bath treatments—including Cleopatra, a milk-and-honey treat that recalls the legendary beauty's preferred ritual—can be drawn up in your tub which overlooks the lagoon. Or you can choose to cuddle up with your partner in a jacuzzi in the spa.

The Six Senses Spa, also located over the lagoon, faces sunrise over the Indian Ocean. Fashioned from plantation teak, cedar and bamboo, the spa is accented with copper and metallic details and hues that echo the multiple shades of the surrounding waters.

In the air-conditioned comfort of the treatment room, unwind to recordings ranging from classical strains to the call of dolphins. Alternatively, leave the glass doors open to hear the waves and the wind. As you peer through the opening in the massage couch into the rectangular glass opening in the floor while your back is kneaded, let your thoughts flit as freely as the tropical fish about the coral below.

Jet Lag Recovery (a full body and scalp massage served with a glass of fresh fruit juice which gives an energy kick) is a popular treatment. Loving twosomes can Indulge the Senses with an aromatherapy massage. The aphrodisiac is not just in the blend of essential oils or the complimentary bottle of champagne—rather, it's in the time that this romantic treatment takes place: at sunset or under the stars.

SPA STATISTICS

SPA AREA
300 sq m (3,229 sq ft)

FACILITIES
5 treatment rooms; 2 sauna and steam rooms (separate for men and women), 1 jacuzzi; 1 gymnasium; spa boutique

SIGNATURE TREATMENTS
Indulge the Senses, Jet Lag Recovery, Maldivian Sand Massage

OTHER TREATMENTS AND THERAPIES
Beauty treatments, Decléor face and body treatments, massages, reflexology, scalp treatments, treatment baths (in guest's room or spa), packages (detoxifying, destressing, rejuvenating)

PROVISIONS FOR COUPLES
Indulge the Senses; 1 double open-air treatment room with ocean view

ACTIVITIES
Massage workshops; island hopping/cultural excursions, private island picnics; badminton, beach volleyball, *boules*, canoeing, fishing, hobicat sailing, jogging, scuba diving, snorkelling, table tennis, tennis, windsurfing; yoga

SERVICES
Day use rooms, general health consultations, skincare consultations; tricycles available free of charge on request

SPA CUISINE
Available at all times and in-room. A health juice and tea menu is available in the spa and F&B outlets. Hay, vegetarian, ovo vegetarian, ovo lacto vegetarian, and pescetarian diets are available on request and following a consultation with the Executive Chef

CONTACT
Lankanfushi Island, North Malé Atoll
The Maldives
Tel: (960) 440 304
Fax: (960) 440 305
Email: sonresa@soneva.com.mv
Website: www.six-senses.com

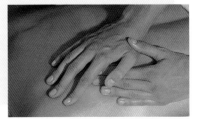

Mogambo Springs: The Spa at Plantation Bay

CEBU, THE PHILIPPINES

ABOVE: Get an invigorating shoulder and back massage at the freshwater pool.

OPPOSITE TOP: The saltwater springs are especially romantic in the evenings.

OPPOSITE BELOW CENTRE: A *cogon* roof and *bagakay* (young bamboo) fence give the spa its native feel.

OPPOSITE FAR RIGHT: Beyond the wooden beaded curtains at the changing room, walls are covered with *banig*.

he waterways that comprise half of the three-hectare (seven-acre) resort are manmade.

If you're not content with soaking in the view from your room—or exploring the Caribbean-like plantation village on foot, bicycle or rollerblades—jump into the meandering saltwater lagoon from selected balconies, slither in on a slide or plunge in from a diving rock. Other watering holes include fishing ponds

(where you can catch your own lunch or leave the fishy work to the chef) and cold springs near the beach.

The 1,600-square metre (17,000-square foot) free-form freshwater swimming pool—with eight whirlpools—is almost totally embraced by the lagoon.

Mogambo Springs is a tranquil haven behind Mogambo Falls (named for a 1950s movie). The fan-cooled structure has an Asian yet almost Japanese feel, with adobe walls and local *cogon* (reed)

roofing, wooden beaded curtains at locker room entrances and colourful *banig* (woven mats traditionally used as sleeping mats) covering the walls.

The spa's pool area resembles a canyon—with rock formations, pathways of river stones and a gurgling brook.

The misty atmosphere comes from a machine that cools the surrounding temperature. A trio of pools—black hot pool, grey saltwater pool and pink cold pool—resemble gems.

The spa's star treatment, the Pool Massage—where head, shoulders, arms and hands are massaged while you soak—features in various spa packages.

From their Head To Foot Body Scrubs, pick Fruit Delicious (lime and mint shower gel, kiwi and grape exfoliating scrub, facial mist, and lime and mint body lotion).

Treatments primarily use The Body Shop's products, while the Italian-made Comfort Zone are used in facials.

No tipping is required so you can focus on selecting your treatments—and where to enjoy them.

For a nominal fee, you can have a massage at three locations outside the spa: at the pool deck, the gazebo by the lagoon or in your room.

SPA STATISTICS

SPA AREA
560 sq m (6,028 sq ft)

FACILITIES
1 double private villa with whirlpool, 3 double treatment rooms, 1 single treatment room; 1 hot pool, 1 saltwater pool; 1 cold pool with swim-up bar, water spouts, needle shower and waterfalls; 1 scrub room; 1 dry sauna; 1 beauty salon; spa retail corner

SIGNATURE TREATMENT
Pool Massage

OTHER TREATMENTS AND THERAPIES
Body scrubs, body wraps, chair massage (using wooden chairs bought from local markets and modified for comfort), facial treatments, foot therapy, massage therapies, reflexology, salon services (eyebrow shaping, haircut/styling, colouring, hot oil/cellophane, manicures/pedicures, curling/straightening, waxing)

PROVISIONS FOR COUPLES
1 double private villa with whirlpool, 3 double treatment rooms

ACTIVITIES
Archery, aerobics, aquaerobics, biking, croquet, cruises, fishing, hobicat sailing, jet-skiing, kayaking, para-sailing, putting green, scuba diving, teambuilding activities, tennis, volleyball, water-skiing, banana boat, wall-climbing, table tennis, billiards

SERVICES
Butler services; baby-sitting, Children's Centre; free airport shuttle services

SPA CUISINE
Not available; special dietary needs can be catered to on request

ADMISSION
Admission fee is waived if treatments are taken up

CONTACT
Marigondon
Mactan Island
Cebu 6015
The Philippines
Tel: (63-32) 340 5900
Fax: (63-32) 340 5988
Email: spa@plantationbay.com
Website: www.plantationbay.com

Amrita Spa at Raffles Hotel

SINGAPORE

ABOVE: Like the spa, the pool, located in a courtyard on the third floor of the hotel, is the sole domain of hotel guests.

RIGHT: The elegant Raffles Hotel, established in 1887, was designated a national monument a century later.

Somerset Maugham—whose spirit is very much alive in a Personality Suite that bears his name and is decorated with his books and photos—described Raffles Hotel as a symbol of 'all the fables of the Exotic East'. James A Michener—who was known to have taken his hotel key when he checked out—wrote, 'To have been young and had a room at Raffles was life at its best'.

These days, to stay in one of the 103 suites is to possibly reside in the same elegant space as royalty, heads of state and other luminaries.

Residents at this hotel—established in 1887 and now a national monument—are assigned personal valets who will see to all their needs, including making reservations at Amrita Spa.

The intimate spa, reflecting the classical architecture of the hotel, is decorated with oriental carpets and antiques from Southeast Asia. Just as visitors to Singapore would go to the Raffles for the Singapore Sling (the cocktail made famous by the hotel), residents visiting the spa would savour the Raffles Signature Body Treatment Experience. This begins with an invigorating salt and essential oil scrub, followed by an aromatherapy mineral bath and an aromatherapy massage.

Another house speciality, the Herbal Kur, begins with a camomile body scrub that prepares the skin for the healing

effect of the Krauter Herbal Bath (infused with pine, wildflowers, Melissa or camomile), and ends with a 30-minute revitalising body massage with lavender oil.

Spa Ritual Packages are available for those with more time. Essence of Raffles, a package for couples, includes an Aromatherapy Facial for her, a Gentlemen's Facial for him and a Raffles Signature Body Treatment for both.

The treatments take place in the Rafflesiana Suite which has an in-room jacuzzi and direct access to the relaxation verandah. European and American guests in particular enjoy toasting themselves in the warm sun on the relaxation verandah overlooking the hotel's Palm Garden.

Spa cuisine is available at the Pool Bar on the third floor of the hotel.

The swimming pool and the gymnasium are open 24 hours a day for the benefit of residents who require a pre-bedtime workout.

Like Amrita Spa, the pool, Pool Bar and the gymnasium are devoted solely to the use of hotel residents.

ABOVE LEFT: The Rafflesiana VIP suite is a favourite with honeymooners. This treatment room has direct access to the relaxation area.

ABOVE RIGHT: The spa's relaxation verandah overlooks the Palm Garden. Guests can listen to music through headphones or bask in the sun.

SPA STATISTICS

SPA AREA
929 sq m (10,000 sq ft)

FACILITIES
1 VIP suite, 1 double treatment room, 4 single treatment rooms; 2 steam rooms and saunas; 1 manicure/pedicure room with hair care station; 24-hour gymnasium and swimming pool

SIGNATURE TREATMENTS
Amrita Spa 'Total Indulgence', Raffles Signature Body Treatment, Herbal Kur, Camomile Body Scrub, Herbal Bliss, Raffles Classic, Essence of Raffles (designed for couples only), Gentlemen's Executive Rescue (specifically designed for men)

OTHER TREATMENTS AND THERAPIES
Ayurvedic Pancha Karma, body massages, body scrubs, body wraps, eyebrow shaping, facial treatments, hand and foot care, shampoo and blow dry, waxing

PROVISIONS FOR COUPLES
Essence of Raffles, Herbal Kur, Raffles Signature Body Treatment; 1 VIP suite with private jacuzzi and steam bath, 1 double treatment room

SPA CUISINE
Available at the Pool Bar; special dietary needs can be catered to on request

SERVICES
Signature homemade tea of a special blend offered prior to treatments; health tips and total wellness of the body, mind and soul consultation by professional spa therapists

ADMISSION
For the exclusive use of in-house guests

CONTACT
1 Beach Road
Singapore 189673
Tel: (65) 6337 1886
Fax: (65) 6337 7650
Email: raffles@raffles.com
Website: www.raffleshotel.com

Amrita Spa at Raffles The Plaza

SINGAPORE

Among Asia's largest luxury spas, the flagship Amrita Spa occupies the 6th, 7th and 8th levels at Raffles The Plaza. Raffles The Plaza hotel is part of the Raffles City complex which also hosts offices, shops and an underground link to the Marina Bay area.

The spa's name—Amrita—is inspired by a Sanskrit legend about a magical elixir for eternal youth. You'll hear the sound of running water before you reach the waiting lounge where water ripples are reflected onto the ceiling. The adjoining boutique retails Amrita Spa Private Label botanical-based products from Australia.

While male and female treatment areas are segregated, couples celebrating a special occasion typically opt for the VIP suites—fitted with jacuzzi, aromatherapy steam room and mini-bar.

Should the two of you wish to spend half a day using the hotel's facilities, a good alternative is the Pavilion Suite which opens directly into the pool area. Spa cuisine—which come with calorie, protein, carbohydrate and fat counts—is served by the poolside Alligator Pear restaurant or for in-suite dining (see 'Cosmopolitan Cuisine', pp118–21).

The treatments combine the age-old traditions of East and West with modern technology. The spa has a special focus on marine-inspired body wraps and masks—the Thermal Kur, for example, consists of a Moor Mud Wrap, Thermal

RIGHT: The separate wet treatment areas for men and women include a cool plunge pool and jacuzzi.

FAR RIGHT: The state-of-the-art cardio theatre has more than 20 machines to work the heart muscles. Each machine has its own headset for the viewing of private business channels.

BELOW: Hot Stone Therapy is one of the specialised massage techniques the spa offers.

OPPOSITE TOP: The swimming pool appears as an oasis dwarfed by the towers that make up Raffles City.

OPPOSITE BELOW LEFT: The Amrita Pavilion opens directly into the pool area.

OPPOSITE BELOW RIGHT: The spa's choice of body scrubs helps detoxify and destress.

Mineral bath and massage. Spa Ritual Packages can be enjoyed individually or as a twosome. Couple favourites include Day Spa Escape (an 85-minute session including aroma hydrofusion, anti-stress back, neck and scalp massage, and facial) and Total Body Wellness (a three-hour-35-minute treatment involving a Sea Salt Scrub, Sea Mud Wrap, Sea Mud Hair Treatment with face and scalp acupressure point massage, body massage and aromatherapy facial).

For those who wish to get away without having to go away, you need not look further than checking into this pampering and integrated spa.

You may also check into the hotels, which offer various room and spa packages for overnight stays.

SPA STATISTICS

SPA AREA
4,645 sq m (50,000 sq ft)

FACILITIES
35 treatment rooms (2 double Amrita Pavilions, 3 double VIP Suites, 26 individual treatment suites), 2 Dermalife rooms, 2 Hydrotone rooms; 2 cool plunge pools, 2 jacuzzis, 2 saunas, 2 steam rooms, 2 warm plunge pools; 2 meditation alcoves, 2 relaxation lounges, 1 yoga pavilion; 1 state-of-the-art cardio theatre, 1 gymnasium, 2 swimming pools, 6 tennis courts; 1 lifestyle boutique

SIGNATURE TREATMENTS
Amrita Signature Massage, Herbal Kur, Thermal Kur, Moor Mud Wrap including customised and wedding packages

OTHER TREATMENTS AND THERAPIES
Ayurvedic Pancha Karma, body bronzing, body scrubs, body wraps, facial treatments, foot and leg massage, manicures/pedicures, massage therapies, pre- and post-natal massage

PROVISIONS FOR COUPLES
Day Spa Escape, Total Body Wellness; use of couple treatment suites with a minimum amount of treatments booked, in-suite dining for spa cuisine

SPA CUISINE
Signature spa cuisine is available at the Alligator Pear restaurant

ACTIVITIES
Tennis clinics, wellness talks; Pilates, workout programmes; yoga, members' activities

SERVICES
Gift certificates; fitness assessments, nutritional consultations, personal training

ADMISSION
Exclusively for in-house guests and members; treatments are also available to non-members

CONTACT
2 Stamford Road
Level 6 Raffles The Plaza
Singapore 178882
Tel: (65) 6336 4477
Fax: (65) 6336 1161
Email: rafflescity@amritaspas.com
Website: www.amritaspas.com

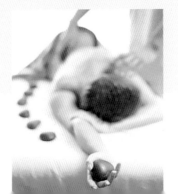

Amrita Spa at Swissôtel Merchant Court

SINGAPORE

ABOVE: Swissôtel Merchant Court sits on the banks of the historic Singapore River.

RIGHT: The swimming pool spells holiday resort rather than city hotel.

Located along the banks of the Singapore River, Swissôtel Merchant Court is within walking distance of the business and financial districts of Raffles Place and Shenton Way, Chinatown, and the restaurant and pub hubs of Clarke Quay, Boat Quay and Mohamed Sultan Road.

Resort-like facilities include the lagoon-like pool—complete with water spouts and slides—which spills over into the children's pool. Non-hotel guests and non-members can use the spa facilities, pool, outdoor jacuzzi and gymnasium for a nominal day fee.

Each treatment room at Amrita Spa is decorated with an oriental wood carving. Interestingly, when lying face down, you'll see a lotus flower on a bed of iridescent stones through the hole in your massage couch.

The Body Wrap room has a heated gel-filled bed to relax the body, maximising the effects of ingredients applied during treatments, which include the Aroma Stress Relief Wrap (using an aloe vera-based body mask) and Purifying Sea Mud Wrap.

The spa offers a range of skincare, back care, massage, hydrotherapies and spa packages, but is perhaps best known for its Ayurvedic treatments such as the Ayurvedic Shiro Dhara and Herbal Wrap. The last includes an Ayurvedic *marma* point face-and-scalp massage

ABOVE LEFT: The wall fountain adds to the relaxing surroundings.

ABOVE CENTRE: In the Ayurvedic Shiro Dhara, a fine stream of warm oil drizzles on to your forehead, calming the body and mind. This is an ideal treatment for sinusitis and insomnia.

ABOVE RIGHT: In the Ayurvedic Herbal Wrap, steaming herbal-soaked linen towels are wrapped around your body. Inhale the steam while a *marma* point massage is performed on your head and scalp.

while you're wrapped in steaming herbal-soaked linen. The treatment encourages detoxification and reduces muscle tension. The 30-minute Anti-Stress massage focuses on the back, shoulders and scalp, and provides a quick dose of bliss. Your therapist will tailor the best blend of essential oils for your needs.

The Invigorate blend is a pick-me-up should you be heading for a meeting straight after. In addition to Amrita Spa Private Label products, the spa uses Dermalogica skin care in its facials.

The spa also offers Bridal Spa Retreats. For her: a Classical Facial, Herbal Body Glow or Mineral Salt, Clarifying Back Treatment or Botanical Back Glow, and manicure and pedicure. For him: a Classical Facial, Herbal Body Glow or Mineral Salt, and a full body massage.

SPA STATISTICS

SPA AREA
560 sq m (6,028 sq ft)

FACILITIES
9 individual treatment rooms, 1 body wrap room, 1 hydrotherapy room; 1 outdoor jacuzzi, 1 sauna, 2 steam rooms; 1 manicure/pedicure station; 1 gymnasium with fitness studio, 1 swimming pool

SIGNATURE TREATMENTS
Aroma Stress Relief Wrap, Ayurvedic Shiro Dhara, Herbal Wrap, Purifying Sea Mud Wrap

OTHER TREATMENTS AND THERAPIES
Back treatments, body scrubs, body wraps, eyebrow shaping, eye treatments, facial treatments, hydrotherapies, manicures/pedicures, massage therapies, waxing

PROVISIONS FOR COUPLES
Bridal Spa Retreat, fitness membership for couples

SPA CUISINE
Available at the Pool Terrace and Bar

ACTIVITIES
Fitness classes

SERVICES
Personal training

ADMISSION
Non-members and non-residents have to pay a fee to use the pool, jacuzzi and gymnasium

CONTACT
20 Merchant Road
Singapore 058281
Tel: (65) 6239 1780
Fax: (65) 6239 1781
Email: amrita.merchantcourt@swissotel.com
Website: www.swissotel.com

Renewal Club Spa at Meritus Negara Hotel

SINGAPORE

In fast-paced Singapore, it's difficult to find a quiet place to rest and relax. But Renewal Club Spa at Meritus Negara Hotel provides just that, and more. Located on the fourth level, the spa is an urban escape set within the beauty and serenity of a tropical Asian retreat. A soothing ambience and a professional team are just two elements that work together to help rejuvenate and refresh tired bodies.

The third, and definitely the most important, element is the range of innovative and creative treatments the spa offers, drawn from the rich herbal traditions of Asia to enhance your health.

Step into the Yuan Room and you'll discover the Tree of Life, a wall mural with mosaic leaves that reflects the spa's respect for Mother Earth. A fitting tribute since the spa prides itself on offering a wide variety of Thai and Chinese herbal treatments. The ingredients for the Thai treatments are selected daily by the spa's Thai trainer, who then prepares traditional formulations to promote blood circulation, relax tired muscles, or exfoliate and moisturise the skin. The trainer is also responsible for preparing a fresh flavour of body scrub every month.

The Chinese treatments are based on principles of traditional Chinese medicine, a world first by Renewal. The treatments, formulated to provide health and beauty benefits, use ingredients

such as ginseng and pearl powder to help detoxify or relieve heatiness.

You can enjoy the benefits of the herbal treatments through an extensive spa menu that includes body wraps, body scrubs, bath infusions and a range of herbal teas.

Signature Chinese treatments include Gui Fei's Ritual and the Chinese Herbology Facial.

The spa experience doesn't just start and end with your treatment. Rather, it begins with a traditional Asian greeting and continues during your herbal

RIGHT: The Yuan Room for couples features a wall painting called the Tree of Life, a lasting reminder of Renewal Club Spa's deep appreciation for fresh, natural herbs.

OPPOSITE TOP: Relax in the Chiang Mai lounge before and after treatments.

OPPOSITE BELOW CENTRE: Nocturnal Bliss is performed at the candle-lit poolside by two therapists.

OPPOSITE BELOW RIGHT: Besides Chinese herbal treatments, the spa offers therapies using Thai herbs and spices (pictured).

treatment, ending with the appropriate herbal tea. The teas—Thai if you had a Thai herbal treatment and Chinese if you had a Chinese treatment—can be enjoyed in the Chiang Mai Relaxation Lounge which faces the pool.

While sipping your tea, you can read up about the herbs just used on your body through the books thoughtfully provided in the lounge. Or you can just lie back and let your eyes rest on the calm waters of the pool.

Another highlight on the menu is the Rose Hip Wrap. The wrap uses oil distilled from seeds of wild roses from the mountains of British Columbia, Canada. Renewal Club Spa is the first and only spa in Singapore to import rose hip oil fresh from the source. The result is a sensory experience that is out of this world and skin that feels moisturised and pampered like never before.

The Thai and Chinese trainers are constantly challenged to create new formulations to ensure that each visit is a whole New Asia Spa experience.

SPA STATISTICS

SPA AREA
418 sq m (4,500 sq ft)

FACILITIES
1 couple's suite, 1 poolside treatment area, 4 single treatment rooms, 1 Thai massage room; 1 consultation corner; 1 jacuzzi, 1 steam room, 1 sauna; retail corner

SIGNATURE TREATMENTS
Chinese Herbology Facial, Flavour of the Month Scrub, Gui Fei's Ritual, Hot Stone Therapy, Nocturnal Bliss, Rose Hip Wrap, Spa à Trois, Tang Royal Spa Experience

OTHER TREATMENTS AND THERAPIES
Back facial treatments, body scrubs, body wraps, foot treatments, lymphobiology, massage therapies, pre- and post-natal massages, sports massage, Remedial Massage, reflexology, slimming/firming treatments, facial treatments, traditional Thai therapies, Trigger-Point Therapy, Movement Therapy, waxing

PROVISIONS FOR COUPLES
Special monthly packages; 1 couple's suite

SPA CUISINE
Not available

ACTIVITIES
Spa appreciation parties, talks; Movement Therapy and fitness programmes

SERVICES
Organising private spa parties, private Movement Therapy and fitness programmes; facilities membership

ADMISSION
Membership not required but available

CONTACT
Level 4
10 Claymore Road
(off Orchard Road)
Singapore 229540
Tel: (65) 6736 3097
Fax: (65) 6736 3098
Email: info@renewal.com.sg
Website: www.renewal.com.sg

Renewal Day Spa at Tong Building

SINGAPORE

Renewal Day Spa could be mistaken for a restful Provençal retreat with its beautifully painted *trompe l'oeils* inspired by the lovely French countryside. But the spa is 17 levels above the heart of busy Orchard Road.

Opened in 1995, it brought the authentic day spa concept to busy executives who couldn't afford the time for a spa vacation. Since then, Renewal has maintained its progressiveness by incorporating treatments beyond the usual scrubs and massages.

Besides relaxation and detoxification therapies not unlike those found in top European spas, Renewal also offers clinical restorative therapies. For example, Myo-fascial Release Therapy is a type of massage that uses various techniques to stretch and strengthen the fascia, a connective tissue that runs through the entire body. This helps to relieve recurring pain caused by a past injury or poor posture. Another hallmark of the spa is its paramedical range of

TOP: Massage therapies are prescribed after a session with one of the spa's counsellors.

FAR LEFT: Lymphobiology combines massage with the use of biological products.

LEFT: The jet streams in the tub help promote circulation and remove toxins via the lymphatic system.

specialised face and body aesthetic programmes. The spa's professional team is made up of experienced paramedical aestheticians working closely with a distinguished American dermatologist. Together, they are able to treat skin conditions such as acne-scarring, hyper pigmentation and premature ageing.

Skin care products—made from pharmaceutical grade ingredients—come from the US and Europe. Renewal carefully selects products that have been extensively researched and tested to ensure their efficacy.

Proving that it does not rest on its laurels, Renewal has also introduced an Integrative Holistic Therapy Programme, the first and only Singapore spa to do so. Combining the best of homeopathy, Movement Therapy and conventional spa therapies, the programme is a complete health plan to improve your physical, emotional and mental well-being. Homeopathy, for instance, treats the person as a whole rather than focusing on the affected parts or organs of the body. It strives to heal by strengthening the immune system, thus reducing recurring illnesses.

The programme offers specific therapies to manage weight, ageing and stress, three of the most common concerns facing today's busy executives. For example, the Age Management Programme delays and reduces menopausal or andropausal symptoms. This is done through a series of sessions comprising homeopathic consultations and supplements, Movement Therapy and specialised massage therapies.

Renewal prides itself on its professional difference. Its counsellors and therapists are trained regularly to ensure a high standard of knowledge and expertise. This is vital to ensure the best service is given to each client.

ABOVE: Hand-painted *trompe l'oeil* murals create the provincial ambience of southern France.

SPA STATISTICS

SPA AREA
334 sq m (3,600 sq ft)

FACILITIES
11 single treatment rooms; 1 aroma sauna, 1 hydrobath, 1 steam room, 1 Vichy shower, 2 consultation rooms; 1 pedicure/manicure corner; 1 deluxe room with manicure/pedicure chair; spa boutique.

SIGNATURE TREATMENTS
Aromatherapy Massage, Balneotherapy, Bio Light Laser Therapy, Micro Current Therapy, Micro Lift Therapy, Microdermabrasion, paramedical face and body treatments, Vichy with Massage, Vichy with Scrub

OTHER TREATMENTS AND THERAPIES
Aromassage with in-house blends, anti-cellulite treatments, body scrubs, body wraps, eye care, facial treatments, foot care, homeopathy, hydrotherapy, lymphobiology, manicures/pedicures, Myo-Fascial Release Therapy, pre- and post-natal massages, reflexology, remedial massage therapies, slimming/firming treatments, waxing

PROVISIONS FOR COUPLES
A ladies-only spa; but men may have body treatments on Sundays, and facials any day of the week

SPA CUISINE
Not available

ACTIVITIES
Health talks and workshops; spa appreciation parties

SERVICES
Consultations with homeopathic doctors, gift certificates

ADMISSION
Membership not required but available

CONTACT
302 Orchard Road
#17-02 Tong Building
Singapore 238862
Tel: (65) 6738 0988
Fax: (65) 6733 7956
Email: rds-tb@renewal.com.sg
Website: www.renewal.com.sg

Spa Botanica at The Beaufort Singapore

SINGAPORE

At The Beaufort Singapore, a luxury resort hotel on Sentosa Island, peacocks roam among native plants such as cotton trees and betel nut palms. Romantics as well as conference participants regularly seek refuge here from the hectic pace of the city, just 10 minutes away from the mainland. You will no doubt be tempted also to head for the secluded swimming lagoon and beach.

Spa Botanica, a five-minute walk from the hotel, provides natural garden settings and healing botanical treatments. The indoor facility—in a restored two-storey colonial building—follows a garden theme. The first level houses men's and women's Galaxy Steam Baths; the second, treatment rooms that overlook the garden spa. The garden spa is an oasis that inspires playful treatment as well as quiet contemplation. After immersing your body in warm soak pools, wade into fresh water before making for the mud pool's central pedestal packed with volcanic mud. After slathering your body—or your partner's—with mud, you briefly bake in the sun until the mud dries into a powder. Then brush or rinse off in the invigorating outdoor Tsunami or Vichy Shower.

For a mind-clearing experience, walk the garden's labyrinth. Not to be confused with a maze, the labyrinth is a meditation tool used since ancient times. Walking it is a metaphor for journeying into a universe of understanding. Coming back out signifies spiritual and physical awakening. The spa's signature treatment, the Singapore Flower Ritual, takes place in an outdoor massage pavilion. After a dry deep tissue massage, a paste of local herbs and flowers is slathered on to exfoliate the skin. After the paste is scrubbed off, a cool hydrosol of native flowers is sprayed on. Another deep tissue massage, this time with aromatherapy oil, induces relaxation, as does a soak in a frangipani-filled bath. Signature packages include the Zen-like Mystic Dreams (which comprises yoga, aromatherapy massage and Frangipani Petal Bath). Jungle Rain, performed in the outdoor garden pavilion, combines a mud wrap with the Vichy shower followed by a Chlorophyll Butter massage.

LEFT: Private spa pavilions and a tea house overlook the floating pools with curtain cascades. The labyrinths for meditation are located on either side.

BELOW LEFT CENTRE: You can enjoy a relaxing massage in the great outdoors.

BELOW LEFT: Guests are introduced to the best of botanicals used by the spa.

OPPOSITE: The entrance and main building of Spa Botanica is a charmingly restored two-storey colonial building.

SPA STATISTICS

SPA AREA
6,000 sq m (64,583 sq ft)

FACILITIES
Spa Botanica Suite, Royal Suite, Deluxe Suite, 6 single and couple outdoor massage pavilions with outdoor bath, 9 single facial/massage rooms, 2 wet treatment rooms; 2 cold plunge pools, 2 float pools with curtain cascades, 2 mud pools, 2 Galaxy Steam Baths, 2 whirlpools; 2 labyrinths; 1 movement studio; 1 swimming pool; 1 spa juice bar; 1 beauty salon, 1 manicure room; 1 consultation room; spa boutique

SIGNATURE TREATMENTS
Mystic Dreams, Harmony Spice, Island Delights, Jungle Rain, Singapore Flower Ritual

OTHER TREATMENTS AND THERAPIES
Aromatherapy, body facials, body scrubs, body wraps, facial treatments, hair and makeup services, hair and scalp treatments, hydrotherapies, lymphatic drainage, manicures/pedicures, massage therapies, reflexology, water shiatsu, waxing

PROVISIONS FOR COUPLES
VIP and couple treatment rooms, outdoor couple massage pavilion, outdoor couple wet treatment pavilion

ACTIVITIES
Nature programmes; biking, meditative movement, Pilates mat work, stress management exercises, team building, tennis, water aerobics

SERVICES
Free shuttle services between hotel and World Trade Centre and Paragon Shopping Centre; consultations, personal training

SPA CUISINE
Available at The Terrace at The Beaufort Singapore. A small selection of healthy snacks available at the spa. Vegetarian selections always available. Special dietary requirements can be catered to on request

ADMISSION
Membership not required. Guests of The Beaufort Member Hotels can use the spa facilities.

CONTACT
2 Bukit Manis Road
Sentosa
Singapore 099891
Tel: (65) 6275 0331
Fax: (65) 6275 0228
Email: enquiries@spabotanica.com
Website: www.spabotanica.com
Head Office
79 Anson Road #07-03
Singapore 079906
Tel: (65) 6820 6788
Fax: (65) 6820 3188

Banyan Tree Spa at Banyan Tree Phuket

PHUKET, THAILAND

Situated on Phuket Island's northwestern coast on the edge of a lagoon by Bang Tao Bay, the villas of Banyan Tree Phuket afford guests luxury and seclusion. Each villa, encircled by a high wall, has sunken granite bathtubs in lush gardens which open to the sky.

Spa partners can opt to stay in one of 14 Spa Pool Villas, each with a dedicated outdoor pavilion for treatments by its glassy pool. You can learn how to massage your partner or just enjoy the romance provided. Your king-sized bed— in a glass-encased bed pavilion floating on a lotus pond—is strewn with flowers, the outdoor sunken tub filled with petals, and incense sticks and scented candles lit to contribute to the heady romantic atmosphere. Other bonuses of staying in a Spa Pool Villa include an in-villa spa breakfast, tasty tea canapés and daily delivery of a juice mixer with a selection of vegetables and fruit.

Spa treatments can be enjoyed within private compounds or at the Thai-styled spa pavilions featuring side-by-side treatment beds for couples.

Spa therapists are required to have 430 hours of theoretical and practical training at the Banyan Tree Spa Academy on the island. They specialise in high-touch, low-tech therapies mainly from Thailand and other parts of Asia.

Signature therapies include the Royal Banyan which is based on Thai palace traditions (Thai acupressure massage, Banyan Massage with local herbs and warm sesame oil, herbal bath, mint footbath) and Harmony Banyan (which includes a 90-minute massage by two therapists who are chosen for their complementary physique and temperament, working in synchronised strokes). Both are three-hour treatments.

SPA STATISTICS

SPA AREA
2,800 sq m (30,139 sq ft)

FACILITIES
5 Beauty Garden Rooms (air-conditioned single rooms), 12 Thai-style Pavilions with two treatment beds each (6 with jacuzzis, 2 with sauna rooms, and 10 with steam rooms); 1 fitness centre, 2 swimming pools; 1 beauty salon (for hair care, manicures/pedicures); spa boutique

SIGNATURE TREATMENTS
Harmony Banyan, Royal Banyan, Thai Healer

OTHER TREATMENTS AND THERAPIES
Body scrubs, body wraps, herbal steam healers, facial treatments, manicures/ pedicures, massage therapies, hair services

PROVISIONS FOR COUPLES
14 Spa Pool Villas with private garden spa pavilions, 12 Thai-style pavilions within Banyan Tree Spa Phuket

SPA CUISINE
Light fusion cuisine with local herbs, fruit and spices at Tamarind Spa Restaurant

ACTIVITIES
Cooking and scuba diving classes; dinner cruises on a wooden long tail boat; aerobics, aqua tone, batik painting, canoeing, golf, sailing, tennis, windsurfing, stretching, *tai ji*; meditation, yoga

SERVICES
Baby-sitting; gift certificates for spa treatments

ADMISSION
Open to walk-in guests, but priority is given to in-house guests

CONTACT
33 Moo 4 Srisoonthorn Road
Cherngtalay, Amphur Talang
Phuket 83110, Thailand
Tel: (66-76) 324 374
Fax: (66-76) 324 375
Email: phuket@banyantree.com or spa-phuket@banyantree.com
Website: www.banyantree.com

Other popular options include the circulation-improving Thai Healer (stretching yoga massage, herbal heat treatment, enriching Thai Herbal Wrap with fresh *plai* and ginger bath) and Essence of Yoga (a taught session of yoga postures, followed by a choice of Asian, Balinese, Hawaiian Lomi Lomi or Swedish massage, and ending with a light healthy breakfast).

Treatments begin and end in an unhurried manner. Set aside an additional 30 minutes so you can enjoy a glass of herbal tea, a shower outdoors and a cool minty footbath. Therapists signal the end of your session by walking around gently clinking Tibetan chimes to awaken you.

Spa-goers who want to transplant some of the serene effects—from incense fragrances to spa music—into their own homes can obtain these from the Banyan Tree Gallery.

Both spa and resort have won numerous awards including World's Best Spa Resort 1998 (*Condé Nast Traveller*) and Top Spa & Retreat Experience (Arts & Entertainment Network USA, 1998). In addition, the resort has entertained numerous Asian heads of state, celebrities Jean-Claude Van Damme and Olivia Newton-John, and Japanese football star Koichi Sugiyama.

TOP LEFT: Your villa's sunken bath opens to the sky.

ABOVE RIGHT: A lagoon Spa Pool Villa overlooking the outdoor spa pavilion and glass-edge pool.

BELOW RIGHT: The Tamarind Spa Restaurant is located on the edge of the 40-metre (131-foot) lap pool.

OPPOSITE: The backdrop to a massage in the spa's Thai *sala* (pavilion) is especially dramatic at sundown.

Being Spa

BANGKOK, THAILAND

 t's easy to feel at home at Being Spa. For Thailand's pioneering independent day spa is not located in a hotel or a resort, but in the seclusion of a two-storey house in downtown Bangkok. On leaving your shoes by the door, a cup of warm watermelon tea and a refreshing cold towel greet you in the waiting room, which resembles the living room of a home. Large art books on the coffee table, earthy stone and wood textures, and hues of brown and ochre—right down to the batik sarongs that drape the treatment couches—add to the homey atmosphere, as do Asian handicrafts such as antique doors from Chiang Mai, teak floors from Ayutthaya and Balinese monster shower heads.

The nine treatment rooms vary in their style and mood but all have shower rooms. Two of the treatment rooms include a Vichy Bed with four water jets shooting from the glazed ceiling overhead, which, like rain plummeting on your back, is a pleasant way to rinse off traces of a scrub.

In a separate wing where foot massages are performed, a row of lounge chairs—each separated by an *ikat* (woven textile) screen for privacy—look out to a neat water garden courtyard that's particularly serene in the evenings.

The spa menu offers a wide gamut of Western and Thai regimes for men who've come to relax, and women

RIGHT: Lying on the Vichy Bed is akin to the calming, relaxing sensation of lying under a shower of warm rain.

BELOW RIGHT: Floral baths are even more charming when enjoyed in a wooden tub.

OPPOSITE TOP: The spa's courtyard looks especially alluring when the sun goes down and the lights come up.

OPPOSITE BELOW LEFT: Spa guests can relax with a drink at this cosy corner.

OPPOSITE BELOW CENTRE: Asian artefacts grace the spa.

OPPOSITE BELOW RIGHT: Handmade ceramic containers for soap, shampoo and moisturiser add to the spa's homely feel.

who've come to be pampered. Several repeat visits are required if you wish to sample the nine facial treatments, 16 body treatments, nine massage therapies and 10 packages.

The spa's signature massage, the Being Ultimate Body Massage, combines aromatherapy, rhythmic touch and pressure point massage to heal and calm. The Siam Herbal Heat Body Massage also employs pressure point massage, but with a steamed muslin parcel of aromatic herbs and spices to relax sore muscles.

Signature scrubs—which sound almost edible—include the Thai Herbal Body Scrub (to hydrate dry skin), Coffee Bean Body Scrub (to give radiance to dull skin) and Thai Pepper Body Scrub (to rejuvenate tired skin). Other house specialities include the Milky Salt Body Wrap (a refreshing experience that

marries the benefits of mineral salts and milk and leaves the skin feeling baby smooth) and Oat Meal Mask Re-Balancing Facial (a hydrating, anti-ageing cocktail of vitamins and proteins that's suitable for all skin types).

Facial treatments also include the Caviar Anti-Ageing Facial (where caviar-based ingredients help revitalise and firm dull, ageing skin) and Whitening Facial (to decrease hyper-pigmentation spots for flawless, fair complexions). There's even one specially designed for males, dubbed the Fitness Facial for Men, which uses aromatic oils to remove roughness and impurities, and a botanical moisturising mask to rehydrate, bring relief and heal damage resulting from overexposure to sunlight and pollution.

Guests with two-and-a-half to three-and-a-half hours to unwind can indulge in various value-for-money treatment packages which cater to slimming, de-stressing and post-sports requirements.

The Being Thai Thai package, especially favoured by couples, includes a Thai Herbal Body Scrub, Floral Milk Bath in a wooden tub, Being Ultimate Body Massage and Whitening Facial Treatment. Therapists are trained to use precise steps for consistency.

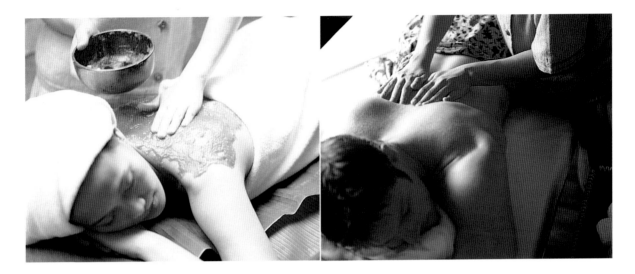

Products used by the spa include Jurlique—produced in South Australia from organically grown herbs and natural ingredients—as well as Decléor and Algotherm from France.

Being Spa is frequented by Thais and expatriates who come in once a week on average to unwind. It also attracts a number of overseas visitors, including guests from many of Bangkok's 5-star hotels. For travellers, an antidote to sore feet is the Tired Legs Cold Wrap (which tones and refreshes with a gel that's rich in marine plant extracts) and the Hot Mud Foot Wrap (where the self-heating marine mud works on the nerve endings of the feet to relax the entire body; it also reduces foot odour and softens the skin). The Being Relaxed package sandwiches the two treatments with a Marine Body Scrub and an Aromatherapy Body Massage.

ABOVE: Spa guests can be pampered with the Papaya and Yogurt Wrap (above) or Being Ultimate Body Massage (right).

BELOW: The spa uses exotic ingredients such as flowers (below) and turmeric (right) in the treatments.

SPA STATISTICS

SPA AREA
825 sq m (8,880 sq ft)

FACILITIES
4 double treatment rooms, 5 single treatment rooms; 1 hand and foot treatment area for 5 people; gift shop

SIGNATURE TREATMENTS
Being Ultimate Body Massage, Coffee Bean Body Scrub, Milky Salt Body Wrap, Oat Meal Mask Re-Balancing Facial, Papaya and Yogurt Wrap, Siam Herbal Heat Body Massage, Thai Herbal Body Scrub, Thai Pepper Body Scrub

OTHER TREATMENTS AND THERAPIES
Body masks, body scrubs, facial treatments, leg and foot treatments, massage therapies, slimming and firming treatments

PROVISIONS FOR COUPLES
4 double treatment rooms

SERVICES
Free *tuk tuk* shuttle services to/from Thong Lo sky-train station

CONTACT
88 Sukhumvit 51
Klongton Neu, Wattana
Bangkok 10110
Thailand
Tel: (66-2) 662 6171
Fax: (66-2) 258 7906
Email: contact@beingspa.com
Website: www.beingspa.com

Chiva-Som International Health Resort

HUA HIN, THAILAND

Chiva-Som International Health Resort is located just a short distance from the king's summer palace in the idyllic holiday town of Hua Hin.

This luxurious three-hectare (seven-acre) 'haven of life' cost US$26 million to construct, and boasts a staff to guest ratio of 5:1.

While succinct, the label 'health resort' doesn't fully indicate Chiva-Som's range of facilities, or its body, mind and spirit approach to wellness.

Forty Western-style guestrooms and suites, located at the far end of the grounds, have a view of the sunrise over the Gulf of Siam, while 17 Thai guest pavilions, clustered in the heart of the grounds, overlook a lake. To maintain the peaceful aura around the property, the use of mobile phones is forbidden.

The room rate includes three low-salt, low-fat meals a day; fat and calorie contents are listed against each serving.

The chef gets his fruit, vegetables and herbs from the resort's organic garden, and vegetarian options are a fixture on the regular menu.

Contrary to popular belief, meat—including kangaroo, turkey and lamb—is available on the menu, as is alcohol. Alcohol, however, is limited to fine wines and champagne, and served only in the evenings.

Whether you're seeking relaxation or require help in overcoming an emotional or health-related hurdle, the experienced medical staff will be able to tailor a programme to your needs.

In addition to practitioners of mainstream and alternative medicine, nutrition, exercise and fitness experts are on hand to provide specialised advice and guidance.

RIGHT: Double Thai massage in a Thai treatment suite.

LEFT: The Turkish-style steam room.

BELOW LEFT: A high-pressure water jet is directed at your body in the Jet Blitz suite.

OPPOSITE: The resort has a peaceful aura. This is maintained by the strict ban on mobile phones, and also the restriction on children below the age of 16.

Some treatments and activities are included in the rack rate; others can be selected from the à la carte menu. These can range from a Swedish massage, Anapanasati Mind Training session, fruit carving class, power walking by the beach, and *muay thai* (Thai kick boxing) workshop to yoga in a garden pavilion.

If you're game for a full-body cardiovascular workout with the bonus of seeing some of Hua Hin's culture and temples, opt for the Adventure Fitness Training which involves exercise activities such as beach biking, kayaking, hiking and personal training. Three-day adventure combinations are also available.

Besides a host of treatment rooms, including special ones for Thai massage and face and body treatments, water features and therapies form a predominant part of the spa.

These include a marble and glass hydrotherapy suite which houses a flotation chamber and six rooms with computerised spa massage baths. Separate heat treatment facilities for male and female guests feature changing rooms, saunas, steam rooms, jacuzzis, cool plunge pools and relaxation lounges overlooking garden courtyards.

Additional waterworks such as a large jacuzzi and cold plunge pool are located in the Bathing Pavilion, a

ABOVE: A heated parcel of herbs is applied to the body in a traditional Thai Herbal Massage.

RIGHT: An aquaerobics session in the Bathing Pavilion's swimming pool.

separate building located on the southern boundaries of the resort.

The centrepiece is an indoor exercise pool where aquaerobics, water Pilates, water *tai ji* and swimming classes are regularly held.

Another highlight is the Kneipp therapy foot bath, which encircles a Turkish-style steam room. When you reach the halfway mark of this pebbled passage filled calf-deep with cold water, stop for a minute in a small foot bath of warm water before completing the circuit. Your soles may hurt deliciously, but your body will feel revitalised from this session which combines the principles of reflexology and water therapy.

Chiva-Som's most popular spa treatments include E'SPA Luxury Facial And Eye Treatment, which revives the skin's natural moisture and luminosity through the application of aromatherapy products and pressure point massage.

RIGHT AND BELOW: Healthy but inspiring food and drinks with vegetables and fruit fresh from the resort's organic garden.

OPPOSITE TOP: A luxurious Western-styled guest room.

The most frequently asked for massages are the traditional Thai and the *Chi nei tsang*. The latter is an internal organ massage that uses the technique of massage directly at the naval and abdominal area, where it is believed stress, tension and negative emotions accummulate, causing the body's energy to be blocked. This blockage slowly weakens the internal organs and decreases energy and vitality. *Chi nei tsang* quickly releases the blockage, bringing relief to the abdomen and energy to the internal organs. It is recommended for digestive problems, and for promoting lymphatic drainage.

The health resort's signature Chiva-Som Experience is a body treatment that combines hydrotherapy and traditional herbs and fruit to exfoliate and nourish the skin. Other signature treatments offered include the Oriental Foot Ritual, a foot massage prefaced with a skin-softening cleansing ritual.

SPA STATISTICS

SPA AREA
1,850 sq m (19,913 sq ft)

FACILITIES
9 Thai massage treatment rooms, 25 wet treatment rooms, 5 holistic treatment rooms; 4 consultation rooms, 1 naturopath/iridology consultation room; 5 hydrotherapy suites, 1 jet blitz suite; 1 flotation chamber; 1 aquatic therapy private pool, 1 cardio theatre/studio, 1 compact tennis court, 2 free-form swimming pools (1 indoor), 1 gymnasium; 1 Pilates studio, 1 *tai ji* pavilion, 1 yoga pavilion

SIGNATURE TREATMENTS
Chiva-Som Experience, Dusk Till Dawn, Pol-la-mai Siam, Oriental Foot Ritual; Thai massage

OTHER TREATMENTS AND THERAPIES
Acupressure reflexology, beauty and facial care, body treatments, body wraps, hair care, hand and foot care, holistic treatments, hydrotherapy, manicures/pedicures, massage therapies (hot stone and aromatherapy); Anapanasati Mind Training, EQ4 Meridian testing; flower remedies, iridology, life coach counselling, naturopathic consultation, reiki

PROVISIONS FOR COUPLES
Couple-designed treatment suite

SPA CUISINE
Available daily at the two restaurants

ACTIVITIES
Cooking, flower arrangement and fruit carving classes, workshops by visiting consultants; aerobics (aqua, regular, step), cardio kick, cardio travel circuit training, Pilates, super stretch, swimming lessons, *tai ji*, Thai hermit stress exercise, Thai kick boxing workshops, *thoi teh*, water Pilates, water *tai ji*; beach biking, pool volleyball, sea kayaking; meditation, yoga

SERVICES
Adventure training; body composition analysis, echocardiography, exercise stress testing, fitness assessment, fitness treatments; aquatic therapy treatments; personal training, private fitness sessions, travel training; weight-management programmes; sightseeing; business facilities

CONTACT
73/4 Petchkasem Road
Hua Hin 77110
Thailand
Tel: (66-32) 536 536
Fax: (66-32) 511 154
Email: reserv@chivasom.com
Website: www.chivasom.com

Devarana Spa at The Dusit Thani Hotel

BANGKOK, THAILAND

 The 500-room, 5-star Dusit Thani is just a short stroll from the Thai capital's business, shopping and entertainment hubs. Facilities include a large ballroom for functions of up to 1,600 people, and eight restaurants serving Chinese, Japanese, Thai, Vietnamese and Western cuisine.

The Tiara restaurant—located on the top floor—affords a panoramic view of the City of Angels fronted by Lumpini Park that faces the hotel.

The spacious Thai-flavoured guest rooms are furnished with materials such as teak and silk, and the suites have individual decorative motifs reflecting different facets of traditional Thai culture.

At Devarana Spa, the globetrotter can select from a buffet of treatments that includes Eastern favourites (such as Thai massage), Western choices (such as Swedish massage), and packaged options (such as the Travellers Recovery Pack comprising a body wrap, face mask and body massage).

The house speciality, the Devarana Massage, combines three Eastern (Ayurvedic, Shiatsu and Thai) and two Western (Aromatherapy and Swedish) massage techniques.

Eastern techniques focusing on the body's energy meridians have a balancing, energising effect, while Western techniques concentrating on the muscle, bone and blood circulation help release muscle tension and reduce stress. Facial therapies are complemented by Jurlique products

derived from organically grown plant-based ingredients, while body scrubs and wraps use Alglotherm products made from seaweed harvested from France's Brittany Coast.

One recommended pre-massage treatment is the skin-cleansing, lung-clearing Aromatic Thai Herbal Steam, one of the water therapies available with any other treatment booked.

In addition to treatments on the spa menu, enquire about sessions with visiting specialists in disciplines such as acupuncture, Ayurveda, traditional Chinese medicine and herbal medicine.

Should you wish to transplant the tinkling refrains of the classical Thai melodies into your own home, recordings are available from the Devarana Spa Gallery, along with other spa products which include candles, clothing, incense and herb soaps.

Devarana, which translates as 'garden in heaven' from the ancient Thai literary work, *Traibhumikatha* by Phraya Lithai, will open at least two more spas later in 2002 at Dusit Resort and Polo Club in Cha-Am/Hua Hin and Dusit Resort in Pattaya.

ABOVE LEFT: Meditate or do yoga in the yoga room.

ABOVE RIGHT: For an hourly premium, enjoy a milk-and-rose bath or other treatments in the grand suite (pictured).

BELOW RIGHT: Lemon grass tea, served before and after treatments, aids digestion.

OPPOSITE TOP: The spa's reception area with day beds overlooking a long reflecting pond.

OPPOSITE BELOW LEFT: Candles (pictured), incense, soaps, shampoos and massage oils from the Devarana Spa Gallery make 'scentsational' gifts.

OPPOSITE BELOW CENTRE: Fresh local herbs are used in the Aromatic Thai Herbal Steam Treatment to cleanse the skin and clear the lungs.

OPPOSITE BELOW RIGHT: Mud is used in two 60-minute wraps: Thai Herbal Mud Wrap and Thermoactive Mud Wrap.

SPA STATISTICS

SPA AREA
1,300 sq m (13,993 sq ft)

FACILITIES
4 deluxe suites, 1 grand suite, 9 single suites; 1 meditation and yoga room, 1 relaxation area; spa gallery

SIGNATURE TREATMENT
Devarana Massage

OTHER TREATMENTS AND THERAPIES
Body scrubs, body wraps, facial treatments, hand and foot treatments, massages, reflexology, water treatments, waxing; spa packages

PROVISIONS FOR COUPLES
Couples can have their treatments in the deluxe suite (which has a shower room with built-in steam, massage area, lounge area and a tub) at no extra charge. The grand suite, available for an hourly surcharge, has a separate steam facility

SPA CUISINE
Healthy, low-calorie meals served at the spa's relaxation area

SERVICES
Personal consultation before each treatment, skin analysis before facial

CONTACT
946 Rama IV Road
Bangkok 10500
Thailand
Tel: (66-2) 636 3596
Fax: (66-2) 636 3597
Email: bangkok@devarana.com
Website: www.devarana.com

Six Senses Spa at The Evason Hua Hin

PRANBURI, PRACHUAP KHIRI KHAN, THAILAND

ABOVE: The spa, which was designed along *feng shui* principles, has an open plan which encourages a better energy flow.

BELOW: Flowers are used in an exotic bath in the Romance package for couples.

The Evason Hua Hin is a short 20-minute drive south of the beach resort town of Hua Hin. Facing the Gulf of Siam, it is set among lotus ponds and waterways in an eight-hectare (20-acre) landscaped garden. Hua Hin became established as a beach resort in 1926 when King Rama VII built the Klai Kangwon beach palace here. Thai royalty still spend vacations in these parts.

Resort guest rooms feature a chic and simple décor of raw wood with a predominance of whites that emphasise space and airiness.

Studios and suites have balconies with outdoor furniture sheltered by a canopy and mosquito net, so you'll have the alternative of sleeping under the stars on a balmy night. Each Evason Pool Villa has a private pool and outdoor bathtub in a garden surrounded by a lotus pond.

Like other sister Six Senses Spas, a *feng shui* expert had advised on the design of the spa. Its open plan encourages a better flow of energy. It is also surrounded by healing water.

The outdoor *salas* (pavilions), accessed by a wooden bridge, are a calming place for a relaxing treatment.

Sala floors are lower than the surrounding water, so while lying on the treatment couch, you're at eye level with what appears to be a miniature waterfall.

The continuous sound of water running over the edge of the *sala* and

RIGHT: *Qi gong* is just one of the many activities guests can take part in.

BELOW: Couples can enjoy a Swedish massage in the outdoor *salas*.

SPA STATISTICS

SPA AREA
2,120 sq m (22,819 sq ft)

FACILITIES
2 double indoor treatment rooms with *yin-yang* jacuzzis, 6 outdoor *salas*, 3 single indoor treatment rooms; 2 sauna and steam rooms; 1 gymnasium, 1 swimming pool; spa boutique

SIGNATURE TREATMENTS
Holistic Massage, Natural Thai Facial, Energy Chair Massage, Oriental Body Glow, Sunburn Retreat

OTHER TREATMENTS AND THERAPIES
Bath treatments (in spa and guest rooms), beauty treatments, body scrubs, Decléor face and body treatments, foot treatments, massage therapies, traditional Thai therapies, manicures/pedicures

PROVISIONS FOR COUPLES
Indulgence and Romance packages; 2 double treatment rooms, 6 outdoor *salas*

SPA CUISINE
A specialised health juice and tea menu is available in the spa and the resort's F&B outlets. Hay, vegetarian, ovo vegetarian, ovo lacto vegetarian, pescetarian and grass-eater diets can be catered to on request, following a consultation with the Executive Chef

ACTIVITIES
Asian fusion and Thai cooking classes, batik and fabric painting classes, fruit and ice carving classes, massage and skincare classes, educational talks; Do-In Meridian Stretching; kayaking, mountain biking, *qi gong*, tennis, sailing, water skiing, wind surfing, yoga

SERVICES
Baby-sitting and Kids Club; consultations (general health, skincare); shuttle services to and from Hua Hin; corporate adventure training programmes, customised eco adventures

ADMISSION
Open to in-house and walk-in guests. Day membership not required for the spa, but required for the gymnasium and pool

CONTACT
9 Paknampran Beach
Pranburi
Prachuap Khiri Khan 77220
Thailand
Tel: (66-32) 632 111
Fax: (66-32) 632 112
Email: rsvn@evasonhuahin.com
Website: www.six-senses.com

flowing away through the white stones that line the area also lulls you.

Couples can ask for one of two double treatment rooms that lead out to beautiful open gardens with double *yin-yang* baths. Packages include Romance (an Exotic Flower Bath followed by a holistic body, face and scalp massage) and Indulgence (a special Aphrodite massage plus a bottle of sparkling wine to complete the experience).

The therapists—of European and Asian origins—are experts in their respective fields. Their pooled expertise has resulted in the highly popular signature Holistic Massage, using techniques from aromatherapy, Shiatsu, Hawaiian Lomi Lomi, and Swedish and Thai massages.

The resort offers a comprehensive list of activities including eco adventures such as mountain biking between temples. It also has access to the Thanarat Military Camp, which offers activities such as obstacle courses and tower parachute jumps.

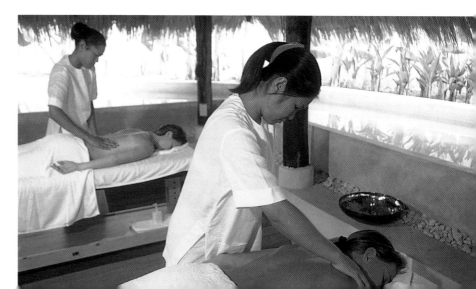

Six Senses Spa at The Evason Phuket

PHUKET, THAILAND

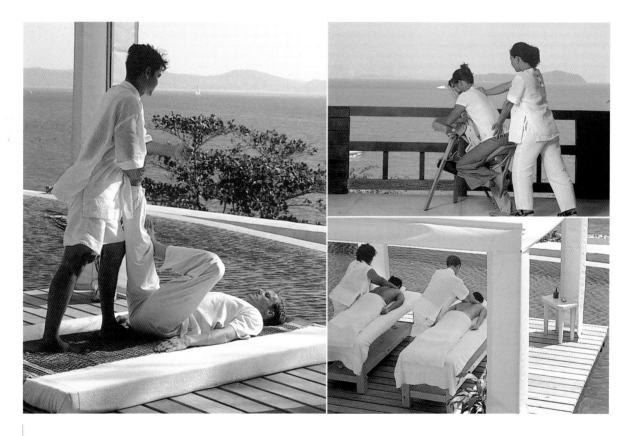

ABOVE: Thai massage in an outdoor *sala* by the sea.

TOP RIGHT: An Energy Chair Massage provides a quick pick-me-up.

ABOVE RIGHT: Couples can enjoy a Swedish massage together in an outdoor *sala* facing the sea.

Tucked within a 21-hectare (64-acre) hillside garden on the edge of the Andaman Sea, The Evason Phuket is a convenient base from which to explore the area's aquatic beauty. The resort offers several options for doing just this—from above as well as below sea level.

It also owns a private island, Bon Island, where guests can suntan on its white sands or snorkel in the clear waters. A 15-minute free shuttle boat ride away, Bon Island has specialities such as back-to-nature dining and showers.

The resort itself is both family and couple friendly. Facilities for the family include a Kids Club and adjacent family pool. A second pool and the Six Senses Spa are closer to the sea.

Treatment rooms in the two-storey spa building—ladies occupy the ground level, while men take the first—have sea views. Guests wanting a tan can

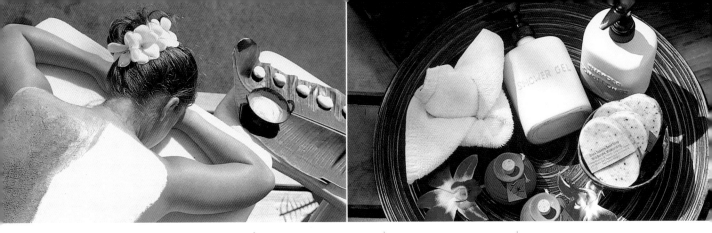

sunbathe on the building's private rooftop. Facilities for couples include four roofed outdoor *salas* (pavilions) which face the sea, as well as three double treatment rooms. Each double treatment room comes with a Yin and Yang jacuzzi, which is used during a bath treatment such as the flower-filled Vanilla Bath.

The aphrodisiac is in the vanilla essential oil in the water and also in the glass of sparkling wine you and your partner sip during the treatment.

Spa packages for couples include Romance (an exotic flower bath to calm the senses plus a holistic body, face and scalp massage) and Indulgence (a holistic massage using a special aphrodisiac mix of essential oils).

Like the Vanilla Bath, Indulgence serves up a bottle of sparkling wine. Couples wishing to take home massage techniques can pick these up from a 170-minute massage workshop.

The spa's speciality is the Holistic Massage, which blends techniques from aromatherapy, Shiatsu, Swedish and Thai massages, and Hawaiian Lomi Lomi.

Therapists are encouraged to use their 'sixth sense' to personalise their treatments. In the grounds of the spa, there is a herb garden which is looked after by the therapists who use the herbs in their treatments.

ABOVE LEFT: Treatments use ingredients ranging from white mud to local herbs.

ABOVE RIGHT: Spa amenities such as soaps, lotions and essential oils can be bought from the spa boutique.

BELOW: Incense, colourful herbal pouches and coconut pots contribute to the spa's earthy, tropical feel.

SPA STATISTICS

SPA AREA
1,248 sq m (13,433 sq ft)

FACILITIES
2 floors, 3 double treatment rooms with Yin and Yang jacuzzis, 6 single treatment rooms, 4 outdoor *salas*; 2 saunas, 2 steam rooms; 1 gymnasium, 2 swimming pools; spa boutique

SIGNATURE TREATMENTS
Holistic Massage, Natural Thai Facial, Energy Chair Massage, Oriental Body Glow, Sunburn Retreat

OTHER TREATMENTS AND THERAPIES
Beauty treatments, body scrubs, Decléor face and body treatments, Wise (Swedish) facial treatments, foot treatments, massage therapies, treatment baths (in guest room and spa), manicures/pedicures, reiki healing

PROVISIONS FOR COUPLES
Indulgence Package, Romance Package, Vanilla Bath; massage workshops; 3 double treatment rooms, 4 outdoor *salas*

SPA CUISINE
A specialised health juice and tea menu is available in the spa and the resort's F&B outlets. Hay, vegetarian, ovo vegetarian, ovo lacto vegetarian, pescetarian and grass-eater diets can be catered to on request, following a consultation with the Executive Chef

ACTIVITIES
Massage and skincare classes, educational talks; boat trips, fishing, island hopping/island safari; aikido, beach volleyball, canoeing, darts, jogging, *qi gong*, sailing, scuba diving, snooker, snorkelling, table tennis, windsurfing, yoga

SERVICES
General health consultations, personal training, skincare consultations; free shuttle transfers between the resort and Phuket town and neighbouring resorts

ADMISSION
Open to in-house and walk-in guests. Day membership not required for the spa, but required for the gymnasium and pool

CONTACT
100 Vised Road, Rawai Beach
Muang District
Phuket 83110
Thailand
Tel: (66-76) 381 011
Fax: (66-76) 381 018
Email: info@evasonphuket.com
Website: www.six-senses.com

The Spa at Hilton Hua Hin

HUA HIN, THAILAND

The winding streets of the charming coastal town lead to The Hilton Hua Hin Resort & Spa, set in a garden by the beach.

Its view of local fishing fleets bobbing on the Gulf of Siam is especially picturesque at sunrise.

While the golfer can tee off at one of six courses five to 30 minutes away from the resort, the restless need not wander far for a dip in the lagoon-like pool or a game of tennis or squash. The spa's contemporary Thai décor, of sandstone walls, Thai silks and Khmer artwork, recalls the ancient Khmer capital at Angkor Wat in Cambodia.

The Spa at Hilton Hua Hin offers traditional Thai therapies as well as those from other cultures.

Natural products such as fresh fruit and herbs, Thai honey, and mineral-rich salts and muds are used.

Signature treatments include Rice Body Polish (exfoliation with ground rice blended with herbs and honey) and Thai Traditional Facial (a skin-brightening treatment using fresh Thai fruit and traditional white clay). Each treatment lasts an hour.

Besides the 90-minute Royal Massage, which is a combination of Swedish, Aromatherapy, Thai and Ayurvedic traditions, the two-hour Touch of Heaven, which includes a massage and facial of your choice, is a popular option. Each component within a package can be prolonged for up to 90 minutes at an additional charge.

The spa caters to couples with double treatment rooms. A special Thai/Japanese room features two Thai

LEFT: Treatment rooms have a meditative air to them.

ABOVE: A single treatment room with simple but chic furnishings.

BELOW: A Swedish massage in the outdoor Thai *sala* is accompanied by the sound of the waves.

OPPOSITE: Guests at The Spa are welcomed with a *Sawadee ka*.

massage beds and a romantically veiled wooden tub for two to enjoy a floral or mineral bath together.

Therapies where you are clothed—such as the Thai massage, Shiatsu and foot reflexology—can be enjoyed outdoors in one of three Thai *salas* (pavilions).

SPA STATISTICS

SPA AREA
1,200 sq m (12,917 sq ft)

FACILITIES
6 double treatment rooms (3 with jacuzzis), 1 Thai/Japanese-style double treatment room with Japanese bath, 3 single treatment rooms; 1 aerobics room, 1 gymnasium, 1 outdoor free-form swimming pool; 3 outdoor Thai *salas*, 1 hair and beauty salon

SIGNATURE TREATMENTS
Royal Massage, Thai Traditional Facial, Rice Body Polish

OTHER TREATMENTS AND THERAPIES
Bath treatments, body scrubs, body wraps, facial treatments, hair services, manicures/pedicures, massage therapies, reflexology, waxing,

PROVISIONS FOR COUPLES
7 double treatment rooms

ACTIVITIES
Thai cooking classes, spa workshop weekends; billiards, *petanque*, squash, table tennis, tennis; beach games, sailing, windsurfing

SERVICES
Baby-sitting, kids club

ADMISSION
Membership not required but available

CONTACT
33 Naresdamri Road
Hua Hin 77110
Thailand
Tel: (66-32) 512 888 ext 1890
Fax: (66-32) 511 053
Email: thespa_huahin@hilton.com
Website: www.huahin.hilton.com

Spa Botanica at The Sukhothai

BANGKOK, THAILAND

A palm-lined driveway just off Bangkok's Embassy Row leads to The Sukhothai, named after Thailand's 13th century capital. Set in a garden of flowers, the symmetry, courtyards and lotus ponds recall the elegant palaces of the Sukhothai period, considered the golden age of Thai art and architecture. The gracious culture continues on to the adjacent Spa Botanica, blending seamlessly with nature's beauty and waterscape.

Like its sister spa at The Beaufort Singapore, the setting and treatments revolve around the healing benefits of plant and water.

The spa takes a holistic approach to wellness, augmenting treatments with special cuisine as well as programmes ranging from positive thinking to homeopathy. Cleansing and purification rituals that include baths and sprays play an especially big role in this garden spa.

Water facilities include hot and cold pools, hydromassage tubs, footbaths, waterfall showers and Vichy showers. The Botanical Bath Ritual follows a circuit in bath houses within the female and male changing rooms. In the steam bath

ABOVE: Pilates is one of the many programmes offered by Spa Botanica.

RIGHT: Visitors to the spa are greeted by the lotus, a symbol of longevity.

ABOVE: Sukhothai's King Ram Khamhaeng would frequently grant audiences to his subjects, who rang bells like these at his palace gates.

BELOW RIGHT: Just off Bangkok's Embassy Row is an oasis of rejuvenation that is Spa Botanica Bangkok.

house—which is infused with fresh herbs and essential oils—you begin the ritual by applying special botanical pastes to your hair, face and body—such as chamomile for the face and eucalyptus for arms and legs—from a palette on a pedestal. After resting in steam on heated tile seats for about 20 minutes, you will move on to the Monsoon shower area for a scrub and invigorating shower.

Bathing rituals are best enjoyed in conjunction with a massage or facial in one of two VIP Suites made special with tubs cast in traditional mould. Made of bell metal, a tub is hammered into shape and then polished by hand for 14 days to bring out its gleam. Each tub is large enough to be shared with a partner.

Signature treatments include the sea-inspired Herbal Delights (Citrus Guava Salt Scrub, Flower Essence Body Treatment, Aromatherapy Massage and Protective Hair & Scalp Treatment) and Jungle Rain (Chlorophyll Body Butter Massage, Body & Hair Mud Wrap and Cascade Deluge Shower).

SPA STATISTICS

OPENING
End 2003

SPA AREA
10,000 sq m (107,639 sq ft)

FACILITIES
2 VIP Suites, 2 deluxe double treatment rooms, 8 superior double treatment rooms, 14 single facial/massage rooms, 4 wet treatment rooms (2 with hydrotherapy bath and 2 Vichy shower facility), 4 spa pavilions; 2 male and female lounges, 2 male and female changing rooms and lockers; 2 bath houses, 2 float pools, 2 steam baths, 2 male and female saunas, 1 wellness centre; 2 labyrinths; 1 gymnasium, 1 movement studio, 1 swimming pool; 1 function room; 1 beauty salon; 1 spa café; 1 retail pavilion; spa boutique

SIGNATURE TREATMENTS
Botanical Bath Ritual, Harmony Spice, Herbal Delights, Jungle Rain, Mystic Dreams

OTHER TREATMENTS AND THERAPIES
Body facial treatments, body scrubs, body wraps, facial treatments, hair and makeup services, hair and scalp treatments, hydrotherapies, lymphatic drainage, manicures/pedicures, massage therapies, reflexology, water shiatsu, waxing

PROVISIONS FOR COUPLES
2 VIP suites, 2 deluxe double treatment rooms, 8 superior double treatment rooms

ACTIVITIES
Programmes and seminars related to wellness and health such as reiki, meditation, nutrition, herbalism, meditative movement, Pilates mat work, stress management exercises; tennis, water aerobics

SERVICES
Consultations, personal training

SPA CUISINE
Available at the hotel. Special dietary needs can be catered to on request

ADMISSION
Membership available but not required. Guests of The Beaufort Member Hotels can use the spa facilities

CONTACT
79 Anson Road #07-03
Singapore 079906
Tel: (65) 6820 6788
Fax: (65) 6820 3188
Email: spaplanner@spabotanica.com
Website: www.spabotanica.com

Six Senses Spa at Ana Mandara Resort

NHA TRANG, VIETNAM

ABOVE: The swimming pool by the sea is open from dawn to midnight.

LEFT: Guests can rinse sand off their feet with water scooped from an earthen vat with a coconut ladle.

A na Mandara (which means 'beautiful house' in the ancient Cham language) lures romantics to this garden paradise near the sea.

Couples inspired to say 'I do' can do so on the palm-lined beach or at a picturesque church in the mountains. A wedding package comes with a Vietnamese herbal bath in your villa and a Vietnamese or Swedish massage.

The spa, surrounded by a grove of pine trees, is composed of private *salas* (pavilions) with grass or slate roofs. Indoor treatment *salas* comprise a double (with outdoor jacuzzi and two outdoor showers) and two singles (one for Shiatsu, Thai and Ayurvedic therapies, with outdoor wooden Japanese bath and shower; the other, a multi-purpose area with outdoor bamboo Vichy shower).

The four outdoor *salas*—two for Oriental therapies and two for European therapies—appear sunken into the surrounding ponds. When you lie on a treatment bed, you are at eye level with water gently spilling into the *sala*, a visually and aurally soothing component in your spa treatment.

The spa's treatments, especially Asian ones, use indigenous Vietnamese ingredients whenever possible. For something local, opt for the Vietnamese massage (a pressure point massage using a moisturising and relaxing blend of essential oils, said to encourage circulation and muscle-toning).

Signature treatments include Adam for men (power-cleansing mini facial, pressure point massage, scalp massage, manicure and pedicure) and Eve for women (deep cleansing and exfoliation, aromatherapy pressure point massage, manicure and pedicure).

You might want to arrive early for treatments as you'll be tempted to linger in the Eden-like male or female changing areas. Each includes a sauna and steam room nestled among trees and lush vegetation, a bamboo walk-through shower and two rainshowers. A pebbled path massages the soles of your bare feet as you pad along.

Leave some time after your treatment to lounge on the floor mattresses and traditional cushions in one of four double relaxation *salas* on stilts.

SPA STATISTICS

OPENING
End January 2003

SPA AREA
1,680 sq m (18,083 sq ft)

FACILITIES
3 double indoor treatment rooms with outdoor jacuzzi and outdoor shower, double Japanese bath and bamboo Vichy shower; 3 outdoor sunken *salas*, 3 relaxation *salas*; 2 saunas, 2 steam rooms; 1 gymnasium, 1 swimming pool; spa boutique; herb garden

SIGNATURE TREATMENTS
Vietnamese Fruit Body Smoother, Vietnamese Massage, Natural Vietnamese Facial

OTHER TREATMENTS AND THERAPIES
Bath treatments, beauty treatments, body scrubs, body wraps, eye treatments, facial treatments, foot treatments, manicures/pedicures, massage therapies, waxing

PROVISIONS FOR COUPLES
3 double indoor treatment rooms, 2 double outdoor treatment *salas*

SPA CUISINE
Chefs will discuss guests' dietary requirements upon check-in for customised meals

ACTIVITIES
Basic Vietnamese language classes, Vietnamese cooking classes; cultural excursions and marketplace tours, island hopping, picnics on deserted islands; bicycle and motorcycle rental, boat charters, beach volleyball, pool table, tennis, trekking; hobicat sailing, fishing, parasailing, snorkelling, scuba diving, windsurfing

SERVICES
Baby-sitting, sleepover programmes for children; free shuttle services within Nha Trang

CONTACT
Beachside Tran Phu Boulevard
Nha Trang
Vietnam
Tel: (84-58) 829 829
Fax: (84-58) 829 629
Email: resvana@dng.vnn.vn
Website: www.six-senses.com/ana-mandara

ABOVE: Spa amenities such as soaps and lotions can be bought from the spa boutique.

LEFT: Couples will love the romantic Ana Mandara Suite.

BELOW: The bathroom in the Ana Mandara Suite opens on to a private walled garden.

Spa Speak

A glossary of common spa, treatment and fitness terms. Variations may be offered, so it's best to check with the respective spas when you make your booking.

Abyhanga Ayurvedic gentle, rhythmic massage in which therapists work warm oil into the body to help enhance the immune system and encourage the removal of accumulated toxins.

Acupoints Points along the meridian channels where the life force—*qi* (Chinese), *prana* (Indian) and *ki* (Japanese)—accumulates. Also known as *sên* (Thai).

Acupressure Application of fingertip (and sometimes palm, elbow, knee and foot) pressure on the body's acupoints to improve the flow of *qi* throughout the body, release muscle tension and promote healing.

Acupuncture Ancient Chinese healing technique in which fine needles are inserted into acupoints along the body's meridians to maintain health and correct any imbalance that causes illness.

Aerobics Fitness routine that involves a series of rhythmic exercises usually performed to music. Promotes cardiovascular fitness, improves the body's use of oxygen, burns calories and increases endurance.

Aerobics studio Area used for floor exercises.

Affusion shower massage Massage given as you lie under a relaxing, rain-like, warm shower of water or seawater. Increases blood circulation.

After-sun treatment Treatment that soothes skin that has been over-exposed to the sun, and cools the over-heated body. May include a cooling bath and a gentle massage with a lotion of soothing ingredients such as cucumber and aloe vera.

Aikido Japanese martial art that uses techniques such as locks and throws, and focuses on using the opponent's own energy against himself.

Algotherapy Use of algae in treatments such as baths, scrubs, wraps and skin care.

Anapanasati Mind Training Meditation practice that involves breathing exercises that promote greater consciousness of the body, mind and spirit to maximise efficiency, and calm and clear the mind to find peace and happiness.

Anti-cellulite treatment Treatment that contours the body and reduces cellulite at various parts of the body.

Anti-stress massage Typically a 30-minute introductory massage, or one for those with limited time and who suffer from high levels of stress. Focuses on tension areas such as the back, face, neck and shoulders.

Aquaerobics Aerobic exercises performed in a swimming pool where the water provides support and resistance to increase stamina, and stretch and strengthen muscles.

Aquamedic pool Pool with specially positioned therapeutic jets for benefits such as relaxation and improving muscle tone.

Aromatherapy Ancient healing art that dates back to 4,500 BC. Refers to the use of essential oils from plants and flowers in treatments such as facials, massages, body wraps, foot baths and hydrobaths.

Aromatherapy massage Massage in which essential oils—either pre-blended or specially mixed for your needs—are applied to the body, typically with Swedish massage techniques.

Asanas Yoga postures.

Ayurveda Holistic system of healing in India that encompasses diet, massage, exercise and yoga.

Ayurvedic massage Massage performed by one or more therapists directly on the skin to loosen the excess *doshas*. Promotes circulation, increases flexibility, and relieves pain and stiffness. Applied with herbal oil.

Baby massage Infant massage that focuses on the special needs of newborns. Relaxes, improves circulation and relieves common infant ailments. Nurtures and bonds when performed by the infant's parent.

Back treatment Deep cleansing skin treatment for the back, neck and shoulders that removes impurities and excess oils, eases tension, and leaves the skin soft and smooth. Also known as **clarifying back treatment** or **purifying back treatment**.

Balinese *boreh* Traditional warming Balinese scrub made from herbs and spices which improve circulation and skin suppleness. The paste is lightly applied to the body which is then wrapped in a blanket. The spices produce a sensation of deep heat.

Balinese coffee scrub Exfoliating scrub in which finely ground Balinese coffee beans are applied to the skin.

Balinese massage Relaxing traditional massage of Bali that uses rolling, long strokes, and finger and palm pressure. Applied with oil.

Balneotherapy Water treatments that use hot springs, mineral water or seawater to improve circulation, restore and revitalise the body, and relieve pain and stress. Also an invigorating, re-mineralising treatment for muscles that uses water jets and a localised massage in a tub with a special hose administered by a therapist.

Bath Soaking or cleansing the body in water that is typically infused with salt, flowers, minerals or essential oils. May serve as a prelude to, or conclude a treatment.

Blisswork Deep tissue exercise that lengthens the body and seeks to restore it to its original design.

Blitz shower Standing body massage in which a high-pressure shower jet is directed at the body or specific parts of the body by a therapist who is about 3 metres away. Has a deep massaging effect which increases circulation. Also known as **douche au jet**, **jet blitz** or **jet massage**.

Beauty treatment Treatment provided by spas to enhance beauty and overall well-being. Includes facials, makeovers, manicures, pedicures and waxing.

Body bronzing Tanning treatment without the sun. May begin with a scrub to smooth the skin, which allows for an even tan.

Body composition analysis Evaluation of lean body mass to determine the percentage of body fat for the purpose of tailoring a nutrition and exercise programme.

Body mask Regenerating treatment in which the body is slathered with clay. The minerals in the clay—which may be mixed with essential oils—detoxify and hydrate the skin, leaving it radiant.

Body scrub Exfoliating body treatment, using products such as salt or herbs, that removes dry, dead skin cells and improves blood circulation. Softens the skin and gives it a healthier glow. Often used for preparing the skin to receive the benefits of massages and wraps. Also known as **body polish**.

Body treatment General term that denotes treatments for the body.

Body wrap Treatment in which the body is wrapped in linen soaked in a herbal solution for about 20 minutes, and sometimes kept under a heated blanket. May be preceded by an application of fruit, herbs, mud or seaweed, and accompanied by a face, head and scalp massage. Detoxifies the system, soothes tired muscles and hydrates the skin.

Bodywork Therapeutic touching or manipulation of the body that uses massage or exercise to relax, ease tension and pain, and treat illnesses. May involve lessons in proper posture or movement. Some modes may treat both the body and mind.

Brush and tone Use of a loofah, special brush or rough cloth to rapidly brush the body to remove dead skin cells and impurities. Often used to prepare the body for treatments such as masks and bronzing. Also known as **dry brushing**.

Bust treatment Treatment to firm and tone the bust and décolleté.

Chair massage Massage performed on you while you remain clothed and seated on a specially designed massage chair. The chair is portable so the massage can be performed almost anywhere. The massage typically concentrates on the back, neck, scalp and shoulders.

Chakras The seven energy centres in the body that are associated with the flow of the body's subtle energy.

Chi nei tsang Internal organ massage that focuses on the navel and surrounding abdominal area where stress, tension and negative emotions accumulate. Relieves illnesses, and releases negative emotions and tensions, bringing relief to the abdomen and vital energy to the internal organs. Effective in eliminating toxins in the gastrointestinal tract, promoting lymphatic drainage and treating digestive problems such as irritable bowel syndrome, bloating and constipation.

Coconut *mangir* Exfoliating and hydrating Indonesian scrub made from a paste of flowers, spices, ground rice and grated coconut.

Cold plunge pool Small pool filled with chilled water to stimulate blood and cool the body quickly, especially after a sauna.

Colour therapy Use of colour to bring about balance.

Complementary therapy Health care system not traditionally utilised by conventional Western medical practitioners, and which may complement orthodox treatments. Also known as **alternative therapy**.

Crème bath Hair and scalp conditioning treatment in which a rich cream is applied to the hair section by section. The hair may be steamed before being rinsed. May include a neck, scalp and shoulder massage.

Cupping Chinese treatment where small glass cups are attached to the skin by a vacuum that is created by placing a lighted match inside each cup to burn up the oxygen. The suction increases the circulation of *qi* and blood.

Dance movement therapy Dance as a therapy, with or without music, to help those with emotional problems. The therapist may suggest movements and encourage the participants to innovate their own to express themselves.

Dancercise Aerobic exercise derived from modified modern dance steps and movements.

Dead Sea mud treatment Application of mineral-rich mud from the Dead Sea. Detoxifies the skin and body and relieves rheumatic and arthritic pain.

Deep tissue massage Firm and deep massage using specific techniques to release tensions, blockages and knots that have built up over time. Believed to release emotional tension. May be adapted to a specific area of tension.

Do-in System of exercise resembling yoga postures that encourages physical and spiritual development. Balances the flow of energy through the meridian system.

Doshas In Ayurveda, the three humours that make up the physical body. Also describes the three constitutional types.

Echocardiography Technique for diagnosing cardiovascular illness by examining the heart and its vessels using non-invasive equipment.

Effleurage Long, even strokes in the direction of the heart which helps push along the flow of blood and lymph.

Endermologie Massage therapy using the Cellu M6 machine to reduce the appearance of cellulite and refine the figure.

Energy balancing General term to describe a variety of practices aimed at balancing the flow of energy in and around the body. Practitioners generally try to remove blockages, and balance and amplify this energy flow.

EQ4 meridian testing Combination of traditional Chinese medicine, homeopathy, kinesiology, medical research and modern computing. A probe is applied to the acupoints to determine the areas that require treatment. It is believed that allergens, food and environmental stresses that weaken the body are reflected in energy levels that are higher or lower than normal.

Equilibropathy Treatment that encourages the body to function properly by relaxing tense muscle groups in order to regulate the body's systems and ensure they work together harmoniously. It begins with an examination of the spinal column and associated muscle groups to determine the cause of health problems and reveal asymptomatic illnesses. A modified acupuncture technique is then used to help release tense and knotted muscle groups. Breathing exercises are taught to stimulate the muscles to release tension and correct the body's structures.

Essential oils Oils, extracted from plants and flowers, that have specific characteristics that determine their use. They may be sedative or stimulating, and have antibacterial and therapeutic qualities. Usually inhaled or used in treatments such as massages, where they are absorbed by the skin.

Exfoliation Removal of dry, dead skin cells and impurities that impede oxygenation, using products such as salt or herbs, or techniques such as dry brushing.

Eyebrow shaping Grooming of the eyebrows, typically by tweezing, to suit the facial features.

Eye treatment Treatment that focuses on the delicate eye area, generally to combat signs of premature ageing, relieve tired eyes, and reduce puffiness and dryness.

Facial Treatment that cleanses and improves the complexion of the face using products that best suit a specific skin type. May include gentle exfoliation, steaming to open pores for extractions, application of a facial mask and moisturiser, and a facial massage. Types of facials include aromatic, oxygenating, whitening and deep cleansing facials.

Facial mask Cleansing facial treatment where products are applied on the face and left on for a period of time to cleanse pores and slough off dead skin.

Facial scrub Exfoliating face treatment that uses products with abrasive ingredients to remove dry, dead skin cells and improve blood circulation. Softens the skin and gives it a healthier glow.

Fitness facial for men Facial that addresses men's skin types and needs, including shaving burn. May include a face, neck and shoulder massage.

Flotation therapy Treatment where you float on salt and mineral water at body temperature in an enclosed flotation tank (also known as an isolation tank). The feeling of weightlessness, and the isolation from external sensations and stimuli provide a deep feeling of relaxation and sensory awareness. May be done in complete silence and darkness, or with music and videos.

Floral bath Bath filled with flowers and essential oils.

Four-handed massage Massage performed by two therapists. Often uses a blend of massage techniques.

G5 vibro massage Deep vibrating massage using a G5 machine that relaxes, stimulates circulation and breaks down fatty deposits.

Glycolic facial Facial that uses glycolic acid to break down the bond which holds dry skin on to the face. Exfoliates the top layer, smoothes the skin and softens lines.

Golden spoons facial Facial using alternating hot and cold 23-karat gold-plated spoons to open and close the pores. Stimulates circulation and helps the skin absorb creams and lotions.

Gommage Massage-like treatment using creams to cleanse and moisturise.

Gong fu Generic term for martial arts that originated in China.

Grass-eater Vegan who does not eat food derived from animals, or processed with animal-derived products.

Gymnasium Workout room with weights, and a range of high-tech cardio and variable resistance equipment.

Hair services Services for the hair, including cutting, styling, deep conditioning, hair colouring, and washing and blowing dry.

Hay diet Diet, devised by American physician Dr William Howard, that recommends that carbohydrates are eaten at separate mealtimes from proteins and acidic fruit. Carbohydrates and proteins are not to be eaten within four hours of each other. Pulses and peanuts are not included in this diet.

Herbal bolus treatment Treatment where a heated muslin or cotton parcel of herbs and spices are placed on various parts of the body to relieve sore muscles, boost circulation and refresh the skin. The herbal packs are also used in place of hands to massage the body. Also known as **herbal heat revival**.

Herbal medicine Use of medicinal herbs and plant-based medicine to prevent and cure illnesses. Some healing systems, traditional Chinese medicine for instance, use mineral- and animal-based ingredients in herbal medicine. Herbal medicine is used by many complementary health disciplines including Ayurveda, homeopathy, naturopathy, and Chinese, Indonesian and Japanese medicines. It may be prepared for internal and external uses through various forms such as pills, teas, oils or compresses. Also known as **herbalism**.

Herbal steam infusion Steaming with herbs. The heat, moisture and fragrance of the herbs help to open the pores and promote relaxation.

Herbal wrap Treatment where the body is wrapped in hot cloth sheets soaked in a herbal solution. Eliminates impurities, softens the skin, and detoxifies and relaxes the body.

Herbology Therapeutic use of herbs in treatments and diets.

High-impact aerobics Aerobics involving jumping, jogging and hopping movements where both feet loose contact with the ground.

Holistic approach Integrated approach to health and fitness that takes into account your lifestyle, and mental, physical and spiritual well-being.

Homeopathy Holistic health care practice, based on the concept of 'like cures like', that treats diseases by using minute doses of natural substances that in a healthy person would produce symptoms similar to what is already being experienced. Developed by German physician Dr Samuel Hahnemann (1755–1843).

Hot plunge pool Pool of hot water that helps open the capillaries.

Hot spring Natural, sometimes volcanic, spring of hot mineral water.

Hot tub Wooden tub of hot or cool water to soak the body.

Hydrobath Bathtub with water jets that pummel all parts of the body. Seawater may be used, or the water may be infused with essential oils or mineral salts. Relaxes, and stimulates muscle tone and circulation.

Hydromassage Underwater massage in a hydrobath equipped with high-pressure jets and hand-manipulated hoses to stimulate the blood and lymphatic circulations.

Hydropool Pool fitted with various high-pressure jets and fountains.

Hydrotherapy Therapeutic use of water which includes baths, steam baths, steam inhalation, in- and under-water massage, soaking in hot springs, and the use of hot, cold or alternating shower sprays.

Indonesian massage Traditional massage of Indonesia that uses deep pressure and specially blended massage oils to ease tension and improve circulation.

Intimacy care Cleansing treatment for the vagina after intercourse, urination or giving birth.

Iridology Analysis of the marks and changes on the iris, which is divided into areas linked to specific body parts and functions, to diagnose a problem, or spot early signs of trouble, in order to recommend appropriate action.

Jamu Indonesian traditional herbal medicine.

Javanese *lulur* Traditional fragrant scrub originating from the royal palaces of Java. A blend of powdered spices, including turmeric and sandalwood, is rubbed on to the body. After the vibrantly coloured paste dries, it is removed with a gentle massage. The skin is then moisturised with yogurt. The *lulur* is often used to clean and pamper the bride during the week leading up to her wedding.

Jet lag treatment Treatment that eases travel-associated aches, pains and stiffness, and helps the body to adjust to the new time zone.

Jin Shin Do Bodymind Acupressure Body-mind healing approach that combines gentle but deep finger pressure on the acupoints to help release physical and emotional tension. The practitioner may suggest that you participate though breathing or focusing techniques.

Kanpō Japanese traditional herbal medicine. Less commonly used to refer to the Japanese traditional healing system.

Kinesiology Use of fingertip pressure to locate weakness in specific muscles and diagnose a problem or asymptomatic illnesses. The fingertips are used to massage the appropriate points to disperse toxins and revitalise the flow of energy.

Kneipp baths Herbal or mineral baths of varying temperatures combined with diet and exercise. Kneipp therapy uses hot and cold hydrotherapy treatments to improve circulation.

Kur Course of daily treatments using natural resources, such as algae and thermal mineral water, to re-mineralise and balance the body.

Labyrinth Ancient meditation tool in which a single winding path leads to a central goal and back out again. Walking it is a metaphor for journeying to the centre of understanding and returning with a broadened outlook.

Lap pool Swimming pool with exercise lanes. Standard lap pools are 50 metres in length.

Life coach counselling Counselling sessions that help to solve daily problems, develop harmony with the self and contribute to understanding life's natural philosophy.

Light therapy Use of natural or artificial light to heal.

Lomi Lomi Massage originating in Hawaii that uses the forearms and elbows, rhythmical rocking movements, and long and broad strokes.

Low-impact aerobics Form of aerobics with side-to-side marching or gliding movements which spare the body from excessive stress and possible injuries.

Lymphatic drainage massage Massage that uses a gentle pumping technique to stimulate lymphatic circulation, and thus reduce water retention and remove toxins. Lymph drainage can be achieved through manual massage or hydromassage. May be performed on the face and neck, or on the body.

Lymphobiology Treatment that combines a massage with an application of biological products to improve the skin's condition. Provides a radiant glow, reduces cellulite, restores hydration, controls acne, balances oily or dry skin, minimises lines and wrinkles, and corrects post-surgical bruising and swelling.

Macrobiotics Diet that aims to balance foods by their *yin-yang* qualities and according to your needs.

Malay massage Traditional massage that uses pressure and long, kneading strokes that focus on the body. May be applied with herbal oil.

Manicure Treatment that beautifies the hands and nails. Hands are soaked and exfoliated with a scrub to remove dead skin cells, cuticles are groomed, and nails are trimmed and shaped. Nails may be buffed to a shine or coated with a polish. May include a hand massage.

Manuluve Hand and arm treatment comprising a scrub and heated seaweed massage.

Marine aerosol treatment Inhalation of ionic seawater mist to cleanse the respiratory system. Alleviates breathing problems caused by asthma or smoking.

***Marma* point massage** Ayurvedic massage in which the *marma* points are massaged with the thumb or index fingers in clockwise circles. Focuses on the face, neck, scalp and shoulders.

***Marma* points** In Ayurveda, the body's vital energy points. It is believed that the dysfunction of any of these points leads to illness.

Massage Therapy that uses manipulative and soft tissue techniques that are generally based on concepts of the anatomy, physiology and human function. Relaxes, creates a sense of well-being, eases strain and tension, mobilises stiff joints, improves blood circulation, improves the digestive system, and encourages the removal of toxins from the body. Generally delivered by hand, though machines and high-powered water-jets are also used.

Masseur Male massage therapist.

Masseuse Female massage therapist.

Meditation Method of deep breathing, mental concentration and contemplation. During meditation, breathing, brain activity, and heart and pulse rates slow, encouraging the body to relax and achieve a greater sense of inner balance and peace. Relieves stress, removes pain and reduces blood pressure.

Meridians Pathways or channels through which the vital energy circulates throughout the body. All illnesses are believed to result from an imbalance or blockage of this flow.

Meridian stretching Stretching exercises designed to encourage physical and mental flexibility, for the body and mind to perform at their peak. Combines exercise, yoga and traditional Chinese medicine.

Microdermabrasion Clinical skin-resurfacing procedure where a jet of fine crystals is vacuumed across the surface of the face to remove the topmost layer of skin.

Mineralise Supply of minerals to the body.

Moxibustion Burning of the dried herb moxa around the acupoints to relieve pain. Applied using cones of moxa directly on the skin, or indirectly with an insulating layer of other herbs.

Muay Thai Thai boxing that involves the use of the upper and lower bodies. A cardiovascular and fat-burning exercise that helps relief stress.

Mud pool Pool with a central pedestal of volcanic mud.The mud is self-applied to the body and left to cake in the sun before being rinsed off.

Mud treatment Mineral-rich mud used to detoxify, loosen muscles and stimulate circulation.

Myofacial release Use of the fingers, palms, forearms and elbows in long, deliberate, gliding strokes to stretch and mobilise the fascia (connective tissue that surrounds and supports the muscles, organs and bones) to provide long-term relief of pain and promote well-being.

Nail art Beautification of the nails with patterns, paintings or other decorative motifs.

Nasya Use of nasal medicated drops to clear the nasal passages to help allergies. One of the five purification techniques in *panchakarma*.

Naturopathy Holistic approach that believes in the body's ability to heal itself. Uses treatments not to alleviate symptoms, but to encourage the body's self-healing mechanism. Symptoms are viewed not as a part of the illness, but as the body's way of ridding itself of the problem. Also known as **natural medicine**.

Njavarakizhi Ayurvedic massage using small linen bags—filled with rice cooked in milk mixed with a herbal blend—to induce sweat. Applied with medicated oil. Strengthens and rejuvenates.

Nutritional consultation Consultation with a qualified nutritional practitioner to review eating habits and dietary needs. Taking into account your lifestyle, food intolerance, appetite control and weight goals, the nutritionist may compile a nutritionally balanced programme to help you attain optimal health and weight.

Onsen Japanese natural hot springs.

Organic food Food grown without the use of pesticides or other chemicals.

Ovo lacto vegetarian Vegan who consumes milk and egg products.

Ovo vegetarian Vegan who consumes egg products.

Panchakarma Ayurvedic therapy (*vamana, virechana, vasti, nasya* and *raktamokshana*) that helps rid the body of its toxins.

Paraffin treatment Application of warm paraffin wax on the hands and feet to the skin to absorb toxins. Leaves the skin silky soft.

Pedicure Treatment that beautifies the feet and nails. Feet are soaked and exfoliated with a scrub to remove dead skin cells, cuticles are groomed, and nails are trimmed and shaped. Nails may be buffed to a shine or coated with a polish. May include a foot and calf massage.

Pediluve Treatment in which feet and legs are dipped in alternate tubs of bubbling jets of warm and cold seawater to improve blood circulation.

Personal fitness assessment Programme that assesses your current fitness levels to recommend a suitable exercise programme. May include tests for aerobic capacity, body composition, blood pressure, heart rate, and muscular endurance and strength.

Personal training One-on-one personalised workout with a qualified instructor.

Pescetarian Vegetarian who consumes fish.

Physiotherapy Rehabilitative therapy that helps recovery from injury, surgery or disease. Treatments—which include massage, traction, hydrotherapy, corrective exercise and electrical stimulation—help relieve pain, increase strength and improve the range of motion.

Pilates Exercise comprising slow, precise movements with special exercise equipment that engage the body and mind, and increase flexibility and strength without building bulk.

Pizhichil Ayurvedic massage in which lukewarm herbal oils are gently and rhythmically applied to the body by two to four therapists.

Pregnancy massage Pre-natal massage that deals with the special needs of a mother-to-be, and anti-natal massages that deal with her needs after she has delivered Some spas have massage tables with a hole in the centre to accommodate a pregnant woman.

Pressotherapy Computerised pressure massage that uses a specially designed airbag that compresses and deflates to improve the circulation throughout the feet and legs.

Purvakarma Two Ayurvedic treatments (*snehana* and *svedana*) that soften and cleanse the skin in preparation for *panchakarma*.

Qi gong Chinese physical exercise of working with or mastering *qi*. Uses breathing and body movement to help develop a powerful *qi*.

Qi 'Vital energy' or 'life force' of the universe and the body. Also known as *ki* (Japanese) and *prana* (Indian).

Raktamokshana Blood purification treatment for illnesses such as skin problems using surgical instruments or leeches. One of the five purification techniques in *panchakarma*.

Reflexology Application of finger-point pressure to reflex zones on the feet—and to a lesser extent, hands—to improve circulation, ease pain, relax the body and re-establish the flow of energy through the body. Its underlying theory is that specific areas on the feet and hands correspond with specific body parts, organs and glands, and that the manipulation of specific areas can bring about change associated with the corresponding parts.

Reiki Healing technique based on ancient Tibetan teachings. The practitioner places his palms over or on various areas of the body for a few minutes each to energise and balance the body, mind and spirit. Helps treat physical problems, heal emotional stresses and encourage personal transformation.

Salt glow Exfoliating treatment where the body is rubbed with a mixture of coarse salt and essential oils to remove dry, dead skin cells and stimulate circulation.

Sauna Dry heat, wood-lined treatment room. The heat brings on sweating to help cleanse the body of impurities and relax the muscles. Usually followed by a cold plunge or shower.

Shiatsu Massage that uses finger pressure—and also the hands, forearms, elbows, knees and feet—on acupoints. Calms and relaxes.

Shirodhara Ayurvedic massage in which warmed medicated oil steadily drips on the forehead. Relieves mental tension and calms the mind.

Signature treatment Treatment specially created by a spa or spa group, often using indigenous ingredients.

Shirovasthi Ayurvedic treatment in which warm herbal medicated oil is massaged on to the head after which a closely fitted cap is worn for a while to retain the therapeutic benefits.

Snehana Ayurvedic oil therapy in which a mixture of herbs, oils and natural ingredients are massaged on to the body. The oils may also be taken orally or introduced as enemas. One of the two preparatory treatments in *purvakarma*.

Spa Term, originating from the name of a town in Belgium where people flocked to in the 17th century for its healing waters, that refers to anything from a mineral spring to an establishment which provides facilities and services that helps you achieve a sense of well-being. Many spas also provide fitness activities, classes on well-being and spa cuisine. Types of spas include day spas (spas for day use); hotel or resort spas (spas located within hotels or resorts); destination spas (spas with an all-round emphasis on a healthy lifestyle, and include on-site accommodation, treatments, programmes and spa cuisine); and mineral springs spas (spas with a natural source of mineral or thermal waters, or seawater).

Spa cuisine Light, healthy meals served at spas. Typically low in calories, fat and salt.

Spa menu Selection of treatments and therapies offered by a spa.

Spa package Two or more treatments offered together. Often longer in length and good value.

Sports massage Deep tissue massage directed at muscles used in athletic activities to help the body achieve its maximum physical efficiency. Before physical exertion, it buffers against pain and injury; after, it helps remove lactic acid and restore muscle tone and range of movement.

Steaming Use of hot steam—often infused with essential oils or herbs—to relax the body, soften the skin, and open up the pores to prepare the face or body for treatment. Hair may also be steamed by wrapping it in a hot towel or exposing it to steam.

Steam room Tiled room with benches in which steam is generated at high pressure and temperature. The steam opens the pores, eliminates toxins, cleanses the skin and relaxes the body.

Step aerobics Aerobic sessions done with a small platform for stepping up and down.

Stress management Techniques to deal with stress and anxiety.

Stretching Flexibility workout where various parts of the body are stretched by assuming different positions. Helps increase flexibility, and relieve stress and tension.

Svedana Body purification method to cleanse and relax through sweat therapy. One of the two preparatory treatments in *purvakarma*.

Swedish massage Massage in which oils are applied to the body with techniques such as gliding, kneading, rubbing, tapping and shaking. Relieves stress, tension and muscle pain; improves circulation; increases flexibility; and induces relaxation.

Tai ji Graceful movement that combines mental concentration with deep, controlled breathing. Regular practice brings about relaxation and good health. Stimulates the body's energy systems and enhances mental functions.

Thai herbal massage Massage using a warmed pouch of steamed Thai herbs pressed against the body's meridians.

Thai massage Traditional massage of Thailand, influenced by Chinese and Indian healing arts, that involves a combination of stretching and gentle rocking, and uses a range of motions and acupressure techniques. The massage is oil-free, and performed on a traditional Thai mattress on the floor. Loose pajamas are worn.

Thalassotherapy Treatments that harness mineral- and vitamin-rich seawater and seaweed for curative and preventive purposes. True thalassotherapy centres are located no more than 800 metres (2,625 feet) from the shore, and constantly pump fresh seawater filtered through large canals for use in the treatments.

Thermal bath Therapeutic use of thermal water rich in salts and minerals.

Traditional Chinese medicine (TCM) Holistic system of care that sees the body and mind as a whole. Treatments include herbal medicine, physical and mental exercises, and therapies such as acupuncture and moxibustion.

Treatments for couples Typically treatments that a couple can enjoy together with a therapist pampering each person. Treatments specially designed for couples usually use an aphrodisiac blend of essential oils.

Tui na Chinese system of manual therapy used to treat specific illnesses of an internal nature and musculoskeletal ailments. Principal hand strokes include pushing (*tui*), grasping (*na*), pressing (*an*), rubbing (*mo*), rolling (*gun*), pulling (*qian*), beating (*da*) and shaking (*dou*). The hands, arms, elbows and feet may be used.

Turkish bath Series of hot and humid steam rooms, each of which increases in heat. You spend several minutes in each room and finish with a cool shower.

Vamana The consumption of potions to induce vomiting to treat bronchitis, and throat, chest and heart problems. One of the five purification techniques in *panchakarma*.

Vasti Use of enemas to calm nerves and treat fatigue, dry skin and digestive imbalances.One of the five purification techniques in *panchakarma*.

Vegan Person who exclusively consumes a vegetable and fruit diet, and does not eat animal products such as butter, cheese, eggs and milk.

Vegetarian Person who consumes mainly vegetables, fruit, nuts, pulses and grains, and who does not eat meat or fish, but eats animal products such as butter, cheese, eggs and milk.

Vichy shower Spray of water from five micro-jets fixed to a horizontal rail which rain down on you while you lie on a table below. May also include a massage. Also known as **affusion shower** or **rain shower**.

Vietnamese massage Invigorating massage that uses a combination of deep stroking and percussive movements. Benefits include stimulating the blood and lymphatic circulation, improving the skin texture and tone, and warming and relaxing the muscle tissue.

Virechana Drinking a herb tea to help flush out elements that may clog the digestive tract. One of the five purification techniques in *panchakarma*.

Visualisation Technique that involves focusing the mind by consciously creating a mental image of a desired condition to bring about change. May be self-directed or therapist guided. Also known as **imaging**.

Warm stone massage Massage where warmed smooth stones are rubbed in long, flowing strokes on to the oiled body, then placed on energy points to ease away tension. Also known as **hot stone massage** or **la stone therapy**.

Watsu Therapy where you float in a swimming pool, supported by a therapist who manipulates your body with stretches, rhythmic movements and pressure point massage to bring deep relaxation.

Waxing Temporary hair removal method. Warm or cool wax, usually honeycomb blended with oils, is applied on to areas of unwanted hair. A cloth is smoothed on to the area and quickly whisked off, pulling the hair off with the wax.

Wet area Area in a spa where jacuzzis, saunas, cold tubs, hot tubs, steam baths and pressure showers are located.

Whirlpool Tub of hot water with high-pressure jets on the sides and bottom that circulate the water. Massages muscles and relaxes the body.

Whitening treatment Treatment that brightens the skin, restores lost radiance and tones pigmentation marks.

Yin and yang *Yin* is the universal energy force whose characteristics are feminine, cold, dark, quiet, static and wet. *Yang* is masculine, warm, bright, dynamic and dry. In traditional Chinese medicine, true balance and health are achieved when these two opposing forces are in balance. Also known as **in** and **yo** (Japanese).

Yoga Ancient Hindu practice comprising focused deep breathing, and stretching and toning the body using various postures. The ultimate goal is to reach your full physical, mental and spiritual potential. Relaxes, and improves circulation, flexibility and strength.

Spa Directory

A comprehensive listing of the spas in the book and their sister spas in Asia. Page references indicate where the entries appear in the book.

CAMBODIA

Phnom Penh
Amrita Spa (pp126–7)
Raffles Hotel Le Royal
92 Rukhak Vithei Daun Penh
Sangkat Wat Phnom
Phnom Penh, Cambodia
Tel: (855-23) 981 888
Fax: (855-23) 981 168
Email: raffles.hlr.ghda@bigpond.com.kh
Website: www.amritaspas.com

Siem Reap
Amrita Spa (pp124–5)
Raffles Grand Hotel d'Angkor
1 Vithei Charles De Gaulle
Khum Svay Dang Kum
Siem Reap, Cambodia
Tel: (855-63) 963 888
Fax: (855-63) 963 168
Email: raffles.grand@bigpond.com.kh
Website: www.amritaspas.com

CHINA

Beijing
The Spa at China Life Tower
16 Chao Yang Men Wai Street
Chaoyang District
Beijing 100020, China
Tel: (86-10) 8525 1818/9
Fax: (86-10) 8525 1817
Email: ahjelmeland@sportathlon.com
Website: www.thespahealthclubs.com

The St. Regis Spa & Club (pp132–3)
21 Jian Guo Men Wai Da Jie
Beijing 100020, China
Tel: (86-10) 6460 6688
Fax: (86-10) 6460 3299
Email: beijing.stregis@stregis.com
Website: www.stregis.com/beijing

Hong Kong
The Spa at Exchange Square
37th Level, One Exchange Square
Central
Hong Kong
Tel: (852) 2525 2900
Fax: (852) 2845 2478
Email: cng@sportathlon.com
Website: www.thespahealthclubs.com

The Spa at The Excelsior
The Excelsior Hotel
Causeway Bay
Hong Kong
Tel: (852) 2837 6837
Fax: (852) 2881 8449
Email: hwelburn@sportathlon.com
Website: www.thespahealthclubs.com

The Spa at The Sheraton
Sheraton Hotel & Towers
20 Nathan Road
Kowloon, Hong Kong
Tel: (852) 2732 6801
Fax: (852) 2311 7995
Email: vtong@sportathlon.com
Website: www.thespahealthclubs.com

Shanghai
Club Oasis (pp128–9)
Grand Hyatt Shanghai
Jin Mao Tower
88 Century Boulevard, Pudong
Shanghai 200121, China
Tel: (86-21) 5049 1234
Fax: (86-21) 5049 1111
Email: info@hyattshanghai.com
Website: www.shanghai.hyatt.com

The Spa at The Hilton (pp130–1)
Hilton Shanghai
250 Hua Shan Road
Shanghai 200040, China
Tel: (86-21) 6248 0000 ext 2600
Fax: (86-21) 6248 3848
Email: spa_shanghai@hilton.com
Website: www.thespahealthclubs.com

The St. Regis Spa Shanghai (pp134–5)
889 Dong Fang Road, Pudong
Shanghai 200122, China
Tel: (86-21) 5050 4567
Fax: (86-21) 6875 6789
Email: stregis.shanghai@starwoodhotels.com
Website: www.stregis.com

INDIA

Bangalore
Angsana Oasis Spa & Resort Bangalore
Northwest Country
Main Doddaballapur Road, Rajankunte
Bangalore 560064, India
Tel: (91-80) 846 8893
Fax: (91-80) 846 8897
Email: spa-bangalore@angsana.com
Website: www.angsana.com

Kerala
Somatheeram Ayurvedic Beach Resort (pp140–1)
Chowara, South of Kovalam, Via Balarampuram
Trivandrum 695501
Kerala, South India
Tel: (91-471) 268 101
Fax: (91-471) 267 600
Email: somatheeram@vsnl.com
Website: www.somatheeram.com

Uttaranchal
Ananda-In the Himalayas Destination Spa (pp136–9)
The Palace Estate
Narendra Nagar, District Tehri-Garhwal
Uttaranchal 249175, India
Sales & Reservation Office
Tel: (91-11) 689 9999
Fax: (91-11) 613 1066
Email: administrator@anandaspa.com
Website: www.anandaspa.com

INDONESIA

Bali
Chavana Spa
Nikko Bali Resort & Spa
Jalan Raya Nusa Dua Selatan
Nusa Dua
Bali 80363, Indonesia
Tel: (62-361) 773 377
Fax: (62-361) 773 388
Email: sales@nikkobali.com
Website: www.nikkobali.com

Club Med Spa
Club Med
Kawasan Wisata Nusa Dua
Bali 80363, Indonesia
Tel: (62-361) 771 521
Fax: (62-361) 771 835
Email: balcplan01@clubmed.com
Website: www.clubmed.com

Jamu Traditional Spa (pp146–7)
AlamKulKul Resort
Jalan Pantai Kuta
Legian
Bali 80361, Indonesia
Tel: (62-361) 752 750
Fax: (62-361) 752 519
Email: jamubali@jamutraditionalspa.com
Website: www.jamutraditionalspa.com

Mandara Spa
Hotel Imperial Bali
Jalan Abimanyu Legian Beach
Bali 80361, Indonesia
Tel: (62-361) 730 730
Fax: (62-361) 730 545
Email: impbali@indosat.net.id
Website: www.bali-imperial.com

Mandara Spa
Hotel Padma Bali
1 Jalan Padma
Legian
Bali 80361, Indonesia
Tel: (62-361) 752 111
Fax: (62-361) 752 140
Email: sales@hotelpadmabali.com
Website: www.hotelpadma.com

Mandara Spa
Hotel Sanur Beach
Jalan Danau Tamblingan
Sanur
Bali 80032, Indonesia
Tel: (62-361) 288 011
Fax: (62-361) 287 566
Email: sanurbch@indosat.net.id
Website: www.aerowisata.co.id/sanur

Mandara Spa
Ibah Luxury Villas
Jalan Raya Campuhan
Ubud
Bali 80571, Indonesia
Tel: (62-361) 974 466
Fax: (62-361) 974 467
Email: ibah@denpasar.wasantara.net.id
Website: www.ibahbali.com

Mandara Spa
The Serai
Buitan Manggis, Karangasem
Bali 80871, Indonesia
Tel: (62-363) 41 011
Fax: (62-363) 41 015
Email: seraimanggis@ghmhotels.com
Website: ghmhotels.com/h_serai

Parwathi Spa (pp150–1)
Matahari Beach Resort & Spa
Pemuteran Village, Singaraja
Bali 81155, Indonesia
Tel: (62-362) 92 312
Fax: (62-362) 92 313
Email: mbr-bali@indo.net.id
Website: www.matahari-beach-resort.com

Pita Maha Spa (pp152–3)
Pita Maha A Tjampuhan Resort & Spa
Jalan Sanggingan, Ubud
Bali 80571, Indonesia
Tel: (62-361) 974 330
Fax: (62-361) 974 329
Email: pitamaha@dps.mega.net.id
Website: www.pitamaha-bali.com

Spa at Maya (pp154–5)
Maya Ubud Resort & Spa
Jalan Gunung Sari
Banjar Ambengan, Ubud
Bali 80571, Indonesia
Tel: (62-361) 977 888
Fax: (62-361) 977 555
Email: spa@mayaubud.com
Website: www.mayaubud.com

The Spa
Bali Golf & Country Club
Kawasan Wisata Nusa Dua
Bali 80363, Indonesia
Tel: (62-361) 771 791
Fax: (62-361) 771 797
Email: baligolf@denpasar.wasantara.net.id
Website: www.baligolfandcountryclub.com

The Spa (pp156–7)
The Chedi
Desa Melinggih Kelod
Payangan, Gianyar
Bali 80572, Indonesia
Tel: (62-361) 975 963
Fax: (62-361) 975 968
Email: chediubd@ghmhotels.com
Website: www.mandaraspa-asia.com

The Spa (pp158–9)
The Legian
Jalan Laksmana
Seminyak Beach
Bali 80361, Indonesia
Tel: (62-361) 730 622
Fax: (62-361) 730 623
Email: legian@ghmhotels.com
Website: www.ghmhotels.com

The Spa
Waterbom Park & Spa
Jalan Kartika Plaza
Tuban
Bali 80361, Indonesia
Tel: (62-361) 758 241
Fax: (62-361) 753 517
Email: info@waterbom.co.id
Website: www.waterbom.com

Thalasso Bali (pp162–3)
Grand Mirage Resort
Jalan Pratama 72–4
Tanjung Benoa, Nusa Dua
Bali 80363, Indonesia
Tel: (62-361) 773 883
Fax: (62-361) 772 247
Email: thalasso@denpasar.wasantara.net.id
Website: www.thalassobali.com

Tjampuhan Spa (pp164–5)
Hotel Tjampuhan & Spa
Jalan Raya Campuhan
Ubud
Bali 80571, Indonesia
Tel: (62-361) 975 368
Fax: (62-361) 975 137
Email: tjampuan@indo.net.id
Website: www.indo.com/hotels/tjampuhan

Waroeng Djamoe Spa (pp166–7)
Hotel Tugu Bali
Jalan Pantai Balu Bolong
Canggu
Bali 80351, Indonesia
Tel: (62-361) 731 701
Fax: (62-361) 731 704
Email: bali@tuguhotels.com
Website: www.tuguhotels.com

Bintan Island, Riau
Angsana Spa Bintan
Angsana Resort & Spa Bintan
Site A4, Lagoi
Bintan Island, Indonesia
Tel: (62-770) 693 111
Fax: (62-770) 693 222
Email: spa-bintan@angsana.com
Website: www.angsana.com

Asmara at Nirwana
Nirwana Resort Hotel
Nirwana Gardens, Bintan Utara
Riau 29152, Indonesia
Tel: (62-770) 692 566
Fax: (62-770) 692 602
Email: enquiries@asmaraspas.com
Website: www.asmaraspas.com

Asmara Ria
Ria Bintan Golf Club
Jalan Perigi Raja, Parcel A11
Lagoi, Bintan Utara
Riau 29152, Indonesia
Tel: (62-770) 692 851
Fax: (62-770) 692 602
Email: enquiries@asmaraspas.com
Website: www.asmaraspas.com

Asmara Tropical Spas (pp144–5)
Mayang Sari Beach Resort
Bintan Utara
Riau 29152, Indonesia
Tel: (62-770) 692 565
Fax: (62-770) 692 602
Email: asmaras@indosat.net.id
Website: www.asmaraspas.com

Banyan Tree Spa Bintan
Banyan Tree Bintan
Site A4, Lagoi
Bintan Island, Indonesia
Tel: (62-770) 693 100
Fax: (62-770) 693 200
Email: spa-bintan@banyantree.com
Website: www.banyantree.com

Lombok, Nusa Tenggara Barat
Mandara Spa
Novotel Coralia Lombok
Mandalika Resort
Pantai Putri Nyale
Pujut, Lombok Tengah 83111
Nusa Tenggara Barat, Indonesia
Tel: (62-370) 653 333
Fax: (62-370) 653 555
Email: hotel@novotel-lombok.com
Website: wwwl.novotel-lombok.com

Mandara Spa
Senggigi Beach Hotel
Jalan Pantai Senggigi
Lombok 83101, Indonesia
Tel: (62-370) 693 210/9
Fax: (62-370) 693 200/339
Email: hsa@mataram.wasantara.net.id
Website: www.aerowisata.co.id/seng.html

East Java
Apsara Residence & Spa (pp142–3)
Hotel Tugu Malang
Jalan Tugu Number 3
Malang 65119
East Java, Indonesia
Tel: (62-341) 363 891
Fax: (62-341) 362 747
Email: malang@tuguhotels.com
Website: www.tuguhotels.com

Jakarta
Jamu Body Treatments
Jalan Cipete VII Number 82A
Jakarta Selatan 12410, Indonesia
Tel: (62-21) 765 9691
Fax: (62-21) 765 9693
Email: jamujkt@cbn.net.id
Website: www.jamutraditionalspa.com

Taman Sari Royal Heritage Spa (pp160–1)
Jalan K H Wahid Hasyim Number 133
Jakarta Pusat 10240, Indonesia
Tel: (62-21) 314 3585
Fax: (62-21) 330 100
Email: spa@mustika-ratu.co.id
Website: www.mustika-ratu.co.id

Java
Jamu Island Spa
AlamKotok Island Resort
Pulau Seribu 14450
Java, Indonesia
Tel: (62-21) 720 9625
Fax: (62-21) 725 6302
Email: kotok@alamresorts.com
Website: www.alamresorts.com

West Java
Javana Spa (pp148–9)
Cangkuang-Cidahu, Sukabumi
West Java, Indonesia
Tel: (62-21) 719 8327/8
Fax: (62-21) 719 5555
Email: javana@indo.net.id
Website: www.javanaspa.com

The Malya
56–8 Jalan Ranca Bentang
Ciumbuleuit
Bandung 40142
West Java, Indonesia
Tel: (62-22) 203 0333
Fax: (62-22) 203 0633
Email: reservation@malyabandung.com
Website: www.malyabandung.com

Yogyakarta
Taman Sari Royal Heritage Spa
Sheraton Mustika Yogyakarta Resort & Spa
Jalan Laksda Adisucipto KM 8,7
Yogyakarta 55282, Indonesia
Tel: (62-274) 511 588
Fax: (62-274) 511 589
Email: info@sheraton-yogya.com
Website: www.sheraton.com

MALAYSIA

Borneo
Mandara Spa
Magellan Sutera Hotel & Spa
2 Sutera Harbour Boulevard
Sutera harbour 88100
Kota Kinabalu, Sabah
Borneo, East Malaysia
Tel: (60-88) 312 222
Fax: (60-88) 311 136
Email: sutera@suterah.po.my
Website: www.suteraharbour.com

Johor
Mandara Spa
Hotel Sofitel Palm Resort
Jalan Pesiaran Golf
(off Jalan Jumbo)
Senai 81250
Johor Darul Ta'zim, Malaysia
Tel: (60-7) 599 6000
Fax: (60-7) 599 7028
Email: sofitel@palmresort.com
Website: www.palmresort.com

Langkawi Island, Kedah
Chavana Spa
Sheraton Langkawi Beach Resort
Teluk Nibong
07000 Langkawi Island
Kedah Darul Aman, Malaysia
Tel: (60-4) 955 1901
Fax: (60-4) 955 1918
Website: www.sheraton.com

Jamu Nature Spa (pp168–9)
The Andaman Datai Bay
Jalan Teluk Datai
07000 Langkawi Island
Kedah Darul Aman, Malaysia
Tel: (60-4) 959 1088
Fax: (60-4) 959 1168
Email: anda@po.jaring.my
Website: www.theandaman.com

Mandara Spa (pp170–1)
The Datai
Jalan Teluk Datai
07000 Langkawi Island
Kedah Darul Aman, Malaysia
Tel: (60-4) 959 2500
Fax: (60-4) 959 2600
Email: datai@ghmhotels.com
Website: www.mandaraspa-asia.com

The Spa (pp174–5)
Berjaya Langkawi Beach & Spa Resort
Karong Berkunci 200
Burau Bay
07000 Langkawi Island
Kedah Darul Aman, Malaysia
Tel: (60-4) 959 1888 ext 701
Fax: (60-4) 959 1886
Email: resvn@b-langkawi.com.my
Website: www.berjayaresorts.com

Pahang
Club Med Spa
Club Med Malaysia
Holiday Villages of Malaysia
Kuantan 25710
Pahang Darul Makmur, Malaysia
Tel: (60-9) 581 9543
Fax: (60-9) 581 9172
Email: info@mandaraspa-asia.com
Website: www.clubmed.com

Pangkor Laut Island, Perak
Spa Village (pp176–7)
Pangkor Laut Resort
Pangkor Laut Island
32200 Lumut
Perak, Malaysia
Tel: (60-5) 699 1100
Fax: (60-5) 699 1200
Email: plr@po.jaring.my
Website: www.pangkorlautresort.com
Reservation: travelcentre@ytlhotels.com.my

Selangor
Sembunyi Spa (pp172–3)
Cyberview Lodge Resort & Spa
MSC Headquarters
63000 Cyberjaya
Selangor, Malaysia
Tel: (60-3) 8312 7000
Fax: (60-3) 8312 7001
Email: hotline@cyberview-lodge.com.my
Website: www.cyberview-lodge.com

Terengganu
Taman Sari Royal Heritage Spa (pp178–9)
Awana Kijal Golf, Beach & Spa Resort
KM28, Jalan Kemaman-Dungun
24100 Kijal, Kemaman
Terengganu Darul Iman, Malaysia
Tel: (60-9) 864 1188
Fax: (60-9) 864 1688
Email: awanakij@tm.net.my
Website: www.awana.com.my

THE MALDIVES

Baa Atoll
The Nautilus Spa (pp180–1)
Coco Palm Resort & Spa
Dunikolu Island
Baa Atoll, The Maldives
Tel: (960) 230 011
Fax: (960) 230 022
Email: cocopalm@sunland.com.mv
Website: www.mandaraspa-asia.com

Six Senses Spa (pp182–3)
Soneva Fushi Resort & Spa
Kunfunadhoo Island
Baa Atoll, The Maldives
Tel: (960) 230 304
Fax: (960) 230 374
Email: sonresa@soneva.com.mv
Website: www.six-senses.com

Malé
Club Med Spa
Club Med Faru
Farukolufushi Island
Malé, Maldives
Tel: (960) 443 021
Fax: (960) 441 997/2415
Email: info@mandaraspa-asia.com
Website: www.clubmed.com

Club Med Spa
Club Med Kani
Kanifinolhu Island
Malé, The Maldives
Tel: (960) 443 152
Fax: (960) 443 859
Email: info@mandaraspa-asia.com
Website: www.clubmed.com

Meemu Atoll
The Spa
Medhufushi Island Resort
Meemu Atoll, The Maldives
Tel: (960) 460 026
Fax: (960) 460 027
Email: medhu@aaa.com.mv
Website: www.aaa-resortsmaldives.com

North Malé Atoll
Angsana Spa Maldives Ihuru
Angsana Resort & Spa Maldives Ihuru
Ihuru Island
North Malé Atoll, The Maldives
Tel: (960) 443 502
Fax: (960) 445 933
Email: spa-maldives@angsana.com
Website: www.angsana.com

Banyan Tree Spa Maldives Vabbinfaru
Banyan Tree Maldives Vabbinfaru
Vabbinfaru Island
North Malé Atoll, The Maldives
Tel: (960) 443 147
Fax: (960) 443 843
Email: spa-maldives@banyantree.com
Website: www.banyantree.com

Mandara Spa
Taj Coral Reef Resort
Meduziyaaraiy Magu
North Malé Atoll, The Maldives
Tel: (960) 441 948
Fax: (960) 443 884
Email: tajcr@dhivehinet.net.mv
Website: www.mandaraspas-asia.com

Six Senses Spa (pp184–5)
Soneva Gili Resort & Spa
Lankanfushi Island
North Malé Atoll, The Maldives
Tel: (960) 440 304
Fax: (960) 440 305
Email: sonresa@soneva.com.mv
Website: www.six-senses.com

South Malé Atoll
Mandara Spa
Taj Spa by Mandara
Taj Exotica Resort and Spa
Meduziyaaraiy Magu
South Malé Atoll, The Maldives
Tel: (960) 442 200
Fax: (960) 442 211
Email: roomrsvn@tajexotica.com.mv
Website: www.mandaraspas-asia.com

THE PHILIPPINES

Cebu
Mogambo Springs: The Spa (pp186–7)
Plantation Bay Resort and Spa
Marigondon
Mactan Island
Cebu 6015, The Philippines
Tel: (63-32) 340 5900
Fax: (63-32) 340 5988
Email: spa@plantationbay.com
Website: www.plantationbay.com

Manila
The Spa at RCBC
3rd & 4th Levels, RCBC Plaza
Corner Senator Gil Puyat & Ayala Avenues
1200 Makati City
Manila, The Philippines
Tel: (63-2) 845 3480
Fax: (63-2) 845 3590
Email: vaquino@sportathlon.com
Website: www.thespahealthclubs.com

SINGAPORE

Amrita Spa (pp188–9)
Raffles Hotel
1 Beach Road
Singapore 189673
Tel: (65) 6337 1886
Fax: (65) 6337 7650
Email: raffles@raffles.com
Website: www.raffleshotel.com

Amrita Spa (pp190–1)
Raffles The Plaza
2 Stamford Road
Level 6, Raffles The Plaza
Singapore 178882
Tel: (65) 6336 4477
Fax: (65) 6336 1161
Email: www.amritaspas.com
Website: www.amritaspas.com

Amrita Spa (pp192–3)
Swissôtel Merchant Court
20 Merchant Road
Singapore 058281
Tel: (65) 6239 1780
Fax: (65) 6239 1781
Email: amrita.merchantcourt@swissotel.com
Website: www.swissotel.com

Renewal Club Spa (pp194–5)
Meritus Negara Hotel
Level 4, 10 Claymore Road
Singapore 229540
Tel: (65) 6736 3097
Fax: (65) 6736 3098
Email: info@renewal.com.sg
Website: www.renewal.com.sg

Renewal Day Spa (pp196–7)
302 Orchard Road
#17-02 Tong Building
Singapore 238862
Tel: (65) 6738 0988
Fax: (65) 6733 7956
Email: rds-tb@renewal.com.sg
Website: www.renewal.com.sg

Spa Botanica (pp198–9)
The Beaufort Singapore
2 Bukit Manis Road
Sentosa, Singapore 099891
Tel: (65) 6275 0331
Fax: (65) 6275 0228
Email: enquiries@spabotanica.com
Website: www.spabotanica.com

The Spa at Raffles Place
1 Raffles Place
#06-00, OUB Centre
Singapore 048616
Tel: (65) 6534 4333
Fax: (65) 6534 3727
Email: bjong@sportathlon.com
Website: www.thespahealthclubs.com

The Spa at The Capital Tower
168 Robinson Road
#09-00, Capital Tower
Singapore 068912
Tel: (65) 6536 5595
Fax: (65) 6536 5545
Email: npassi@sportathlon.com
Website: www.thespahealthclubs.com

The Spa at The Oriental
The Oriental Singapore
5 Raffles Avenue
Marina Square
Singapore 039797
Tel: (65) 6331 0032
Fax: (65) 6339 4296
Email: rhassan@sportathlon.com
Website: www.thespahealthclubs.com

THAILAND

Bangkok
Banyan Tree Spa Bangkok
Banyan Tree Bangkok
21/100 South Sathon Road
Bangkok 10120, Thailand
Tel: (66-2) 679 1200
Fax: (66-2) 679 1199
Email: spa-bangkok@banyantree.com
Website: www.banyantree.com

Being Spa (pp202–5)
88 Sukhumvit 51
Klongton Neu, Wattana
Bangkok 10110, Thailand
Tel: (66-2) 662 6171
Fax: (66-2) 258 7906
Email: contact@beingspa.com
Website: www.beingspa.com

Devarana Spa (pp210–1)
The Dusit Thani Hotel
946 Rama IV Road
Bangkok 10500, Thailand
Tel: (66-2) 636 3596
Fax: (66-2) 636 3597
Email: bangkok@devarana.com
Website: www.devarana.com

Imperial Mandara Spa
Imperial Queen's Park Hotel
199 Sukhumvit Soi 22
Bangkok 10110, Thailand
Tel: (66-2) 261 9000
Fax: (66-2) 258 2327
Email: imperial@mandaraspa-asia.com
Website: www.imperialqueenpark.com

Mandara Spa
Bangkok Marriott Resort & Spa
257/1-3 Charoen Nakorn Road
At the Krungthep Brigde, Thonburi
Bangkok 10600, Thailand
Tel: (66-2) 476 0021/2
Fax: (66-2) 460 1805
Email: marriottresortspa@minornet.com
Website: www.marriotthotels.com/bkkth

Royal Orchid Mandara Spa
Royal Orchid Sheraton
2 Captain Bush Lane
New Road, Siphya
Bangkok10500, Thailand
Tel: (66-2) 266 0123
Fax: (66-2) 236 8320
Email: ROSHT@mozart.inet.co.th
Website: www.royalorchidsheraton.com

Spa Botanica (pp218–9)
The Sukhothai
79 Anson Road, #07-03
Singapore 079906
Tel: (65) 6820 6788
Fax: (65) 6820 3188
Email: spaplanner@spabotanica.com
Website: www.spabotanica.com

The Spa on Thirty Nine
8th Level, 55 Biohouse Building,
Sukhumvit 39, Klongtonnue, Wattana
Bangkok 10110, Thailand
Tel: (66-2) 262 0520-2
Fax: (66-2) 262 0523
Email: djackson@sportathlon.com
Website: www.thespahealthclubs.com

Chiang Mai
Angsana Spa Allamanda Laguna Phuket
Allamanda Laguna Phuket
29 Moo 4 Srisoonthorn Road
Cherngtalay, Amphur Talang
Phuket 83110, Thailand
Tel: (66-76) 324 359
Fax: (66-76) 324 360
Email: spa-allamandaphuket@angsana.com
Website: www.angsana.com

Angsana Spa Green View – Chiang Mai
Green Valley Country Club
183/1, Chotana Road
Mae Sa-Mae Rim
Chiang Mai 50180, Thailand
Tel: (66-5) 329 8220
Fax: (66-5) 329 7386
Email: spa-greenviewchiangmai@angsana.com
Website: www.angsana.com

Hua Hin
Chiva-Som International Health Resort (pp206–9)
73/4 Petchkasem Road
Hua Hin 77110, Thailand
Tel: (66-32) 536 536
Fax: (66-32) 511 154
Email: reserv@chivasom.com
Website: www.chivasom.com

Mandara Spa
Anantara Resort
43/I Phetkasem Beach Road
Hua Hin 77110, Thailand
Tel: (66-32) 520250-6
Fax: (66-32) 520259/60
Email: info@anantara.com
Website: www.anantara.com

Mandara Spa
Hua Hin Marriott Resort & Spa
107/1 Phetkasem Beach Road
Hua Hin 77110, Thailand
Tel: (66-32) 511 881–4 or 512 410–2
Fax: (66-32) 512 422
Email: marriottresortspa@minornet.com
Website: www.marriotthotels.com

The Spa (pp216–7)
Hilton Hua Hin
33 Naresdamri Road
Hua Hin 77110, Thailand
Tel: (66-32) 512 888 ext 1890
Fax: (66-32) 511 053
Email: thespa_huahin@hilton.com
Website: www.huahin.hilton.com

Phuket

Angsana Spa Dusit Laguna
Dusit Laguna Resort
390 Srisoonthorn Road, Cherngtalay
Amphur Talang, Phuket 83110, Thailand
Tel: (66-76) 324 320
Fax: (66-76) 324 174
Email: spa-dusitphuket@angsana.com
Website: www.angsana.com

Angsana Spa Laguna Beach Resort Phuket
Laguna Beach Resort
323/2 Moo 2, Srisoonthorn Road, Cherngtalay
Amphur Talang, Phuket 83110, Thailand
Tel: (66-76) 325 405
Fax: (66-76) 325 407
Email: spa-lagunabeachphuket@angsana.com
Website: www.angsana.com

Angsana Spa Panwaburi
The Panwaburi
84 Moo 8, Sakdidej Road, Tambon Vichit, Muang
Phuket 83000, Thailand
Tel: (66-76) 200 800
Fax: (66-76) 200 812
Email: spa-panwaburiphuket@angsana.com
Website: www.angsana.com

Angsana Spa Sheraton Grande Laguna Phuket
Sheraton Grande Laguna Phuket
10 Moo 4, Srisoonthorn Road
Cherngtalay, Amphur Talang
Phuket 83110, Thailand
Tel: (66-76) 324 101
Fax: (66-76) 324 368
Email: spa-sheratonphuket@angsana.com
Website: www.angsana.com

Banyan Tree Spa (pp192–3)
Banyan Tree Phuket
33 Moo 4, Srisoonthorn Road
Cherngtalay, Amphur Talang
Phuket 83110, Thailand
Tel: (66-76) 324 374
Fax: (66-76) 324 375
Email: spa-phuket@banyantree.com
Website: www.banyantree.com

Mandara Spa
Pearl Village
Nai Yang Beach and National Park
Phuket 83140, Thailand
Tel: (66-76) 327006/327015
Fax: (66-76) 327338/9
Email: pearlvil@loxinfo.co.th
Website: www.phuket.com/pearlvillage

Mandara Spa
JW Marriott Phuket Resort & Spa
Moo 3, Mai Khao, Talang
Phuket 83140, Thailand
Tel: (66-0) 7633 8000
Fax: (66-0) 7634 8348
Email: jwmp@mandaraspa-asia.com
Website: www.marriott.com

Six Senses Spa (pp214–5)
The Evason Phuket
100 Vised Road
Rawai Beach, Muang District
Phuket 83110, Thailand
Tel: (66-76) 381 011
Fax: (66-76) 381 018
Email: info@evasonphuket.com
Website: www.six-senses.com

The Spa at Phuket City
154 Phang-Nga Road
Amphur Muang
Phuket 83000
Thailand
Tel: (66-76) 233 333
Fax: (66-76) 233 384
Email: spaphuket@sportathlon.com
Website: www.thespahealthclubs.com

Pranburi

Six Senses Spa (pp212–3)
The Evason Hua Hin
9 Paknampran Beach
Pranburi
Prachuap Khiri Khan 77220
Thailand
Tel: (66-32) 632 111
Fax: (66-32) 632 112
Email: rsvn@evasonhuahin.com
Website: www.six-senses.com

VIETNAM

Nha Trang

Six Senses Spa (pp220–1)
Ana Mandara Resort
Beachside
Tran Phu Boulevard
Nha Trang
Vietnam
Tel: (84-58) 829 829
Fax: (84-58) 829 629
Email: resvana@dng.vnn.vn
Website: www.six-senses.com/ana-mandara

Bibliography

Alphen, Jan Van and Aris, Anthony (General Editors), *Oriental Medicine: An Illustrated Guide to the Asian Arts of Healing*, Shambhala Publications, 1995

Archipelago Guides Bali: A Traveller's Companion, Archipelago Press, an imprint of Editions Didier Millet Pte Ltd, 1995

Archipelago Guides Thailand: A Traveller's Companion, Archipelago Press, an imprint of Editions Didier Millet Pte Ltd, 2001

Beers, Susan-Jane, *Jamu: The Ancient Indonesian Art of Herbal Healing*, Periplus Editions (HK) Ltd, 2001

Benge, Sophie, *The Tropical Spa*, Periplus Editions (HK) Ltd, 1999

Cash, Mel, *Sport & Remedial Massage Therapy*, Ebury Press, an imprint of Random House, 1996

Chapman, Jessie, *Yoga: Postures for Body, Mind and Soul*, HarperCollinsPublishers (Australia), 2000

Claire, Thomas, *Bodywork: What Type of Massage to Get and How to Make the Most of it*, Quill, an imprint of William Morrow and Company, Inc., 1995

Cummings, Joe and Martin, Steven, *Thailand*, Lonely Planet Publications, 2001

Dillard, James and Ziporyn, Terra, *Alternative Medicine For Dummies*, IDG Books, 1998

Dr Duo Gao (Consultant Editor), *The Encyclopedia of Chinese Medicine*, Sevenoaks Ltd, 1997

Jonas, Steven M.D. and Gordon, Sandra, *30 Secrets of the World's Healthiest Cuisines*, John Wiley & Sons, Inc., 2000

Mitchell, Stewart, *The Complete Illustrated Guide to Massage*, Element Books Limited, 1997

Nash, Barbara, *From Acupressure to Zen: An Essay of Natural Therapies*, Hunter House, 1996

National Museum of the Republic of Indonesia, *Pusaka: Art of Indonesia*, Archipelago Press, an imprint of Editions Didier Millet Pte Ltd, 1992

Ody, Penelope, with Lyon, Alice Lyon and Vilinac, Dragana, *The Chinese Herbal Cookbook: Healing Foods from East and West*, Kyle Cathie Ltd, 2000

Plants, Indonesian Heritage Series Vol 4, Archipelago Press, an imprint of Editions Didier Millet Pte Ltd, 1996

Purchon, Nerys, *Health and Beauty the Natural Way*, MetroBooks, an imprint of Friedman/ Fairfax Publishers, 1997

Rister, Robert, *Japanese Herbal Medicine: The Healing Art of Kampo*, Avery Publishing Group, Inc., 1999

Ryrie, Charlie, *Healing Energies of Water*, Journey Editions, an imprint of Periplus Editions (HK) Ltd, 1999

Shealy, C Norman, *The Complete Family Guide to Alternative Medicine*, Element Books Ltd, 1996

The Complete Illustrated Encyclopedia of Alternative Healing Therapies: A Complete Guide to Natural Healing, Element Books Ltd, 1999

The Encyclopedia of Alternative Medicine, Journey Editions, an imprint of Charles E Tuttle Co., Inc., 1996

Vyas, Bharti and Warren, Jane, *Simply Ayurveda*, HarperCollinsPublishers (UK), 2000

Warrier, Gopi and Gunawant, Deepika, *The Complete Illustrated Guide to Ayurveda: The Ancient Indian Healing System*, Element Books Ltd, 1997

Woodham, Anne and Dr Peters, David, *Encyclopedia of Natural Healing: The Definitive Home Reference Guide to Treatments for Mind and Body*, Dorling Kindersley Ltd, 2000

Young, Jacqueline, *The Healing Path: The Practical Guide to the Holistic Traditions of China, India, Tibet and Japan*, Thorsons, an imprint of HarperCollinsPublishers (UK), 2001

Index

Page numbers in **bold** type refer to entries in Spa Speak; those in *italic* type refer to an illustration. Readers should refer to individual spa entries for guidance on treatments and therapies offered by the spas.

Picture Credits

The publisher would like to thank the following for permission to reproduce their material:

Amrita Spa 8 centre right
Ananda-In the Himalayas Destination Spa 31, 32 below, 33, 35, 37
Asmara Tropical Spas at Mayang Sari Beach Resort 8 top left, 48
Banyan Tree Spa 2, 5, 8–9 top centre, 69 top right, 84
Bridgeman Art Library 15 top, STC98424: 'An Itinerant Doctor at Tien-Sing', from *China in a Series of Views* by George Newenham Wright (c. 1790–1877), 1843 (coloured engraving) by Thomas Allom (1804–72) (after) Private Collection/The Stapleton Collection, UK/Bridgeman Art Library; 15 below, STC89855: 'An Apothecary', plate 26 from *The Costume of China*, engraved by J Dadley, 1800 (engraving) by Major George Henry Mason (19th century) (after) The Stapleton Collection, UK/Bridgeman Art Library; 29, DND112086: *Vasdya Dhanvantari, Supreme Saint of Ayurveda Medicine*, Private Collection/Dinodia Picture Agency, Bombay, India/Bridgeman Art Library; 32 top, ASC140112: *Indian Doctor Examining A Patient*, c. 1890 (w/c on paper) by Punjabi School (19th century), Royal Asiatic Society, London, UK/Bridgeman Art Library
British Library 28 (Add.24099.fol.118)
Chiva-Som International Health Resort 8 below right, 27, 43, 75, 76, 86
Corbis 41 top right (© Lindsay Hebberd/Corbis), 53 (© Hulton-Deutsch Collections/Corbis), 54 (© Corbis), 55 top right (© Archivo Iconografico, SA/Corbis), 60–1 (© Michael S Yamashita/Corbis), 65 top right (© Michael S Yamashita/Corbis), 70 (© Raoul Minsart/Corbis), 71 (© José Manuel Sanchis Calvere/Corbis), 78 (© Bettmann/Corbis), 79 (© Bettmann/Corbis)
Club Oasis at Grand Hyatt Shanghai 18
Duncan Baird Publishers, London 56 (Matthew Ward/©Duncan Baird Publishers), 58 (Sian Irvine/©Duncan Baird Publishers)
ImageState 52 top
Jamu Nature Spa at The Andaman Datai Bay 44 left
Jamu Traditional Spa at Alam KulKul Resort 8, 42, 45 top centre, 47 below right
John Falconer 40
Joko Sugianto 41 below left
Luca Tettoni Photography 62, 63, 64, 65, 66
Mandara Spa 1, 5, 9 below right, 85
Mary Evans Picture Library 14, 16
National Museum of Ethnology, Leiden, The Netherlands 50 (B226-310), 51 (2602-23)
National Palace Museum, Taipei, Taiwan, Republic of China 17 top
Okky (Laras Magazine) 166–7
Parwathi Spa at Matahari Beach Resort & Spa 73
Renewal Club Spa 19 top left
Science Museum/Science & Society Picture Library 55 below left
Sembunyi Spa at Cyberview Lodge Resort & Spa 46, 47 top left, 49
Six Senses Spa at The Evason Hua Hin 82
Six Senses Spa at The Evason Phuket 26, 67, 68, 74
Six Senses Spa at Soneva Gili Resort & Spa 9 below left
Somatheeram Ayurvedic Beach Resort 34 top left
The Spa at Hilton Hua Hin 36, 87 top right
The St. Regis Spa & Club 23
Taman Sari Royal Heritage Spa at Awana Kijal Golf, Beach & Spa Resort 87 below centre
Tara Sosrowardoyo 38
Thalasso Bali at Grand Mirage Resort 87 below left
Waroeng Djamoe Spa at Tugu Bali 6 below left
The Wellcome Library, London 12, 30
Werner Forman Archive, Shanxi Provincial Museum, Xian 52 below left

Additional photography by Jörg Sundermann and Lai Choon How.

Photographs on pp1–6

p1: Mandara's signature body scrubs are made from aromatic spices, herbs and other fresh ingredients.
p2: Romance couple treatment at Banyan Tree Spa.
p5: The open-air sunken bath at the villa at Banyan Tree Phuket.
p6: Fragrant essential oils at Waroeng Djamoe Spa at Hotel Tugu Bali.

Acknowledgements

The publisher would like to thank the following for their contributions and assistance:

Amrita Spa, The Beaufort Singapore and Renewal Club Spa for the use of their premises, therapists and products; Yin Yang Spa, a member of the Eu Yan Sang group, for the loan of products; Coriander Leaf for the loan of tableware; and Terry Lim for the translation of a kanpō recipe.